Business an

ELEMENTS OF INTERNATIONAL LAW

Series Editors

Mark Janis is William F. Starr Professor of Law at the University of Connecticut.

Douglas Guilfoyle is Professor of International Law and Security at UNSW Canberra.

Stephan Schill is Professor of International and Economic Law and Governance at the University of Amsterdam.

Bruno Simma is Professor of Law at the University of Michigan and a Judge at the Iran–US Claims Tribunal in The Hague.

Kimberley Trapp is Professor of Public International Law at University College London.

Elements of International Law represents a fresh approach in the literature of international law. It is a long series of short books. *Elements* adopts an objective approach to its subject matter, focusing on narrowly defined core topics in international law. Eventually, the series will offer a comprehensive treatment of the whole of the field. At the same time, each individual title will be a reliable go-to source for practicing international lawyers, judges and arbitrators, government and military officers, scholars, teachers, and students engaged in the discipline of international law.

Previously published titles in this series

Treaties
Richard Gardiner

The Law of International Financial Institutions
Daniel D. Bradlow

Occupation in International Law
Eliav Lieblich and Eyal Benvenisti

Arms Control and Disarmament Law
Stuart Casey-Maslen

International Law of Taxation
Peter Hongler

Jus Cogens
Dinah Shelton

The International Tribunal for the Law of the Sea
Kriangsak Kittichaisaree

International Law in the Russian Legal System
William E. Butler

The European Court of Human Rights
Angelika Nussberger

Business and Human Rights

Robert McCorquodale

OXFORD
UNIVERSITY PRESS

Great Clarendon Street, Oxford, OX2 6DP,
United Kingdom

Oxford University Press is a department of the University of Oxford.
It furthers the University's objective of excellence in research, scholarship,
and education by publishing worldwide. Oxford is a registered trade mark of
Oxford University Press in the UK and in certain other countries

© Robert McCorquodale 2024

The moral rights of the author have been asserted

First Edition published in 2024

All rights reserved. No part of this publication may be reproduced, stored in
a retrieval system, or transmitted, in any form or by any means, without the
prior permission in writing of Oxford University Press, or as expressly permitted
by law, by licence or under terms agreed with the appropriate reprographics
rights organization. Enquiries concerning reproduction outside the scope of the
above should be sent to the Rights Department, Oxford University Press, at the
address above

You must not circulate this work in any other form
and you must impose this same condition on any acquirer

Public sector information reproduced under Open Government Licence v3.0
(http://www.nationalarchives.gov.uk/doc/open-government-licence/open-government-licence.htm)

Published in the United States of America by Oxford University Press
198 Madison Avenue, New York, NY 10016, United States of America

British Library Cataloguing in Publication Data
Data available

Library of Congress Control Number: 2023948128

ISBN 978–0–19–285585–5 (hbk.)
ISBN 978–0–19–285586–2 (pbk.)

DOI: 10.1093/law/9780192855855.001.0001

Printed and bound by
CPI Group (UK) Ltd, Croydon, CR0 4YY

Links to third party websites are provided by Oxford in good faith and
for information only. Oxford disclaims any responsibility for the materials
contained in any third party website referenced in this work.

Series Editors' Preface

Elements of International Law represents a fresh approach to the literature of international law. It is a long series of short books. Following the traditional path of an international law textbook, *Elements*, rather than treating the whole of the field in one heavy volume, focuses on more narrowly defined subject matters.

There is nothing like Elements. It treats particular topics of international law much more extensively and in significantly more depth than traditional international law texts or encyclopedias. As each book in the Elements series has a relatively narrow focus, it provides a comprehensive treatment of a specialized subject matter, in comparison to the more limited treatment of the same subject matter in other general works.

Like a classic textbook, Elements aims to provide objective statements of the law. The series does not concern itself with the academic niches filled ably by doctoral theses, nor include works which take an argumentative point of view, already well done by the OUP Monograph series. Except in length and integration, Elements is for substantive topics comparable to OUP's Commentary series on individual treaties. Each book is exhaustively footnoted in respect of international legal practice and scholarship, including treaties, diplomatic practice, decisions by international and municipal courts and arbitral tribunals, resolutions and acts of international organizations, and commentary by the most authoritative jurists.

Elements adopts an objective, non-argumentative approach to its many subject matters and constitutes a reliable go-to source for practising international lawyers, judges and arbitrators, government and military lawyers, and scholars, teachers, and students engaged in the discipline of international law.

Mark Janis
Douglas Guilfoyle
Stephan Schill
Bruno Simma
Kimberley Trapp

Preface

In the early 1990s I gave a seminar to the senior executives of a global extractives company in which I asked them about their responsibilities in relation to a few human rights issues that they might encounter in their activities. They struggled to provide any coherent answers and were puzzled about why they should have responsibilities at all because they considered that human rights issues were a matter for governments alone. It made me think about how international law was failing to deal with corporate actions which have human rights impacts. So I began my research—and subsequent legal practice—into what is now the business and human rights field, though it did not then exist as a field.

Over 30 years later, business and human rights is a recognized and distinct field of scholarship and legal practice. The growth of scholarship (in legal and other disciplines) and of legal and other disputes in this field, and the excellent and insightful people working around the world in it, are astounding. The work of John Ruggie and his team in crafting the United Nations Guiding Principles on Business and Human Rights (UNGPs) has undoubtedly helped to galvanize the issues. Nevertheless, I find it extraordinary that, when the renewal of the mandate of the UN Working Group on Business and Human Rights—which was one consequence of the UNGPs and of which I am now a member—came to a vote in the UN Human Rights Council in July 2023, there were no objections to it by any state. Businesses around the world may resist complaints against their activities but very few now claim that they have no responsibilities at all (legal or otherwise) for their actions which have human rights impacts.

Having seen these amazing changes, I was daunted by the task of drafting a book which aims to explain and explore these developments from the perspective of international law. I have done my best and apologize for the omissions I have had to make to keep the book within a reasonable length and with a necessary focus on public international law, while recognizing that there are many fields of law and other disciplines which have direct effects on the business and human rights field. I have also tried my best to follow the wise advice of Kimberley Trapp, my kind Editor, to set out the different debates and issues which have arisen while not emphasizing my own views. My warm thanks to Samson Daniel for his dedicated research assistance and Lara Blecher for her review of a chapter, and my thanks and appreciation also to Rebecca Lewis and Reyman Dickrose Joseph and Caroline Valia-Kollery at OUP.

I am enormously grateful to the many people from around the globe who have assisted me in my professional journey in this field. Without them, my research would have been diminished, my ideas more limited, my legal practice possibly disappeared, and my encounters with businesses, civil society, law firms, academics, governments, and international organizations much less fruitful. I was supported by the British Institute of International and Comparative Law, for which I had the honour of serving as its Director for 10 years, in ensuring that business and human rights became a key part of their activities and that it included lawyers from across many areas of practice and sectors. The University of Nottingham, where I taught Business and Human Rights with fabulous colleagues and inspiring students, and Brick Court Chambers, where my legal practice was enabled, and the members of, and the fabulous team supporting, the Working Group on Business and Human Rights, were also key to my continuing interest in this field.

I particularly thank very warmly those who have been my co-authors and editors in this field, all of whom—without exception—have been a delight to work with and have expanded my knowledge. There is just one person to whom I want to add a special note of thanks, and that is Penelope Simons, as she has helped me from the very early days in this field to grapple with so many of these ideas and gently encouraged me in our challenge to a state-based approach to international law.

There are four people to whom I am most appreciative for all their unstinting support: my wife, Kate, and our three children, Rory, Ella, and Flora. Without their encouragement, considerable patience, kind understanding, and ongoing enthusiasm, as well as their love, I could not have done what I have in my professional career. Thank you, thank you. I dedicate this book to them.

Cambridge, UK
July 2023

Contents

List of Abbreviations   xiii

1. Development of Business and Human Rights Law   1
    1. Context   1
    2. Definitions   4
    3. History   6
       a. Background   6
       b. International Legal Developments   7
    4. Conclusions   14

2. International Law and Business   15
    1. Context   15
    2. Business and International Law   16
    3. State Responsibility for Business   18
    4. Roles of Business in International Law   20
    5. Business in International Law   23
       a. International Investment Law   23
       b. International Humanitarian Law   26
       c. International Environmental Law   28
    6. Conclusions   29

3. International Regulation of Business Concerning Human Rights Issues   31
    1. Context   31
    2. The UN Guiding Principles   32
    3. Influence of the UNGPs on International Regulation   35
       a. OECD Guidelines   35
       b. ILO Multinational Enterprises Declaration   37
       c. IFC Performance Standards and the Equator Principles   38
    4. Influence on National Regulation   40
    5. Legal Nature of International Regulation   42
    6. Conclusions   47

4. State Obligations Concerning Business and Human Rights   48
  1. Context   48
  2. State Responsibility   50
    a. Attribution by Elements of Government Authority   52
    b. Attribution by Acting under the Instructions, Direction, or Control   53
    c. Attribution by Adoption of Actions   56
    d. Complicity   56
  3. State Obligations and Human Rights   59
  4. Actions Beyond a State's Territory   63
  5. Domicile of a Business   70
  6. Other Aspects of State Obligations   71
    a. Regulation   71
    b. Policies and Oversight   73
    c. State-Owned Entities   76
  7. Conclusions   79

5. Corporate Responsibilities and Human Rights Due Diligence   81
  1. Context   81
  2. Corporate Responsibility   83
    a. Definition   83
    b. Respect   85
    c. Distinction from State Obligations   86
  3. Business Enterprises   89
  4. Human Rights   91
  5. Human Rights Impacts   94
  6. Types of Conduct   95
    a. Cause, Contribute to, and Directly Linked   95
    b. Leverage   101
  7. Human Rights Due Diligence   103
    a. Definition   103
    b. Application   108
      i. Human Rights Impact Assessment   108
      ii. Integration   111
      iii. Tracking   114
      iv. Communication   117
    c. Breadth of HRDD   119
  8. Conclusions   123

6. **Access to Remedies for Victims** — 124
   1. Context — 124
   2. International Legal Obligations on States to Provide Remedies — 126
      a. Right to a Remedy — 126
      b. Transnational/Extraterritorial — 127
   3. Remedy — 129
      a. Definition — 129
      b. Operational Grievance Mechanisms — 132
   4. Judicial Mechanisms — 133
      a. Types of Judicial Mechanism — 133
      b. Barriers to Judicial Remedies — 135
      c. Case Law — 137
         i. United States of America — 137
         ii. United Kingdom — 138
         iii. Other States — 141
         iv. Criminal Law — 143
      d. Human Rights — 144
   5. State-Based Non-Judicial Mechanisms — 145
   6. Business Operational Grievance Mechanisms — 151
   7. Conclusions — 155

7. **National Regulation of International Human Rights Responsibilities of Business** — 157
   1. Context — 157
   2. Examples of Legislation Prior to the UNGPs — 160
      a. South Africa Broad-Based Black Empowerment Act 2003 — 160
      b. Brazil Decree No. 540/2004 ('Dirty List') — 161
      c. California Transparency in Supply Chains Act 2010 — 161
   3. Examples of HRDD Legislation Subsequent to the UNGPs — 162
      a. French Duty of Vigilance Act 2017 — 162
      b. The Netherlands Child Labour Due Diligence Act 2019 — 164
      c. German Corporate Due Diligence Obligations in Supply Chains Act 2021 — 166
      d. Norwegian Transparency Act 2021 — 167
      e. EU Draft Corporate Sustainability Due Diligence Directive 2022 — 168
   4. Examples of Specific Legislation Relating to Business and Human Rights — 171
   5. Conclusions — 173

8. Future Developments in Business and Human Rights Law — 176
1. Context — 176
2. Reviewing Progress — 178
3. Climate Change — 180
4. Technology — 185
5. Business and Human Rights Treaty — 188
   a. Reasons for a Treaty — 189
   b. Process — 191
   c. Issues — 192
6. Conclusions — 195

9. Conclusions: International Law, Business, and Human Rights — 197
1. Context — 197
2. Business and Human Rights as Part of International Law — 198
3. Business, Human Rights, and International Law — 199

Bibliography — 203
Index — 221

List of Abbreviations

ACHPR	African Charter on Human and Peoples' Rights
AI	artificial intelligence
ARSIWA	ILC Articles on the Responsibility of States for Internationally Wrongful Acts
BHRRC	Business and Human Rights Resource Centre
BIT	bilateral investment treaty
CESCR	Committee on Economic, Social and Cultural Rights
CHRB	Corporate Human Rights Benchmark
CRC	Convention on the Rights of the Child
CRPD	Convention on the Rights of Persons with Disabilities
CSDDD	Draft Directive on Corporate Sustainability Due Diligence
CSR	Corporate Social Responsibility
DRC	Democratic Republic of Congo
EC	European Commission
ECtHR	European Court of Human Rights
EU	European Union
GNI	Global Network Initiative
HRC	UN Human Rights Committee
HRDD	human rights due diligence
HRIA	human rights impact assessment
ICCPR	International Covenant on Civil and Political Rights
ICESCR	International Covenant on Economic, Social and Cultural Rights
ICJ	International Court of Justice
ICT	information and communications technology
IFC	International Finance Corporation
IHL	International humanitarian law
IHRB	Institute for Human Rights and Business
ILC	International Law Commission
ILO	International Labour Organization
mHRDD	mandatory human rights due diligence
MNC	multinational corporation
MNE	multinational enterprise
NAP	National Action Plan
NCPs	National Contact Points

List of Abbreviations

OECD	Organisation for Economic Co-operation and Development
OGM'	operational-level grievance mechanism
OHCHR	Office of the UN High Commissioner for Human Rights
OPT	Occupied Palestinian Territories
SOE	State-owned enterprise
SRSC	Special Representative of the Secretary-General of the UN on the Issue of Human Rights and Transnational Corporations and Other Business Enterprises
TNC	transnational corporation
TRIPS	Agreement on Trade-Related Aspects of Intellectual Property Rights
TVPA	Torture Victim Protection Act
TWAIL	Third World Approaches to International Law
UDHR	Universal Declaration on Human Rights
UK	United Kingdom of Great Britain and Northern Ireland
UN	United Nations
UNCTNC	Commission on Transnational Corporations
UNFCCC	UN Framework Convention on Climate Change
UNGC	UN Global Compact
UNGPs	UN Guiding Principles on Business and Human Rights
US	United States
WGBHR	Working Group on Business and Human Rights

1
Development of Business and Human Rights Law

1. Context

On 3 December 1984, in the densely populated Indian city of Bhopal, there was a major explosion in a factory producing methyl isocyanate gas—a highly toxic substance used in rubber and adhesives—which released 47 tons of the gas into the air.[1] It is estimated that this leak caused more than 7,000 people to die within days and a further 15,000 people to die in the years which followed. More than 100,000 people have continued to suffer from chronic and debilitating illness.[2] The leak also contaminated the groundwater, which continues to this day to affect the quality of life of the people in the region.[3] The scale of this impact on human rights was vast and was described by one judge as the largest ever peacetime industrial disaster.[4]

This factory was owned by Union Carbide India Ltd (UCI), which was an operationally controlled subsidiary of Union Carbide Corporation (UCC), a chemical company headquartered in the United States of America (US). It quickly became clear that UCI had no assets of any value (as they had allegedly been transferred to UCC),[5] and no legal aid was available in the US to the Indian claimants. They could not, therefore, pursue the claim against UCC in the US. As a consequence, the Indian government passed

---

[1] Dominique Lapierre and Javier Moro, *Five Past Midnight in Bhopal* (Grand Central Publishing, 2003).
[2] Amnesty International, *Clouds of Justice* (Amnesty International Publications, 2014) www.amnesty.org/download/Documents/96000/asa200152004en.pdf, 5.
[3] Surya Deva, 'Bhopal: The Saga Continues 31 Years on' in Dorothée Baumann-Pauly and Justine Nolan (eds), *Business and Human Rights From Principles to Practice* (Routledge, 2016) [Deva, Bhopal], 22.
[4] Judge Keenan of the US Southern District Court of New York in *In re Union Carbide Corp. Bhopal Gas Plant Disaster*, 634 F. Supp. 842 (S.D.N.Y. 1986).
[5] Amnesty International, note 2.

legislation in 1985, which enabled the Indian government to become the sole entity to represent the victims[6] of the disaster in all legal proceedings within and outside India.[7] In its claim against UCC in the US, the Indian government argued that UCC operated as one multinational enterprise and that:

> A multinational corporation has a primary, absolute and non-delegable duty to the persons and country in which it has in any manner caused to be undertaken any ultrahazardous or inherently dangerous activity. This includes a duty to provide that all ultrahazardous or inherently dangerous activities are conducted with the highest standards of safety and to provide all necessary information and warnings regarding the activity involved.[8]

The US District Court dismissed the claim in May 1986 on the ground of *forum non conveniens* (i.e. that a US court was not the appropriate forum to consider the case as the damage occurred in India and the victims were in India).[9] On a judicial recommendation, UCC consented to the jurisdiction of the Indian courts.[10]

Accordingly, the Indian government brought a claim against UCC and UCI in the District Court of Bhopal in September 1986 in the amount equivalent to US$3billion.[11] UCC maintained the position that it was not liable because UCI was a separate legal entity, even though UCC owned and controlled UCI, and supplied technology and trained staff who worked at UCI. The proceedings continued until February 1989, when the Indian Supreme Court approved a settlement of US$470million to the Indian

---

[6] In relation to the terminology of 'victim', Upendra Baxi has argued: 'The terminology of "victims" denies the violated of any agency or capacity to act as "militant subject"; it denies them a history and future of their own; it obscures the fact that, as in Bhopal, the "victims" are re-victimized by the corporate state': Upendra Baxi 'Human Rights Responsibility of Multinational Corporations, Political Ecology of Injustice: Learning from Bhopal Thirty Plus?' (2015) 1 *Business and Human Rights Journal* 21, 26.

[7] The Bhopal Gas Leak Disaster (Processing of Claims) Act, 1985 (India), s. 3.

[8] *In re Union Carbide Corp. Bhopal Gas Plant Disaster*, 634 F. Supp. 842 (S.D.N.Y. 1986): Baxi, note 6, 37.

[9] The principle of *forum non conveniens* is discussed in Chapter 6.

[10] *In re Union Carbide Corp. Bhopal Gas Plant Disaster*, note 8. Note that later civil claims were brought in the US and were all dismissed by the same judge who decided the first case: Judge Keenan. Also Jayanth K. Krishnan, 'Bhopal in the Federal Courts: How Indian Victims failed to get Justice in the United States' (2020) 72 *Rutgers University Law Review* 101.

[11] *Union of India v. Union Carbide Corporation Case* No. 1113, District Court of Bhopal, India.

government on the condition that the civil and criminal cases were discontinued.[12] This decision was criticized as being made without giving sufficient reasons and that the settlement was deeply unfair to the victims, who would receive approximately US$300–500 per person, which in most instances would not cover all their medical expenses.[13] Indeed, it appears that many of the victims did not receive their compensation at all, due to a heavily bureaucratic approach by the responsible officials.[14]

The criminal claims were later reinstated and in June 2010—26 years after the explosion—the Chief Judicial Magistrate Court in Madhya Pradesh in India convicted UCI and seven of its executives of criminal negligence.[15] The court determined that 'an American corporation cynically used a third world country to escape from the increasingly strict safety standards imposed at home. Safety procedures were minimal and neither the American owners nor the local management seemed to regard them as necessary'.[16]

Today the factory site at Bhopal is still contaminated and Dow Chemicals, which acquired UCC in 2001, denies any legal responsibility.[17] As Surya Deva notes:

> Bhopal was, and remains, a stark reminder of the difficulties that victims of corporate human rights abuses experience in seeking justice, especially when an MNC [multinational corporation] is involved and both the home and the host governments lack the political will or capacity to pursue all means to hold the MNC accountable.[18]

It is in the context of such actions by businesses which have caused human rights impacts without providing any effective remedy, as in Bhopal, that the development of business and human rights law should be understood.

In order to explore the development of business and human rights within international law, and its consequences for international law, this book will begin with the history of these developments, especially the

---

[12] *Union Carbide Corporation v. Union of India* SLP (Civ.) 13080 of 1988.
[13] Deva, Bhopal, note 3, 23 and Amnesty International, note 2, 60–1.
[14] Baxi, note 6, 30 calls it '[t]he multifarious, even nefarious, "bureaucratization of justice" practised by the tribunals established for the disbursement of compensation [which] re-victimized the already traumatized victims'.
[15] *State of Madhya Pradesh v. Anderson*, Criminal Case No. 8460/1996.
[16] Ibid., para. 216.
[17] Dow Chemicals, Bhopal | Issues | Dow Corporate. https://corporate.dow.com/en-us/about/legal/issues/bhopal/tragedy.html (last accessed 8 November 2023)
[18] Deva, Bhopal, note 3, 24.

ground-breaking change created by the United Nations Guiding Principles on Business and Human Rights 2011 (UNGPs). It will show how international law, with its traditional approach focused on state actions and state sovereignty, has struggled to deal with the rise, and increasing direct involvement, of businesses in the international legal order. This book will follow the three-pillar structure of the UNGPs to consider the extent of the state's international legal obligations to protect the human rights of persons adversely affected by business activities, and it will then analyse the corporate responsibility to respect human rights. The third pillar of the UNGPs concerns access to remedies for those adversely affected by business activities, such as the victims in Bhopal, and, after close examination of this pillar, the book indicates how national regulation and case law are now beginning to introduce some accountability for business and some remedies for victims. The book ends with examples of where this dynamic area of law is possibly headed. Throughout this book, there are many indications as to how many areas of international law are affected—and challenged—by these developments in business and human rights.

2. Definitions

Business and human rights law has generally focused on the legal aspects of corporate responsibilities for human rights impacts, including their nature, scope, and extent; the clarification of those to whom these legal responsibilities might be owed, such as local communities and workers; and the means and methods of any liability and enforcement. While the terminology of 'business and human rights' has undergone change over time,[19] these legal issues remain central to these rights.

In particular, the focus of business and human rights law is on legal standards and legal issues. This does not mean that this is the only focus of the business and human rights field, as there are many important disciplines, such as international relations, corporate management, business ethics, financial management, and organizational studies, which bring vital engagement in, and insights on, issues of business and human rights.[20]

---

[19] Surya Deva, 'From "Business or Human Rights" to "Business and Human Rights": What Next?' in Surya Deva and David Birchall (eds), *Research Handbook on Business and Human Rights* (Edward Elgar, 2020) [Deva and Birchall, BHR] and Nadia Bernaz, *Business and Human Rights: History, Law and Policy-Bridging the Accountability Gap* (Routledge, 2016).

[20] For example, Karin Buhmann, *Human Rights: A Key Idea for Business and Society* (Routledge, 2022); Axel Marx, Geert Van Calster, Jan Wouters with Karin Otteburn and Diana

3. History

a. Background

The development of the field of business and human rights primarily arose out of the difficulty of both domestic and international law in dealing with the effects of businesses operating transnationally. This was because businesses were no longer only undertaking their activities (such as buying and selling goods and services) within the boundaries of the state in which they had been incorporated (i.e. registered). It was not clear in those circumstances whether the domestic law of that state was the only relevant law and, if that state applied its laws to the activities of the business—being a corporate 'national' of that state—outside that state, whether it would infringe international law with its strict jurisdictional limits of a state's powers (discussed in the next chapter).

Further, an ongoing issue is whether international law even applies to the activities of an entity which is not a state (discussed in Chapter 3). As a consequence, if neither international law nor domestic law applies, there is a possibility that this would lead to a 'governance gap':

> The root cause of the business and human rights predicament today lies in the governance gaps created by globalization—between the scope and impact of economic forces and actors, and the capacity of societies to manage their adverse consequences. These governance gaps provide the permissive environment for wrongful acts by companies of all kinds without adequate sanctioning or reparation. How to narrow and ultimately bridge the gaps in relation to human rights is our fundamental challenge.[23]

Hence, a key motivation in the development of business and human rights law has been to reduce or end this governance gap so that businesses operating transnationally are accountable in law.

Examples of such businesses operating transnationally can be found as early as the seventeenth century. The English East India Company began

---

[23] Special Rapporteur for the Secretary General on Business and Human Rights (SRSG), 'Report of the Special Representative of the Secretary-General on the issue of human rights and transnational corporations and other business enterprises' Human Rights Council Eighth Session, UN Doc. A/HRC/8/5 (7 April 2008), www.reports-and-materials.org/Ruggie-report-7-Apr-2008.pdf, para. 3.

These areas will be considered in places in this book, although the book's focus is on the legal aspects of the field of business and human rights, with emphasis on the international legal elements of this field, as this book forms part of a series on the elements of international law.

It would, however, be misleading to understand business and human rights law as being a subset of international human rights law. While international human rights law is a relevant framework for considering the rights and responsibilities of actors in the international community,[21] the legal position of businesses within states and within the international system, as well as the likelihood that those who claim to have legal rights and those who might have legal responsibilities in this field are located in different states, is such that a much wider viewpoint is required. This means that the areas of public international law which can be relevant to business and human rights law are, for example, international investment law, international humanitarian law, international criminal law, international environmental law, and international legal theory, as well as many of the general principles of public international law such as state responsibility and state sovereignty. In addition, there are many areas of domestic law which require engagement with business and human rights at times, especially in regulation and litigation. This includes domestic corporate law, domestic criminal law, tort/obligations and contract law, domestic human rights law, domestic environmental law, and domestic constitutional law, as well as private international law and comparative law.[22]

The terminology used in this book includes the term 'business' and 'businesses'. This is used here for convenience to cover all types of corporate entities, including companies, corporations, joint ventures, partnerships, franchises, and others, no matter their size, ownership, or location, and irrespective of whether they have transnational activities. In a similar way, the UNGPs —discussed below—use the term 'business enterprises' to encompass all corporate entities.

Lica, *Research Handbook on Global Governance, Business and Human Rights* (Edward Elgar, 2022); and Florian Wettstein, *Business and Human Rights: Ethical, Legal, and Managerial Perspectives* (CUP, 2022).

[21] On the breadth of scope of international law: Robert McCorquodale, 'An Inclusive International Legal System' (2004) 17 *Leiden Journal of International Law* 477–504.

[22] For some examples as to how these areas of law affect litigation in domestic courts against transnational corporations: Robert McCorquodale, 'The Litigation Landscape of Business and Human Rights' in Richard Meeran and Jahan Meeran (eds), *Human Rights Litigation against Multinationals in Practice* (OUP, 2021).

its existence in 1600 with a charter from the British monarch, Elizabeth I. It quickly expanded its activities, so that it is claimed that its operations accounted for half the world's trade from the mid-1700s to the early 1800s.[24] Further, across the seventeenth and early eighteenth centuries it had considerable military, political, and social power in India, with the parliamentarian and philosopher Edmund Burke claiming in the British Parliament in 1788:

> [The East India Company appears] more like an army going to pillage the people under the pretence of commerce than anything else ... [Their business is] more like robbery than trade.[25]

Another example is the Dutch East India company, founded by the government of the Netherlands in 1602 with a monopoly on trade in Asia, and with state-like powers to wage war, imprison and execute convicts, negotiate treaties, and establish colonies.[26] In 1670 the Hudson's Bay Company was founded in England to undertake all trade in the far north of North America and it grew to control trade across most of modern-day Canada, with vast economic, political, and legal powers.[27]

b. International Legal Developments

Many writers date the beginning of an understanding for a need for international law to be applied to businesses, due to their human rights impacts, in the 1970s with the 'Sullivan Principles', which sought to pressure businesses to disengage from apartheid South Africa,[28] and when Ken Saro-Wiwa and others from the Ogoni people began leading protests against the pollution and environmental degradation they alleged were caused by

---

[24] Anthony Farringdon, *Trading Places: The East India Company and Asia 1600–1834* (British Library, 2002).
[25] William Dalrymple, *The Anarchy: The Relentless Rise of the East India Company* (Bloomsbury, 2019), 310.
[26] Pepijn Brandon, 'Between Company and State: The Dutch East and West Indies Companies as Brokers between War and Profits' in Grietje Baars and Andre Spicer (eds), *The Corporation: A Critical, Multidisciplinary Handbook* (CUP, 2017), 215.
[27] Stephen Brown, *The Company: The Rise and Fall of the Hudson's Bay Empire* (Doubleday, 2020).
[28] Michael Santoro, 'Sullivan Principles or Ruggie Principles? Applying the Fair Share Theory to Determine the Extent and Limits of Business Responsibility for Human Rights' (2012) XXVIII/106 *Notizie di Politeia* 171.

businesses in Nigeria's Niger Delta.[29] The latter became international news in the 1990s, especially with the death of Saro-Wiwa allegedly at the hands of the Nigerian military government.[30]

However, Antony Angie, in his analysis of the development of international law during the colonial era from the fifteenth century onwards, argues that businesses have been operating transnationally since long before the 1970s.[31] He considers that international law was deliberately framed in colonial times to justify the gaining of control over natural resources around the world, and to promote and protect the economic interests of the businesses based in the colonial states.[32] Indeed, Penelope Simons, in her excellent critique of the role of business in international law, notes:

> [T]he root causes of corporate impunity for violations of human rights are deeply embedded in the international legal system. International law has been used progressively since colonial times to protect and facilitate foreign investment and trade activity while at the same time undermining the ability of Third World states to control and regulate transnational corporate actors. The policies and practices of international financial institutions have played a central role in this process.[33]

Therefore, there is a long history of the interaction between business and international law.

It was, though, only in the 1970s that there began concerted attempts at international regulation of business activity affecting human rights, which reflected some rejection of the colonial situation. In 1976 the United Nations (UN) Commission on Transnational Corporations (UNCTNC) was created, which arose out of the pressure from Global South states for a reordering of the international legal order.[34] A key document emanating

---

[29] See the introduction to Chapter 4.
[30] Florian Wettstein, 'The History of "Business and Human Rights" and its Relationship with Corporate Social Responsibility' in Deva and Birchall, BHR, note 19, 23, 25.
[31] Antony Anghie, *Imperialism, Sovereignty and the Making of International Law* (CUP, 2005). Also Sundhya Pahuja, *Decolonizing International Law* (CUP, 2011).
[32] Anghie, note 31, 211ff.
[33] Penelope Simons, 'International Law's Invisible Hand and the Future of Corporate Accountability for Violations of Human Rights' (2012) 3 *Journal of Human Rights and the Environment* 5, 35.
[34] For further detail, see Michelle Staggs Kelsall, '"Poisonous Flowers on the Dust-heap of a Dying Capitalism": The United Nations Code of Conduct on Transnational Corporations, Contingency and Failure in International Law' in Kevin Heller and Ingo Venzke (eds), *Contingency in International Law: On the Possibility of Different Legal Histories* (OUP, 2021).

from this pressure was the passing by the UN General Assembly of the Charter of Economic Rights and Duties of States 1974, which provided:

> Each State has the right ... to regulate and supervise activities of transnational corporations within its jurisdiction and take measures to ensure that such activities comply with its law, rules and regulations and conform to its economic and social policies. Transnational corporations shall not intervene in the internal affairs of a host State. Every State should, with full regard to its sovereign rights, cooperate with other states in the exercise of the right set forth in this paragraph.[35]

The UNCTNC comprised 48 individual experts as members and had two key responsibilities: to gather information on the political, legal, economic, and social aspects of transnational corporations through the UN Centre on Transnational Corporations; and to produce a Code of Conduct on TNCs through an Intergovernmental Working Group. The Code was conceived as a multilateral instrument 'defining the entirety of relations between governments and TNCs',[36] and to include a general code and some specific codes. However, differences between the members of the UNCTNC and states hindered any progress. These differences were primarily about the definition of a TNC (such as whether to include state-owned businesses), how specific would be the Code of Conduct (including whether it should refer to human rights), and, more generally, whether international law would apply at all.[37] In regard to the latter, the Executive Director of the UN Centre on Transnational Corporations wrote in 1984:

> On international law, it was recognized that there existed a fundamental difference of opinion between the OECD countries and the developing countries on the relationship between international law, including customary international law, and the Code. It was also agreed by all sides that the only way of dealing with this matter was to employ language that was sufficiently ambiguous to be interpreted differently by the

---

[35] Charter of Economic Rights and Duties of States, General Assembly Res. 3281 (XXIX), 12 December 1974, Art. 2(2)(b).
[36] Karl Sauvant, 'The Negotiations of the United Nations Code of Conduct for Transnational Corporations: Experiences and Lessons Learned' (2015) 16 *The Journal of World Investment & Trade* 11, 19.
[37] Samuel Asante, 'Doctrinal differences on the Code' in Khalil Hamdani and Lorraine Ruffin (eds), *UN Centre on Transnational Corporations: Corporate Conduct and the Public Interest* (Routledge, 2015), 91.

various groups. Although the need for ambiguity was generally recognized, the search for a formula was unsuccessful. Numerous drafts were considered, but all were viewed by one group or another as compromising its fundamental position of principle.[38]

Accordingly, despite its years of operation, there was no real agreement by the members of the UNCTNC or by states on these matters, and work on the Code was officially suspended in 1992.[39] Interestingly, of these issues, the one about which type of business should be included in international regulation remains a core issue today, as seen in debates about the draft business and human rights treaty discussed in Chapter 8, though there the applicability of international law (even if not its interaction with the domestic level) is largely accepted.

While the UNCTNC was slowly trying to devise Codes of Conduct, two other international organizations acted in this field. First, the Organisation for Economic Cooperation and Development (OECD), being an intergovernmental body of industrialized states, adopted the OECD Guidelines for Multinational Enterprises (OECD Guidelines) in 1976.[40] The text of the OECD Guidelines was negotiated between the governments of the OECD member states, and both employers' and workers' organizations were consulted. It initially dealt mainly with employment and social policy matters before adding environmental issues in a revision in 2000. The OECD Guidelines were an Annex to the OECD Declaration on International Investment and Multinational Enterprises 1976, and the Declaration was intended to encourage a better environment for international investment and raise awareness of the positive contributions of business investment to economic and social development generally. The original OECD Guidelines were thus created to deal with the concern in the mid-1970s that 'actual or potential political or other interference by TNCs in developing

---

[38] Office of the Secretary-General, 'Internal Memorandum from Sidney Dell to the Secretary-General of the United Nations re: Conclusion of the Special Session of the Commission on Transnational Corporations', 11–29 June 1984' (5/07/1984) EO/433, Folder No. S-1048-21, quoted in Michelle Staggs Kelsall, 'Human Rights, Incorporated? Business & Human Rights in an Age of Neoliberalism' (PhD thesis, University of Nottingham, 2019, unpublished, with author).

[39] UNGA Doc. A/47/446 (1992) Report of the President of the General Assembly at its forty-sixth session on a Code of Conduct on Transnational Corporations, which called for 'a fresh approach to the development of a legal framework for direct foreign investment'.

[40] OECD, 'The OECD Guidelines for Multinational Enterprises', OECD Declaration and Decisions on International Investment and Multinational Enterprises: Basic Texts (DAFFE/IME) [OECD Guidelines].

host states in the context of investments that were being promoted by the [OECD] Declaration might lead host states not to impose restrictions on the rights of foreign investors [i.e. OECD businesses]'.[41] This approach by industrialized states in the 1970s in protecting the right of investors under international law is consistent with the earlier analysis relating to protection of investment interests during the colonial period.

Second, the International Labour Organization (ILO) adopted the ILO Tripartite Declaration of Principles concerning Multinational Enterprises and Social Policy (ILO Multinational Enterprises Declaration) in 1977.[42] This was negotiated between the three partners of the ILO, being government delegates, workers' representatives, and employers' representatives, and it intended to establish standards for each group to follow. It was updated in 2000 in order to incorporate the ILO Declaration on Fundamental Principles and Rights at Work 1998 within its provisions. Both international documents were later revised in light of the UNGPs, as is considered in Chapter 3.

The third major step in international regulation came in August 1998, when the UN Sub-Commission on the Promotion and Protection of Human Rights (the Sub-Commission) established a working group on the working methods and activities of TNCs. The Sub-Commission was the main subsidiary body of the UN Commission on Human Rights (now the UN Human Rights Council), and it was established in 1947 with 12 expert members. The working group on the working methods and activities of TNCs comprised five regional experts, who worked from 1999 to 2004, during which time they produced four drafts. This process concluded with the production of the Norms on the Responsibilities of TNCs and Other Business Enterprises with regard to Human Rights in 2003 (the Norms).[43] After considerable debate, the Norms were eventually rejected by the UN

---

[41] Karen Buhmann, *Changing Sustainability Norms through Communication Processes* (Edward Elgar, 2017), 113.

[42] ILO Tripartite Declaration of Principles concerning Multinational Enterprises and Social Policy, adopted by the Governing Body of the International Labour Office at its 204th Session (Geneva, November 1977) and amended at its 279th (November 2000), 295th (March 2006), and 329th (March 2017) Sessions.

[43] ECOSOC, UN Doc. E/CN.4/Sub.2/2003/12(Rev.2) (30 May 2003) 'Draft Norms on the Responsibilities of Transnational Corporations and Other Business Enterprises with Regard to Human Rights' (30 May 2003). Also UNECOSOC, Sub-Commission on Human Rights, Res. 2003/16, and David Weissbrodt and Maria Kruger, 'Norms on the Responsibilities of Transnational Corporations and Other Business Enterprises' (2003) 97 *American Journal of International Law* 901.

Commission on Human Rights in 2004.[44] A key factor in the failure of the Norms to receive approval by states—and so to become a treaty—was that, because the Norms set out international legal obligations directly for TNCs, this was contrary to the traditional view that only states have international legal obligations under international law (including on human rights matters). This is discussed at more length in Chapter 2.

After this strong view taken by states against accepting any international legal obligations on TNCs in relation to human rights in the shape of a treaty or similar, the pressure to have international regulation in this field continued in a different form. In April 2005, a resolution was passed by the UN Commission on Human Rights requesting the appointment of a Special Representative of the Secretary-General of the UN on the Issue of Human Rights and Transnational Corporations and Other Business Enterprises (SRSG).[45] Instead of a Commission comprised of 48 experts, or a working group on the Norms of six experts, there was just one person—Professor John Ruggie, who was a political science academic and who had worked in the UN system for some time, including helping to establish the UN Global Compact.[46]

The UN Global Compact is relevant, as it was a key idea of the then UN Secretary-General, Kofi Annan, to 'initiate a global compact of shared values and principles, which will give a human face to the global market'.[47] The Global Compact established ten principles for businesses to adhere to, which included principles on human rights and labour.[48] It has issued guidance, such as how a business can prioritize its responses where it has more than one actual or potential adverse human rights impact in its supply

---

[44] UNCHR, UN Doc. E/CN.4/2004/116 'Responsibilities of Transnational Corporations and other Business Enterprises with regard to Human Rights' (22 April 2004) 1(c) (affirming that the Norms have 'no legal standing').

[45] UN Commission on Human Rights Resolution 2005/69 of 20 April 2005, UN Doc. E/CN.4/2005/L.10/Add.17. Argentina, India, Nigeria, the Russian Federation, and Norway proposed the resolution, which was passed by 49 votes in favour, 1 abstention, and 3 against (Australia, South Africa, and the United States).

[46] 'Secretary-General appoints John Ruggie of United States Special Representative on issue of human rights, transnational corporations, other business enterprises' UN Doc. SG/A/934 (28 July 2005) https://press.un.org/en/2005/sga934.doc.htm.

[47] UN Office of the Secretary-General, 'Press Release: Secretary-General Proposes Global Compact on Human Rights, Labour, the Environment, in address to World Economic Forum in Davos' UN Doc. SG/SM/6881 (15 February 1999).

[48] UNGC Principles 1 and 2. Over 9,000 companies have signed the Global Compact, in addition to over 4,000 non-business signatories: www.unglobalcompact.org/what-is-gc/participants.

chain.[49] Yet it is not legally binding and has limited compliance mechanisms, though it aspires to be a 'learning platform'.[50]

During his first three-year mandate, the SRSG constructed a conceptual framework (the Framework):[51]

> The Framework rests on three pillars. The first is the State duty to protect against human rights abuses by third parties, including business enterprises, through appropriate policies, regulation, and adjudication. The second is the corporate responsibility to respect human rights, which means that business enterprises should act with due diligence to avoid infringing on the rights of others and to address adverse impacts with which they are involved. The third is the need for greater access by victims to effective remedy, both judicial and non-judicial. Each pillar is an essential component in an inter-related and dynamic system of preventative and remedial measures: the State duty to protect because it lies at the very core of the international human rights regime; the corporate responsibility to respect because it is the basic expectation society has of business in relation to human rights; and access to remedy because even the most concerted efforts cannot prevent all abuse.[52]

In 2008 the (now created) UN Human Rights Council welcomed the Framework and resolved to extend the SRSG's mandate for a further three years in order for him to develop recommendations to 'operationalize' these core principles.[53] These became the UNGPs in 2011, of which there is a detailed analysis in Chapter 3.

---

[49] UN Global Compact Good Practice Note, *A Structured Process to Prioritise Supply Chain Human Rights Risks*, 9 July 2015.

[50] Radu Mares, 'The Limits of Supply Chain Responsibility: A Critical Analysis of Corporate Responsibility Instruments' (2010) 79 *Nordic Journal of International Law* 193, 204.

[51] SRSG, 'Report of the Special Representative of the Secretary-General on the issue of human rights and transnational corporations and other business enterprises, John Ruggie' Human Rights Council Eighth Session (7 April 2008) UN Doc. A/HRC/8/5 www.reports-and-materials.org/Ruggie-report-7-Apr-2008.pdf.

[52] UNGPs, Introduction, para. 6. Also SRSG, 'Report of the Special Representative of the Secretary-General on the issue of human rights and transnational corporations and other business enterprises, Human Rights Council Seventeenth Session (21 March 2011) UN Doc. A/HRC/17/31 www.ohchr.org/Documents/Issues/Business/A-HRC-17-31_AEV.pdf (SRSG 2011), 4

[53] UNHRC, Twenty-eighth Meeting 18 June 2008 'Mandate of the Special Representative of the Secretary-General on the issue of human rights and transnational corporations and other business enterprises' UN Doc. Res. 8/7 http://ap.ohchr.org/documents/E/HRC/resolutions/A_HRC_RES_8_7.pdf, 6.

4. Conclusions

This history shows that there have been continuing efforts by parts of the international community to create clarity about the international legal obligations of business, especially TNCs, for those of their activities which adversely impact on human rights. At various stages there has been a lack of agreement by states, pressure from businesses and others, and uncertainty over the international obligations which apply and how they apply. This is seen in the failure of both the UN Commission on Transnational Corporations and the Norms to obtain agreement by states. In addition, the broader context of the desire of most industrial states to protect their corporate nationals from international legal obligations meant that there remained considerable division among states as to the way forward.

Therefore, most of the efforts that have been successful in this area have been to create non-legally binding international obligations—generally called 'responsibilities'—on businesses, as shown in Chapter 3. Yet all these efforts were aimed at creating international regulation of business activities in the area of human rights.

A key issue remains as to what extent these developments are part of, or relevant to, international law. This will be explored in the next chapter.

2
International Law and Business

1. Context

In 2001–02, Argentina suffered a significant financial crisis.[1] One consequence was that water and sewage services in Buenos Aires, which were provided by a private business under an agreement with the government, were terminated by the Argentinian government. One of the investors in that business, a Spanish business called Urbaser, brought a claim under a bilateral investment treaty (BIT) between Spain and Argentina. These BIT treaties enable an investor to take their claim against a state to an international arbitration tribunal outside the jurisdiction of the state.[2] Argentina brought a counterclaim arguing that there was a failure by the business to provide the necessary level of investment, which had led to violations of the human right to water.

The international arbitration tribunal accepted jurisdiction over the claim and counterclaim, on the basis that the particular BIT allowed reference to international law, amongst other legal systems.[3] The tribunal then considered whether businesses had obligations under international law. It decided that BITs give businesses the capacity to have rights under international law and so businesses must be subject to international law obligations.[4] Further, it held:

> The Tribunal may mention in this respect that international law accepts corporate social responsibility as a standard of crucial importance for companies operating in the field of international commerce. This

---

[1] International Monetary Fund, *The IMF and Argentina 1991–2001: Evaluation Report* (IMF, 2004).
[2] Bilateral investment treaties are discussed in more detail below.
[3] *Urbaser S.A. and Consorcio de Aguas Bilbao Bizkaia, Bilbao Biskaia Ur Partzuergoa v. The Argentine Republic*, ICSID Case No. ARB/07/26, decided 8 December 2016 [*Urbaser v. Argentina*].
[4] Ibid., para. 1194.

standard includes commitments to comply with human rights in the framework of those entities' operations conducted in countries other than the country of their seat of incorporation [providing a reference to the UNGPs]. In light of this more recent development, it can no longer be admitted that companies operating internationally are immune from becoming subjects of international law ...

[and] there is an obligation on all parts, public and private parties, not to engage in activity aimed at destroying such [human] rights.[5]

Ultimately, the tribunal concluded that, in these particular circumstances, '[t]he human right to water entails an obligation of compliance on the part of the State, but it does not contain an obligation for performance on part of any company providing the contractually required service'.[6] Accordingly, the counterclaim failed.[7] Nevertheless, the importance of this quoted statement by the tribunal is that it acknowledges that businesses have obligations under international law, that those obligations include compliance with international human rights law, and that businesses are subjects of international law.

This chapter will consider the relevance of business actions in relation to international law, as was highlighted in *Urbaser v. Argentina*. It will briefly summarize the principal elements of the shifts and debates regarding the status and responsibilities of business in the international legal system.[8] It will then place these views in the context of some relevant international law areas, such as international investment law, international humanitarian law, and international environmental law, and reflect on what this all means in terms of responsibilities by business for human rights impacts.

2. Business and International Law

The activities of a particular type of business have been considered most relevant for international law. This is the transnational corporation (TNC), which is the term used by the United Nations (UN) system, and

---

[5] Ibid., paras 1195, 1199.
[6] Ibid., para. 1208.
[7] Edward Guntrip, '*Urbaser v Argentina*: The Origins of a Host State Human Rights Counterclaim in ICSID Arbitration?' (*EJIL Talk!* 10 February 2017) (ejiltalk.org).
[8] For a detailed review, see *Persons: Individuals and Corporations* in the Elements of International Law series.

which is sometimes known as the multinational enterprise (MNE),[9] which is the term used by the Organisation for Economic Co-operation and Development (OECD). The clearest definition of this type of business is given by the OECD:

> [TNCs/MNEs] usually comprise companies or other entities established in more than one country and so linked that they may coordinate their operations in various ways. While one or more of these entities may be able to exercise a significant influence over the activities of others, their degree of autonomy within the enterprise may vary widely from one multinational enterprise to another. Ownership may be private, State or mixed.[10]

As noted in Chapter 1, there has been a long history of interaction between business and international law. In this, the role of law is crucial to the development of TNCs, as Peter Muchlinski has noted:

> Legal factors represent one of the most visible institutional variables that MNEs confront when organizing their operations. The main functions of law in this respect revolve around two core objectives: facilitation of business activity, and the regulation of its impacts. An underlying element in this process is the generation of trust in the operation of business, through the provision of a stable and predictable business environment and through the control of undesirable economic and social effects. Thus, law performs not only an economic, but also a social function in the growth of MNEs.[11]

It is, therefore, appropriate to consider how the international legal system, in facilitating the economic and social functions and activities of TNCs, treats TNCs as part of international law.

---

[9] They are also often called multinational corporations (MNCs). I will use the term 'TNCs' in this book, unless the context requires otherwise.
[10] OECD Guidelines, Guideline I 'Concepts and Principles' para. 4.
[11] Peter Muchlinski, *Multinational Enterprises and the Law* (OUP, 3rd ed., 2021), 32. Also B.S. Chimni, 'International Institutions Today: An Imperial Global State in the Making (2004) 15 *European Journal of International Law* 1, who argues (p. 14) that 'in the 1970s and 1980s international organizations ... were ... facilitating the further liberalization of international and national markets ... by heavily promoting free trade and export-processing zones of interest to transnational corporations'.

It is also of note that business can rely on international law, even when the state itself may be reluctant to do so. Kishanthi Parella argues that, in some instances, businesses do incorporate parts of international law—especially on climate change, human rights, and sustainable development—into board governance, management decision-making, and contractual relationships, irrespective of their home state's position on that international law.[12] She explains that businesses 'choose to comply with international law for reasons other than legal mandate, such as corporate strategy and purpose, risk management, and stakeholder management' and that, in so doing, businesses 'challeng[e] a traditional view of international law that assumes that the state pathway is a necessary condition for corporations to comply with international law'.[13] Indeed, there are many examples of businesses which expressly proclaim their aim to comply with aspects of international law as part of their corporate policies, including the UN Guiding Principles on Business and Human Rights (UNGPs).[14]

3. State Responsibility for Business

The general international legal principle is that a state only has international legal responsibility for the actions of that state, which includes organs of the state and public officials. The core elements of state responsibility, as set out in the International Law Commission's (ILC) Articles on the Responsibility of States for Internationally Wrongful Acts (ARSIWA), are that every international wrongful act of a state—which is an action or an omission attributable to the state when there is a breach of an international obligation—entails the international responsibility of that state.[15] Many of the articles in ARSIWA, including the ones examined here, can be

---

[12] Kishanthi Parella, 'International Law in the Boardroom' (2023) 108 *Cornell Law Review* 839.
[13] Ibid., 54.
[14] For example, Unilever's Human Rights Policy, Unilever Human Rights Policy Statement, and HM-Group-UNGP-Index-2022.pdf (hmgroup.com).
[15] ILC, *Articles on the Responsibility of States for Internationally Wrongful Acts*, Report of the International Law Commission on the Work of its 53rd session, A/56/10, August 2001, UN GAOR. 56th Sess. Supp. No. 10, UN Doc. A/56/10(SUPP) (2001). These laws on state responsibility have been criticized by some writers as a law developed by states in which states determine their own obligations for certain public acts in relation to other states and how a state can then enforce these obligations against other states: Philip Allott, 'State Responsibility and the Unmaking of International Law' (1988) 29 *Harvard International Law Journal* 1.

considered to represent customary international law,[16] and they have been applied to human rights issues.[17]

There are, though, a few exceptions to this principle set out in ARSIWA, in which a state may have international responsibility for the actions of businesses. ARSIWA identifies four main situations in which the actions of a business (or another non-state actor) can be attributed to the state, for which the state will incur international responsibility where there is a breach of an international obligation (such as an obligation under a human rights treaty).[18] First, a state would be responsible for the actions of a business where the latter was exercising elements of governmental activity, such as with prisons and boundary control.[19] Second, a state would be responsible for the actions of a business that was acting under the instructions or direction or control of the state, such as a private security business.[20] Third, where the state adopts or acknowledges the actions of a business as its own, then that state may incur international responsibility for those actions.[21] Fourth, responsibility is engaged when the state is complicit in enabling actions by businesses which are contrary to international law.[22]

---

[16] Arman Savarian, 'The Ossified Debate on a UN Convention on State Responsibility' (2001) 70 *International and Comparative Law Quarterly* 769.

[17] For example, the Inter-American Court of Human Rights held in *Awas Tingni v. Nicaragua*, I-ACtHR, IHRR (2001), para. 153: '[a]ccording to the rules of law pertaining to the international responsibility of the State and applicable under international human rights law, actions or omissions by any public authority, whatever its hierarchical position, are chargeable to the State which is responsible under the terms set forth in the American Convention [on Human Rights].'

[18] Indeed, the ILC expressly deleted a draft article (Article 11) that had stated that actions by non-state actors could not be attributed to the state: Nicola Jägers, *Corporate Human Rights Obligations: In Search of Accountability* (Intersentia, 2002), 143–5. For a fuller discussion on the area of state responsibility for corporate activity: Robert McCorquodale and Penelope Simons, 'Responsibility Beyond Borders: State Responsibility for Extraterritorial Violations by Corporations of International Human Rights Law' (2007) 70 *Modern Law Review* 599.

[19] ARSIWA, Article 5. The ILC notes, for example, that private 'firms may be contracted to act as prison guards and in that capacity may exercise public powers such as the powers of detention and discipline pursuant to a judicial sentence or to prison regulations': James Crawford, *The International Law Commission's Articles on State Responsibility: Introduction, Text and Commentaries* (CUP, 2002) [ILC Commentaries], note 16, 100.5.

[20] ILC Commentaries, ibid., paras 91.2 and 121. Also *Prosecutor v. Duško Tadić*, Case No. IT-94-1, International Criminal Tribunal for the former ICTY, Appeals Chamber (1999) 38 ILM 1518, 1541, para. 117, and *Ilascu v. Moldova and Russia*, App no. 48787/99 (ECHR, 8 July 2004).

[21] ARSIWA, Article 11 and ILC Commentaries, note 19, paras 121–3. More generally, *Case Concerning United States Diplomatic and Consular Staff in Tehran (United States of America v. Iran)* [1980] ICJ Rep. 3, paras 57, 69–71.

[22] ARSIWA, Article 16.

There is a further situation where a state can incur international responsibility for the actions of a business, though this situation does not arise by means of attribution. This is where the state itself fails to exercise due diligence to prevent the effects of the actions of the business.[23] The legal foundation for this situation is that the state has an international obligation to protect all persons in their jurisdiction. Accordingly, under international human rights law, a state has an obligation to prevent human rights violations by all persons, including businesses, within its jurisdiction.[24] This customary international law obligation is repeated in Guiding Principle 1 of the UNGPs:

> States must protect against human rights abuse within their territory and/or jurisdiction by third parties, including business enterprises. This requires taking appropriate steps to prevent, investigate, punish and redress such abuse through effective policies, legislation, regulations and adjudication.

This is stated to be a 'foundational' principle,[25] and is given as a mandatory legal requirement on states.

Accordingly, states have been found to be in breach of their international human rights obligations in relation to activities of businesses because the acts or omissions by the state enabled the businesses to act as they did so as to lead to human rights violations. In all these cases, the state was in breach of its obligations under the relevant human rights treaty. State responsibility in relation to business activities are discussed in more depth in Chapter 4.

4. Roles of Business in International Law

A starting point for most writers considering the issue of the roles of business in international law is whether businesses (especially TNCs) can be 'subjects' of international law, in the sense of being creators, developers, and

---

[23] Ian Brownlie, *System of the Law of Nations: State Responsibility, Part I* (Clarendon Press, 1983), 161. Also ILC Commentaries, note 19, para. 92.4. This arises from *Velásquez Rodriguez v. Honduras* (1989) 28 ILM 294, which is discussed in Chapter 5.
[24] Andrew Clapham, *Human Rights in the Private Sphere* (Clarendon Press, 1993) and Andrew Clapham, 'Revisiting *Human Rights in the Private Sphere*: Using the ECHR to Protect the Right of Access to the Civil Court' in Craig Scott (ed.), *Torture as Tort* (Hart, 2001), 513.
[25] UNGPs, Part I.A.

enforcers of international law. The dominant approach for a long time was that '[s]ince the Law of Nations is a law between States only and exclusively, States only and exclusively are subjects of the Law of Nations'.[26] What this statement indicates is that only states can be subjects of international law (formerly called the 'Law of Nations'). This approach has been widened during the last century to include international organizations comprised of states and created by states, as confirmed by the International Court of Justice (ICJ) in its *Reparations for Injuries* advisory opinion concerning the international legal personality of the UN itself.[27]

In these approaches, if there is a subject of international law then there must be an 'object' about which international law is concerned. The objects will include territory and commerce, and, in these approaches, they would also include individuals, businesses, and other non-state actors. These dominant approaches mean that any activities of businesses in the international legal system are seen as wholly determined by states and entirely dependent on states' consent, and so cannot form part of the creation, development, or enforcement of international law.[28]

This approach of binary opposition between subject and object has been criticized by a number of writers. Rosalyn Higgins, a former President of the ICJ, has stated:

> [T]he whole notion of 'subjects' and 'objects' has no credible reality, and, in my view, no functional purpose. We have erected an intellectual prison of our own choosing and then declared it to be an unalterable constraint ... It is much more helpful, and closer to perceived reality, to return to the view of international law as a particular decision-making process. Within that process (which is a dynamic and not a static one) there are a variety of participants, making claims across state lines, with the object of maximizing various values ... Now, in this model, there are no 'subjects' and 'objects' but only participants.[29]

---

[26] Lassa Oppenheim, *International Law*, vol. 1 (Longmans, 1905), 341.
[27] *Reparation for Injuries suffered in the Service of the United Nations (Advisory Opinion)* [1949] ICJ Rep. 174.
[28] For a more detailed discussion: Robert McCorquodale, 'An Inclusive International Legal System' (2004) 17 *Leiden Journal of International Law* 477.
[29] Rosalyn Higgins, *Problems and Process: International Law and How We Use It* (OUP, 1994), 49.

Feminist scholars have agreed, noting that the dominant approach privileges the voices of states, since all potential participants are compared to states, and it silences alternative voices.[30] Others agree, with David Bilchitz noting that business obligations in relation to human rights preceded those of the state and so must be included in the international regulation of human rights obligations.[31]

Accordingly, a range of different approaches to determining those who are potential creators of international law have been devised. These include examining the 'participation' in the international legal system of those actually involved in it,[32] looking at the 'functions' of different actors[33] or their 'capacity',[34] and at the management of law.[35] Others take alternative approaches, such as that of global legal pluralism, where there are a number of different normative systems that operate and interact at the international level.[36] These approaches have led Christoph Schreuer to argue that 'we should adjust our intellectual framework to a multi-layered reality consisting of a variety of authoritative structures ... [in which] what matters is not the formal status of a participant'.[37]

In order to explore the reality of what has occurred in international law in relation to business activities, the sections which follow consider the participation of business in a cross-section of areas of international law—international investment law, international humanitarian law, and

---

[30] Hilary Charlesworth and Christine Chinkin, *The Boundaries of International Law: A Feminist Analysis* (Manchester University Press, 2000).
[31] David Bilchitz, *Fundamental Rights and the Legal Obligations of Business* (CUP, 2021).
[32] Karen Knop, *Diversity and Self-Determination in International Law* (CUP, 2002) and Alan Boyle and Christine Chinkin, *The Making of International Law* (OUP, 2007).
[33] Christoph Schreuer, 'The Waning of the Sovereign State: Towards a New Paradigm for International Law' 4 *European Journal of International Law* (1993) 447; International Law Association (ILA), *First Report of the Committee on Non-State Actors* (ILA, 2010), 636 (which also used the term 'actors'); and Steven Ratner, 'Corporations and Human Rights: A Theory of Legal Responsibility' (2001) 111 *Yale Law Journal* 443.
[34] Andrew Clapham, *Human Rights Obligations of Non-State Actors* (OUP, 2006).
[35] Math Nortmann and Cedric Ryngaert (eds), *Non-State Actor Dynamics in International Law: From Law-Takers to Law-Makers* (Ashgate, 2010).
[36] Boaventura de Sousa Santos, *Towards a New Legal Common Sense: Law, Globalization, and Emancipation* (Butterworths, 2002) and Paul Schiff Berman, *Global Legal Pluralism: A Jurisprudence of Law Beyond Borders* (CUP, 2012). For a fuller discussion: Robert McCorquodale, 'Pluralism, Global Law and the Accountability of Corporations for Human Rights Violations' (2013) 2 *Global Constitutionalism* 287.
[37] Schreuer, note 33, p. 453. Also Hersch Lauterpacht, 'The Subjects of the Law of Nations' (1947) 63 *Law Quarterly Review* 438, 444 and Robert McCorquodale, 'Sources and the "Subjects" of International Law: A Plurality of Law-Making Participants' in Jean d'Aspremont and Samantha Besson (eds), *Oxford Handbook on the Sources of International Law* (OUP, 2017), 749.

international environmental law—as being areas relevant to business participation. The substantive aspects of these areas of international law will only be touched on briefly here because each of these areas is covered in other books in this Elements of International Law Series.

5. Business in International Law

a. International Investment Law

International legal regulation over economic issues, including the cross-border economic activities of business, has been evident for centuries, as was highlighted in Chapter 1. In recent decades this has included trade matters, especially with the advent of the World Trade Organization,[38] and intellectual property matters, most clearly seen in the Agreement on Trade-Related Aspects of Intellectual Property Rights (TRIPS).[39] Indeed, John Jackson has argued that 'it is plausible to suggest that ninety per cent of international law work is in reality international economic law in some form or another'.[40]

A key aspect of international legal regulation over economic matters is international investment law, which primarily concerns the rules and mechanisms in relation to direct foreign investment by business (both private and state-owned) into states.[41] These rules and mechanisms are based on an interplay of treaties between states and contracts between businesses and states, as is seen in the example given in the introduction to this chapter. These treaties are BITs, of which there are now over 3,000 globally, and the contracts between states and businesses are many times this number.[42] These BITs enable individual private investors (almost all of whom are businesses) to rely on the provisions of these treaties, both in terms of the standards of treatment of these businesses within domestic law

---

[38] Daniel Bethlehem, Donald McRae, Rodney Neufeld, and Isabelle Van Damme (eds), *The Oxford Handbook of International Trade Law* (OUP, 2nd ed., 2022).
[39] Holger Hestermeyer, *Human Rights and the WTO: The Case of Patents and Access to Medicines* (OUP, 2007).
[40] John Jackson, 'International Economic Law: Reflections on the "Boiler Room" of International Relations' (1995) 10 *American University Law Review* 595, 596.
[41] Ursula Kriebaum, Christoph Schreuer, and Rudolf Dolzer, *Principles of International Investment Law* (OUP, 3rd ed., 2022).
[42] Campbell McLachlan, Laurence Shore, and Matthew Weiniger, *International Investment Arbitration* (OUP, 2nd ed., 2017).

and the choice of forum for the settlement of disputes, the latter of which is primarily through international arbitration before an international tribunal of experts.[43]

The international investment tribunals are often established under an international mechanism, such as the International Centre for the Settlement of Investment Disputes, and are not restricted to applying domestic law. Indeed, the development of these BITs under such mechanisms involves the consent of host states to international arbitration in respect of a wide range of investors, which are unknown and unnamed at the time of the treaty, and these investors can bring a claim before an international tribunal at any time. There are now a range of mechanisms under international investment law by which businesses can bring claims against states, without having first to exhaust domestic remedies.[44]

These developments led Francisco Orrego Vicūna, who was one of the leading Latin American jurists and practitioners in this field, to write:

> What used to be a useful comparison between international law and a separate domestic legal framework—treaties and contracts—has now become a part of a single legal structure which encompasses both contracts and treaties as well as a host of other instruments ... What is interesting to realize is that the closer the interactions between treaties and contracts the greater the nexus between one and the other that will develop. This is noticeable, for example, when states undertake ... to treat breaches of a contract as a breach of a treaty protecting the rights of investors ... Investment contracts are thus linked automatically by the treaty to international arbitration and the standards of treatment laid down by the treaty and international law.[45]

Orrego Vicūna shows how there is a mixing of treaty law and contract law in this legal structure to enable businesses and states to engage in international investment. These legal structures have established procedures, legally binding decision-making bodies, and enforcement procedures.[46]

---

[43] Ibid.
[44] Ludovica Chiussi, 'The Role of International Investment Law in the Business and Human Rights Legal Process' (2019) 21 *International Community Law Review* 35.
[45] Francisco Orrego Vicūna, 'Of Contracts and Treaties in the Global Market' (2004) 8 *Max Planck Yearbook of United Nations Law* 341.
[46] Muthucumaraswamy Sornarajah, 'Power and Justice in Foreign Investment Arbitration' (1997) 14 *Journal of International Arbitration* 103. In the European Union (EU), businesses can bring claims for a breach of EU law direct to the Court of Justice of the EU: Margot Horspool, Matthew Humphreys, and Michael Wells-Greco, *European Union Law* (OUP, 11th ed., 2021).

In the course of a number of decisions by international arbitration tribunals, such as in the *Urbaser v. Argentina* case discussed in the introduction to this chapter, the issue of the extent to which business has distinct international rights and obligations does arise.[47] These include matters such as whether businesses have international human rights obligations under international investment law,[48] though the structures and procedures of international investment law have been considered by one writer as being such as to inhibit the effective implementation of human rights obligations.[49] Indeed, there are wide-ranging critiques of the current international investment law from Third World and feminist scholars and others, which indicate how the development of this law has assisted business at the expense of people.[50]

There remains debate as to whether this high level of participation by businesses in international investment law is still solely dependent on state consent or whether that consent has dissipated due to the demands of international investment. Whatever view is taken, it is evident that, in reality, businesses are participating in international economic law.

---

[47] Fabio Santacroce, 'The Applicability of Human Rights Law in International Investment Disputes' (2019) 34 *ICSID Review—Foreign Investment Law Journal* 136 and Vivian Kube, *EU Human Rights, International Investment Law and Participation* (Springer, 2019), especially 131–98.

[48] Pierre-Marie Dupuy, Francesco Francioni, and Ernst-Ulrich Petersmann, *Human Rights in International Investment Law and Arbitration* (OUP, 2009); Adam McBeth, *International Economic Actors and Human Rights* (Routledge 2010); Susan Karamanian, 'Human Rights Dimensions of Investment Law' in Erika De Wet and Jure Vidmar (eds), *Hierarchy in International Law* (OUP, 2012), 236; and Jun Zhao, 'Human Rights Accountability of Transnational Corporations: A Potential Response From Bilateral Investment Treaties' (2015) 8 *Journal of East Asia & International Law* 47.

[49] Daria Davitti, *Investment and Human Rights in Armed Conflict: Charting an Elusive Intersection* (Hart, 2019). Also Surya Deva and Tara Van Ho, 'Addressing (In)Equality in Redress: Human Rights-Led Reform of the Investor-State Dispute Settlement Mechanism' (2023) 24 *Journal of World Investment & Trade* 398.

[50] Erika George and Elizabeth Thomas, 'Bringing Human Rights into Bilateral Investment Treaties: South Africa and a Different Approach to International Investment Disputes' (2018) 27 *Transnational Law & Contemporary Problems* 403; Penelope Simons, 'International Law's Invisible Hand and the Future of Corporate Accountability for Violations of Human Rights' (2012) 3 *Journal of Human Rights and the Environment* 5; and James Gathii, 'Third World Approaches to International Economic Governance' in Richard Falk, Balakrishnan Rajagopal, and Jacquelin Stevens (eds), *International Law and the Third World: Reshaping Justice* (Routledge, 2008), 255.

b. International Humanitarian Law

International humanitarian law (IHL) concerns the law relating to armed conflicts, both in terms of the regulation and lawfulness of the conduct of the conflict and the protection of those affected by the conflict.[51] The relevant law is most clearly set out in the Geneva Conventions of 1949 and their 1977 Protocols, and IHL has rules with regard to those directly involved in armed conflict, for both states and armed non-state groups, as well as for civilians.[52]

Many armed conflicts involve armed groups which are not state armed forces, as seen in most civil wars. The International Criminal Tribunal for the Former Yugoslavia explained how armed conflicts can include non-state actors:

> [A]n armed conflict exists whenever there is a resort to armed force between States or protracted armed violence between governmental authorities and organized armed groups or between such groups within a State. International humanitarian law applies from the initiation of such armed conflicts and extends beyond the cessation of hostilities until a general conclusion of peace is reached; or, in the case of internal conflicts, a peaceful settlement is achieved. Until that moment, international humanitarian law continues to apply in the whole territory of the warring States or, in the case of internal conflicts, the whole territory under the control of a party, whether or not actual combat takes place there.[53]

As a consequence, in order to ensure regulation of armed conflicts, IHL specifically includes armed groups—which are non-state actors—as 'combatants' with rights and obligations.[54] This was set out as early as 1907 in the Hague Regulations on War:

---

[51] David Turns, 'The Law of Armed Conflict (International Humanitarian Law)' in Malcolm Evans, *International Law* (OUP, 5th ed., 2018), 840.
[52] Ben Saul and Dapo Akande (eds), *The Oxford Guide to International Humanitarian Law* (OUP, 2020).
[53] *Prosecutor v. Duško Tadić*, Case No. IT-94-1-AR72 (2 October 1995), para. 70.
[54] Anthea Roberts and Sandesh Sivakumaran, 'Lawmaking by Nonstate Actors: Engaging Armed Groups in the Creation of International Humanitarian Law' (2012) 37 *Yale Journal of International Law* 107.

The laws, rights, and duties of war apply not only to armies, but also to militia and volunteer corps fulfilling the following conditions:

1. To be commanded by a person responsible for his subordinates;
2. To have a fixed distinctive emblem recognizable at a distance;
3. To carry arms openly; and
4. To conduct their operations in accordance with the laws and customs of war.[55]

Further, these non-state groups can, under IHL, enter agreements with states and with each other, often with the active engagement of other states and international organizations.[56] An example of a non-state actor becoming party to a treaty was when the Polisario Front, on behalf of the people of Western Sahara—which is not recognized generally as a state—made a unilateral declaration to apply the Geneva Conventions 1949 and the Additional Protocol I to the armed conflict between itself and Morocco, and this was accepted by the body with membership responsibility for the Geneva Conventions.[57] International criminal law can also be applied to enforce some of the obligations of non-state actors under IHL.[58]

While business was to some extent included in earlier understandings of IHL, this has not occurred under current IHL or in the related international criminal law regime.[59] This is seen most clearly in the decision taken by states during the drafting of the International Criminal Court Statute in 1998 to limit its jurisdiction to natural persons and specifically not to include businesses committing or complicit in international crimes.[60] This decision was due to a range of factors, including the large number of other issues that needed to be included in the Statute, a wish to focus on natural

---

[55] Hague Regulations respecting the Laws and Customs of War on Land 1907, Article 1.
[56] For examples of such agreements: Sandesh Sivakumaran, *The Law of Non-International Armed Conflict* (OUP, 2012), 124–32.
[57] Katharine Fortin, 'Universal Declaration by Polisario under API Accepted by Swiss Federal Council' [2015] Armed Groups and International Law, http://armedgroups-internationallaw.org/2015/09/02/unilateral-declaration-by-polisario-under-api-accepted-by-swiss-federal-council.
[58] William Schabas, *International Criminal Law* (Edward Elgar, 2012) and Robert Cryer, Hakan Friman, Darryl Robinson, and Elizabeth Wilmshurst, *An Introduction to International Criminal Law and Procedure* (CUP, 3rd ed., 2014).
[59] Dieter Fleck, *The Handbook of International Humanitarian Law* (OUP, 4th ed., 2021) and Emily Crawford and Alison Pert, *International Humanitarian Law* (CUP, 2nd ed., 2020).
[60] Andrew Clapham, 'The Question of Jurisdiction under International Criminal Law over Legal Persons: Lessons from the Rome Conference' in Menno Kamminga and Saman Zia-Zarifi (eds), *Liability of Multinational Corporations under International Law* (Brill, 2000), 139.

persons, a concern that membership of a business by an individual could create liability, and questions of international enforcement over businesses.[61] Nevertheless, there is ongoing debate as to whether businesses can be complicit in international crimes, with jurists such as Andrew Clapham arguing cogently that, as some international crimes such as torture and genocide are also protected under international human rights law and as, increasingly, national criminal laws allow for corporate crimes, it should be accepted that businesses have international criminal obligations.[62] Further, as discussed in Chapter 6, businesses have been prosecuted in domestic courts on the basis of complicity in relation to breaches of IHL.[63]

c. International Environmental Law

International environmental law was initially seen in the context of state responsibility (discussed above and in the next chapter) for matters such as transboundary pollution.[64] It has since developed in response to transboundary issues of air, land, and water pollution; protection of flora and fauna; and global environmental degradation.[65] There is now a vast array of international instruments concerning environmental matters, and all states have agreed to at least one international instrument that contains provisions relating to the protection of the environment.[66]

International environmental law has created customary international law binding on all states, with one example being the precautionary principle, where measures should be taken, even in the absence of conclusive scientific evidence, to anticipate, prevent, or minimize the causes of

---

[61] Joanna Kyriakakis, 'Corporations before International Criminal Courts: Implications for the International Criminal Justice Project' (2017) 30 *Leiden Journal of International Law* 221.

[62] Andrew Clapham, 'Extending International Criminal Law beyond the Individual to Corporations and Armed Opposition Groups' (2008) 6 *Journal of International Criminal Justice* 899.

[63] For example, *French Republic v. LaFarge*, Appeal No. 19-87-367, French Cour de Cassation, decision of 7 September 2021, Decision—Appeal No. 19-87.367 | Court of Cassation (courdecassation.fr); and prosecution in Sweden against Lundin Energy, 11 November 2021; 'Sweden Charges Lundin Energy Executives with Complicity in Sudan War Crimes (Reuters, 11 November 2021) www.reuters.com/world/africa/sweden-charges-lundin-energy-executives-complicity-sudan-war-crimes-2021-11-11/.

[64] *Trail Smelter Arbitration (USA v. Canada)* (1941) 3 RIAA 1905.

[65] Alan Boyle and Catherine Redgwell, *Birnie, Boyle and Redgwell's International Law and the Environment* (OUP, 4th ed., 2021).

[66] Lavanya Rajamani and Jacqueline Peel (eds), *The Oxford Handbook on International Environmental Law* (OUP, 2021).

environmental damage and/or climate change and to mitigate its adverse effects.⁶⁷ Another is the principle of prevention, which the ICJ has clarified:

> The Court points out that the principle of prevention, as a customary rule, has its origins in the due diligence that is required of a State in its territory. It is 'every State's obligation not to allow knowingly its territory to be used for acts contrary to the rights of other States' (*Corfu Channel (United Kingdom v. Albania), Merits, Judgment, I.C.J. Reports 1949*, p. 22). A State is thus obliged to use all the means at its disposal in order to avoid activities which take place in its territory, or in any area under its jurisdiction, causing significant damage to the environment of another State. This Court has established [in *Legality of the Threat or Use of Nuclear Weapons, Advisory Opinion, I.C.J. Reports 1996 (I)*, p. 242, para. 29] that this obligation 'is now part of the corpus of international law relating to the environment.'⁶⁸

Both these principles can be seen in the development of business and human rights law, as will be shown later in this book. For example, an international obligation may arise where a business causes pollution and when a state refuses to take any legislative, judicial, or administrative action against perpetrators of environmental damage.⁶⁹ There are also a considerable number of states that have laws which place obligations on businesses in relation to environmental harm.⁷⁰ Climate change impacts are discussed in Chapter 8.

6. Conclusions

Businesses are engaged in a number of activities within the broad scope of international law. In some instances this has led to the attribution to states

---

⁶⁷ *Responsibilities and Obligations of States Sponsoring Persons and Entities with respect to Activities in the Area*, Case No. 17, Advisory Opinion (2011) 50 ILM 458, Seabed Disputes Chamber of the International Tribunal of the Law of the Sea, 1 February 2011, paras 125–37.
⁶⁸ *Case Concerning Pulp Mills on the River Uruguay (Argentina v. Uruguay) (Merits)* [2010] ICJ Rep. 14, para. 101.
⁶⁹ Sumudu Atapattu and Carmen Gonzalez, 'The North-South Divide in International Environmental Law: Framing the Issues' in Shawkat Alam, Sumudu Atapattu, Carmen Gonzalez, and Jona Razzaque (eds), *International Environmental Law and the Global South* (CUP, 2015).
⁷⁰ Emma Lees and Jorge Viñuales (eds), *The Oxford Handbook of Comparative Environmental Law* (OUP, 2019).

of actions by businesses—as is discussed in Chapter 4—and the development of structures and mechanisms to deal with the role of businesses when the actions are across state borders.

This chapter shows that the international legal system offers a fragmented approach to the role of business.[71] There are parts of it in which businesses have international legal rights of much the same weight as states, and other parts where the legal rights and obligations of businesses have been entirely dependent on state actions. Nevertheless, there is increasing evidence that the reality of business participation in international law is different from what the dominant, state-only approach would seem to indicate. The next chapter traces the steps in the development of an international legal framework on business and human rights.

---

[71] Report of the Study Group of the International Law Commission finalized by Martti Koskenniemi, *Fragmentation of International Law: Difficulties Arising from the Diversification and Expansion of International Law* (13 April 2006) UN Doc. A/CN.4/L.682 http://legal.un.org/ilc/documentation/english/a_cn4_l682.pdf.

3
International Regulation of Business Concerning Human Rights Issues

1. Context

> I am under no illusion that the conclusion of my mandate will bring all business and human rights challenges to an end. But [the UN Human Rights] Council endorsement of the Guiding Principles [on Business and Human Rights] will mark the end of the beginning. Therefore, I very much hope that the Council seizes the opportunity provided by the remarkable consensus and convergence of approaches that has been achieved, endorse the Guiding Principles, and then build on this solid foundation, step by step, in the years ahead. Human rights are at stake—and so, too, is the social sustainability of enterprises and markets as we know them.[1]

This statement by Professor John Ruggie, the Special Representative of the Secretary-General on business and human rights (SRSG), who was the key architect of the UNGPs, was made on 16 June 2011 to the UN Human Rights Council. After his speech, the UNGPs were unanimously endorsed by the Council.[2]

---

[1] John Ruggie, Presentation of Report to UN Human Rights Council, 30 May 2011, Opening Statement to United Nations Human Rights Council (https://media.business-humanrights.org/media/documents/files/media/documents/ruggie-statement-to-un-human-rights-council-30-may-2011.pdf), 6–7.

[2] UN Human Rights Council, 'Human Rights and Transnational Corporations and Other Business Enterprises' UN Doc. A/HRC/RES/17/4 (16 June 2011), 2 www.unglobalcompact.org/docs/issues_doc/human_rights/A.HRC.17.RES.17.4.pdf. The UN Human Rights Council is an elected body of 47 states. In its resolution endorsing the UNGPs, the Council also resolved

John Ruggie called it the 'end of the beginning' because, for more than 30 years—as summarized in Chapter 1—successive efforts to develop universal international standards, dealing with the adverse impacts on human rights connected with the activities of transnational corporation (TNCs) and other business enterprises, had not succeeded.[3] It was his hope that there was now a new way forward due to the UNGPs.

This chapter will consider the UNGPs in general and their influence on international regulation. It will also analyse the legal nature of the UNGPs and related international regulation, and what that means for international legal regulation in the area of business and human rights.

2. The UN Guiding Principles

As noted in Chapter 1, the UNGPs are founded on—and structured to follow—the Framework.[4] There are, accordingly, three 'pillars' to the UNGPs, 'Protect, Respect and Remedy', being:

- Pillar I: States have a duty to protect against human rights abuses committed by business enterprises;
- Pillar II: Business enterprises have a responsibility to respect human rights; and
- Pillar III: Victims of business-related human rights abuses need access to effective remedies.

These pillars are each the subject of a separate chapter in this book.

The UNGPs were intended to provide practical guidance on how states and businesses can enhance 'standards and practices ... so as to achieve tangible results for affected individuals and communities'.[5] There are 31 Guiding Principles (GPs) in total in the UNGPs, each accompanied by a

---

to establish a Working Group on the issue of human rights and transnational corporations and other business enterprises, with a mandate, inter alia, to promote the effective and comprehensive dissemination and implementation of the UNGPs (WGBHR).

[3] César Rodríguez-Garavito (ed.), *Business and Human Rights: Beyond the End of the Beginning* (CUP, 2017).

[4] SRSG, 'Report of the Special Representative of the Secretary-General on the issue of human rights and transnational corporations other business enterprises, John and Ruggie' Human Rights Council Eighth Session, UN Doc. A/HRC/8/5 (7 April 2008), www.reports-and-materials.org/Ruggie-report-7-Apr-2008.pdf [the Framework].

[5] UNGPs, 1.

short Commentary. Further guidance (the Interpretive Guide) elaborating on the UNGPs, in particular the principles relating to businesses' responsibility to respect human rights, was subsequently published by the Office of the UN High Commissioner for Human Rights (OHCHR).[6]

The creation of the UNGPs was a significant achievement of the SRSG and his team. They were developed by a process which John Ruggie called 'principled pragmatism', being 'an unflinching commitment to the principle of strengthening the promotion and protection of human rights as it relates to business, coupled with a pragmatic attachment to what works best in creating change where it matters most—in the daily lives of people'.[7] It also had to survive the rigours of a process through the UN system.

John Ruggie has stated that there were six key strategies which he adopted, as SRSG, which helped to facilitate the UNGPs through this process:

1. Creating a minimum common knowledge base that permits a shared conversation to take place;
2. Ensuring the legitimacy of the mandate process, quite apart from questions of substance;
3. Bringing new players to the table whose insights and influence could advance the agenda;
4. Road testing core proposals to demonstrate that they actually can work on the ground;
5. Having an end-game strategy and effective political leadership to execute it where the opportunities exist or where these can be created;
6. Working towards convergence among standard-setting bodies in order to achieve scale and benefit from the broadest possible portfolio of implementing mechanisms.[8]

Indeed, the process by which the UNGPs were created is often considered a key reason for why they were adopted by states and accepted by many businesses and civil society. As Radu Mares has noted:

---

[6] OHCHR, 'The Corporate Responsibility to Respect Human Rights: An Interpretive Guide' UN Doc. HR/PUB/12/02 (10 October 2012), www.ohchr.org/Documents/Issues/Business/RtRInterpretativeGuide.pdf [Interpretive Guide].

[7] Interim Report of the Special Representative of the Secretary-General on the Issue of Human Rights and Transnational Corporations and Other Business Enterprises, E/CN.4/2006/97, 2006 [SRSG Report 2006], para. 81.

[8] John Ruggie, *Just Business* (Norton, 2013) [Ruggie, Just Business], 129.

Linked to the task of securing stakeholder buy-in, Ruggie employed a participatory approach throughout his mandates. He had arranged seminars, conferences, field studies and other engagement avenues that he used to collect views and communicate his work. Make no mistake, this approach was also clearly outlined in the UN mandate as a reaction to some criticisms that the Draft Norms process had received. Furthermore, Ruggie networked widely and commissioned studies from various organisations, law firms and experts in an attempt to leverage expertise on punctual issues. This approach has generated a remarkable effervescency and engagement in the legal community, for example. Finally, Ruggie engaged with countless individuals, critics and supporters alike, through open letters or private exchanges.[9]

This participatory approach by the SRSG was impressive. It generated considerable interest and engagement in the process by many stakeholders who might have been thought to be sceptical of it, including business, and enabled the final product to be welcomed by many stakeholders, as noted in the quotation above.

This does not mean that the UNGPs are without criticism. There have been many criticisms of its concepts, terminologies, and applications. For example, it has been claimed that the ruling out of extraterritorial obligations on a state with regard to business activities in the UNGPs (discussed in Chapter 4) has 'set the bar clearly below the current state of international human rights law'.[10] It has been argued that it is not clear what is meant by the 'responsibility of a business enterprise', especially as the distinction in terminology between a 'duty' of state (which is a legal obligation) and a business enterprise's 'responsibility' (which is essentially voluntary) can be confusing, not least as one of the core aspects of international law concerns 'state responsibility'—as discussed in Chapter 2 and elaborated on in Chapter 4—which deals with legal obligations.[11] Others criticize

---

[9] Radu Mares, 'Business and Human Rights After Ruggie: Foundations, the Art of Simplification and the Imperative of Cumulative Progress' in Radu Mares (ed.), *The UN Guiding Principles on Business and Human Rights—Foundations and Implementation* (Martinus Nijhoff, 2012), 1, 6–7 (footnotes omitted).

[10] Olivier De Schutter, 'Towards a New Treaty on Business and Human Rights' (2015) 1 *Business and Human Rights Journal* 41, 45.

[11] Radu Mares, '"Respect" Human Rights: Concept and Convergence' in Robert Bird, Daniel Cahoy, and Jamie Darin Prenkert (eds), *Law, Business and Human Rights: Bridging the Gap* (Edward Elgar, 2014).

the UNGPs for not imposing direct legal obligations on businesses,[12] for not looking at broader obligations on states to fulfil human rights and so creating a 'conceptual anarchy' in conflating concepts,[13] and for failing to acknowledge the need for specific protection for women in relation to negative impacts of business activities.[14] The extent to which it is legally binding is also an issue, which is discussed below.

Nevertheless, it is clear that the development and creation of the UNGPs has fundamentally changed the debate about the responsibilities of business for human rights abuses and has provided a framework for analysis. It is now undoubtedly the initial primary location for discussions about this area.

3. Influence of the UNGPs on International Regulation

The UNGPs were directly influential in the inclusion of human rights responsibilities on business in other international instruments. In particular, the UNGPs led to revisions of the OECD Guidelines in 2011, and the ILO Multinational Enterprises Declaration in 2017, as well as the International Finance Corporation's Performance Standards in 2012 and the Equator Principles in 2013, each of which is discussed below. It has also influenced some national and regional legislation, discussed in Chapter 7, and is intricately linked to the draft treaty on business and human rights, which is discussed in Chapter 8.

a. OECD Guidelines

The Organisation for Economic Co-operation and Development (OECD) Guidelines for Multinational Enterprises were revised in 2011 specifically

---

[12] David Bilchitz, *Fundamental Rights and the Legal Obligations of Business* (CUP, 2021) and the general discussion in Chapter 2.

[13] Surya Deva, *Regulation of Corporate Human Rights: Humanising Business* (Routledge, 2014), 110.

[14] Penelope Simons and Melisa Handl, 'Relations of Ruling: A Feminist Critique of the United Nations Guiding Principles on Business and Human Rights and Violence against Women in the Context of Resource Extraction' (2019) 31 *Canadian Journal of Women and the Law* 113.

to align with the UNGPs.¹⁵ John Ruggie stated that the revised OECD Guidelines were 'the first [inter-governmental instrument] to take the Guiding Principles' concept of risk-based due diligence for human rights impacts and extend it to all major areas of business ethics'.¹⁶ The OECD has since published a number of important Responsible Business Conduct Guidance documents in relation to particular sectors and on human rights due diligence more generally.¹⁷ These apply to human rights impacts of business related to, for example, conflict, labour rights, bribery and corruption, disclosure and consumer interests, and in the supply chain more generally.¹⁸

In addition, the OECD extends the responsibilities of business to include the environment, being an aspect that was within its previous revision. The OECD Guidelines now provide:

> [Business] enterprises should, within the framework of laws, regulations and administrative practices in the countries in which they operate, and in consideration of relevant international agreements, principles, objectives, and standards, take due account of the need to protect the environment, public health and safety, and generally to conduct their activities in a manner contributing to the wider goal of sustainable development.¹⁹

This extension to the environment includes encouraging, in their supply chain, '[the] development and provision of products or services that have no undue environmental impacts; are safe in their intended use; reduce greenhouse gas emissions; are efficient in their consumption of energy and natural resources; can be reused, recycled, or disposed of safely'.²⁰ In 2023,

---

[15] Statement by Professor Roel Nieuwenkamp, the Chair of the negotiations which led to the 2011 revision of the OECD Guidelines, as set out in *Expert Letters and Statements on the Application of the OECD Guidelines for Multinational Enterprises and UN Guiding Principles on Business and Human Rights in the Context of the Financial Sector*, June 2014, 18–20.

[16] John Ruggie and Tamaryn Nelson, 'Human Rights and the OECD Guidelines for Multinational Enterprises: Normative Innovations and Implementation Challenges', Corporate Social Responsibility Initiative Working Paper No. 66 (May 2015), 13.

[17] For example, OECD, Due Diligence Guidance for Responsible Supply Chain of Minerals from Conflict-Affected Areas (OECD, 2016); OECD, Responsible Business Conduct for Institutional Investors: Key Considerations for Due Diligence under the OECD Guidelines for MNEs (OECD, 2016).

[18] OECD Guidelines, Commentary on General Policies, para. 14.

[19] OECD Guidelines, Section VI Environment.

[20] Ibid., Art. 6.

the OECD Guidelines were updated to clarify some aspects, including in relation to climate change.[21]

One clear obligation of OECD member states under the OECD Guidelines is to establish National Contact Points (NCPs), in order to promote and implement the Guidelines. A key role of NCPs is to review complaints brought against businesses alleged to be acting contrary to the OECD Guidelines, and so provide a mechanism for non-judicial dispute settlement. This role is discussed in Chapter 6 in relation to access to remedies.

b. ILO Multinational Enterprises Declaration

In March 2017, the International Labour Organization (ILO) Multinational Enterprises Declaration (ILO MNE Declaration) was amended so as to align with the UNGPs.[22] It provides guidance on human rights due diligence processes in achieving decent work, sustainable businesses, more inclusive growth, and better sharing of the benefits of foreign direct investment.[23] For example, it reinforces the UNGPs Commentary to Guiding Principle 12 in providing:

> Enterprises, including multinational enterprises, should carry out due diligence to identify, prevent, mitigate and account for how they address their actual and potential adverse impacts that relate to internationally recognized human rights, understood, at a minimum, as those expressed in the International Bill of Human Rights and the principles concerning fundamental rights set out in the ILO Declaration on Fundamental Principles and Rights at Work.[24]

The ILO MNE Declaration also emphasizes the importance of meaningful consultation with potentially affected groups and other relevant stakeholders, including workers' organizations, in the identification and

---

[21] They were also renamed in 2023 to become the OECD Guidelines for Multinational Enterprises on Responsible Business Conduct , https://mneguidelines.oecd.org/mneguidelines/.

[22] Preamble to 2017 revision, www.ilo.org/empent/areas/mne-declaration/lang--en/index.htm.

[23] ILO, 'Multinational Enterprises and Enterprise Engagement Unit (MULTI) (ENTERPRISES)', www.ilo.org/empent/units/multinational-enterprises/lang--en/index.htm.

[24] ILO MNE Declaration, General Policy 10.

assessment of actual or potential adverse human rights impacts resulting from a business's own activities or from their business relationships.[25]

c. IFC Performance Standards and the Equator Principles

The International Finance Corporation (IFC), which is part of the World Bank, has a range of Environmental and Social Performance Standards, which 'define IFC clients' responsibilities for managing their environmental and social risks'.[26] These are applicable to those to whom the IFC provides finance for specific projects, which are primarily businesses or others in the private sector.

In 2012 the IFC's Performance Standards were revised and now include reference to the UNGPs, with the rationale for this being set out:[27]

> Business should respect human rights, which means to avoid infringing on the human rights of others and address adverse human rights impacts business may cause or contribute to. Each of the Performance Standards has elements related to human rights dimensions that a project may face in the course of its operations. Due diligence against these Performance Standards will enable the client to address many relevant human rights issues in its project.[28]

Compliance with these Performance Standards is made effective through the determination by the IFC as to which business can seek funding from the IFC, as well as oversight by the Compliance Advisor Ombudsperson (CAO) mechanism.[29] This mechanism allows communities affected on

---

[25] Ibid., 10(e). See Jernej Letnar Černič, 'The ILO Tripartite Declaration of Principles Concerning Multinational Enterprises and Social Policy Revisited: Is There a Need for Its Reform?' [2019] *European Yearbook of International Economic Law* 193.

[26] IFC Environmental and Social Performance Standards (2012), www.ifc.org/wps/wcm/connect/Topics_Ext_Content/IFC_External_Corporate_Site/Sustainability-At-IFC/Policies-Standards/Performance-Standards.

[27] Ibid. On the background to this, see the submission to the SGSR prior to the UNGPs from NGOs: *The International Finance Corporation's Performance Standards and The Equator Principles: Respecting Human Rights and Remedying Violations?*, www.ciel.org/wp-content/uploads/2015/05/Ruggie_Submission.pdf.

[28] IFC, Guidance Note 1, 1: www.ifc.org/wps/wcm/connect/9fc3aaef-14c3-4489-acf1-a1c43d7f86ec/GN_English_2012_Full-Document_updated_June-27-2019.pdf?MOD=AJPERES&CVID=mRQmrEJ.

[29] IFC, 'Office of the Compliance Advisor/Ombudsman', www.cao-ombudsman.org/.

the ground by an IFC-funded project to bring a complaint about the IFC funding of a project, though this is limited to a complaint that the IFC did not follow its own processes. There is some evidence that this mechanism can be effective, such as in relation to environmental matters,[30] with possible consequent pressure on the IFC to ensure that borrowers do undertake human rights due diligence. There are, though, critiques of the effectiveness of the CAO mechanism.[31]

The Equator Principles also concern financial provision to private business.[32] They are a 'risk management framework, adopted by financial institutions, for determining, assessing and managing environmental and social risk in projects ... [and] are primarily intended to provide a minimum standard for due diligence and monitoring to support responsible risk decision-making'.[33] Over 100 financial institutions across nearly 40 states have adopted them for use in decisions about certain types of projects in asset finance and investment.[34]

The Equator Principles were amended in 2013, in light of the UNGPs, with these amendments including the introduction of human rights and environmental conditions to those seeking finance.[35] As stated in the revised Preamble to the Equator Principles:

> We recognise the importance of climate change, biodiversity, and human rights, and believe negative impacts on project-affected ecosystems, communities, and the climate should be avoided where possible. If these impacts are unavoidable they should be minimised, mitigated, and/or offset ... We therefore recognise that our role as financiers affords us opportunities to promote responsible environmental stewardship and socially responsible development, including fulfilling our

---

[30] For example, 'Probe Finds IFC Investment in Tata Power Project Breaching Norms' (21 March 2017), www.news18.com/news/business/probe-finds-ifc-investment-in-tata-power-project-breaching-norms-1362325.html and Ademolal Adeyemi, 'Changing the Face of Sustainable Development in Developing Countries: The Role of the International Finance Corporation' [2014] *Environmental Law Review* 91.

[31] Sara Seck, 'Indigenous Rights, Environmental Rights, or Stakeholder Engagement: Comparing FC and OECD Approaches to Implementation of the Business Responsibility to Respect Human Rights' (2016) 12 *McGill International Journal of Sustainable Development, Law and Policy* 53.

[32] The Equator Principles are available at https://equator-principles.com/about/.

[33] Ibid. See John Conley and Cynthia Williams, 'Global Banks as Global Sustainability Regulators?: The Equator Principles' (2011) 33 *Law & Policy* 542.

[34] Equator Principles, https://equator-principles.com/members-reporting/.

[35] The third edition of the Equator Principles (EP III) is available at https://equator-principles.com/about/.

responsibility to respect human rights by undertaking due diligence in accordance with the Equator Principles.[36]

The UNGPs are expressly referred to in a footnote to this statement. However, the lack of an explicit requirement for all borrowers to undertake human rights impact assessments in all circumstances has been criticized as making the impact of the UNGPs—through the Equator Principles—ineffective and uneven at best in this sector.[37] The Equator Principles also lack any effective access to remedy for victims.[38]

4. Influence on National Regulation

The UNGPs and the OECD Guidelines have been referenced in a number of national and regional pieces of legislation. For example, both were referred to during the debate on what became the French Duty of Vigilance Act 2017[39] and the Netherlands Child Labour Due Diligence Act 2019, with part of the title of the latter being taken from the core element of business responsibility under the UNGPs. The UNGPs and the OECD Guidelines were also directly considered in the development of the German Corporate Due Diligence in Supply Chains Act 2021 and the Norwegian Transparency Act 2021. These pieces of legislation are considered more closely in Chapter 7. There are also other pieces of national legislation which are consistent with aspects of the UNGPs but do not make direct reference to it, such as the Sierra Leone's Customary Land Rights Act 2022.[40]

The European Commission proposal for a Corporate Sustainability Due Diligence Directive, issued in February 2022 (also analysed in Chapter 7), refers directly to the UNGPs and the OECD Guidelines many times in its

---

[36] Ibid., Preamble.
[37] Christopher Wright, 'Global Banks, the Environment, and Human Rights: The Impact of the Equator Principles on Lending Policies and Practices' [2012] *Global Environmental Politics* 56.
[38] An independent complaints system has been set up by a civil society organization, BankTrack: https://www.equator-complaints.org/about_us.= On access to remedy, see Chapter 6.
[39] Stéphane Brabant, Elsa Savourey, and Charlotte Michon, 'The Vigilance Plan: Cornerstone of the Corporate Duty of Vigilance Law' *Revue internationale de la compliance et de l'éthique des affaires* (14 December 2017).
[40] Umaru Fofana, 'Sierra Leone Passes New Laws to Boost Landowners' Rights' *Reuters* (8 August 2022).

Introduction and its Preamble.[41] For example, paragraph 12 of the proposed Preamble provides:

> This Directive is in coherence with the EU Action Plan on Human Rights and Democracy 2020–2024. This Action Plan defines as a priority to strengthen the Union's engagement to actively promote the global implementation of the United Nations Guiding Principles on Business and Human Rights and other relevant international guidelines such as the OECD Guidelines for Multinational Enterprises, including by advancing relevant due diligence standards.

Therefore, the UNGPs and OECD Guidelines have provided a clear basis for legislative action at national and regional levels. As discussed in Chapter 7, some states in other regions, including Asia-Pacific, and Latin America and the Caribbean, have not taken legislative action but have shown engagement with the UNGPs, such as producing national action plans on business and human rights.[42]

In relation to case law at the national level, a 2021 report showed that the UNGPs have been increasingly referred to across a wide range of national jurisdictions and international courts and tribunals in diverse matters.[43] For example, a court in South Africa made reference to the UNGPs in relation to state obligations concerning access to remedies for a debtor,[44] as did a court in the Netherlands in relation to an oil business's obligations concerning climate change.[45] These are instances of the effective enforcement of the UNGPs as part of national law considerations.[46]

---

[41] European Commission, Proposal for a Directive on corporate sustainability due diligence and annex: ttps://commission.europa.eu/publications/proposal-directive-corporate-sustainability-due-diligence-and-annex_en.. See, for example, the Introduction pp. 2, 5, and 9; and the Preamble paras 5, 6, and 44. Discussions on the final terms of the Directive are ongoing at the time of writing.

[42] OHCHR, National action plans on business and human rights, https://www.ohchr.org/en/special-procedures/wg-business/national-action-plans-business-and-human-rights.

[43] Debevoise & Plimpton LLP, UN Guiding Principles on Business and Human Rights at 10: The Impact of the UNGPs on Courts and Judicial Mechanisms (2021)..

[44] *In re University of Stellenbosch Legal Aid Clinic et al.*, High Court of South Africa (Western Cape Division, Cape Town), Case No. 16703/14 (8 July 2015), Judgment, para. 11, [2015] ZAWCHC 99, www.saflii.org/za/cases/ZAWCHC/2015/99.html. This part of the decision was not directly considered on appeal.

[45] *Milieudefensie v. Royal Dutch Shell plc* [2021] C/09/571932, ECLI:NL:RBDHA:2021:5339, Rechtbank Den Haag, C/09/571932/HA ZA 19-379. This case is discussed in Chapter 8.

[46] Other courts have not taken this approach, with the UK Supreme Court not referring to the UNGPs in their decisions, even when asked to do so by parties before it: see Intervention (amicus) in *Vedanta Resources Ltd v. Lungowe* [2019] UKSC 20.

In relation to case law at the international level, the UNGPs have been specifically referred to by, for example, the Inter-American Court of Human Rights, in relation to the obligations of the state under the UNGPs to ensure that a human rights impact assessment was conducted.[47] In addition, an international investment arbitration tribunal considered that the UNGPs were 'the basic document' that applies international human rights standards to companies.[48]

5. Legal Nature of International Regulation

One important matter for international law in this area concerns the extent to which these international documents are legal binding and, if so, on which actors. The UNGPs state in their introduction:

These Guiding Principles are grounded in recognition of:
(a) States' *existing* obligations to respect, protect and fulfil human rights and fundamental freedoms;
(b) The role of business enterprises as specialized organs of society performing specialized functions, required to comply with all applicable laws and to respect human rights;
(c) The need for rights and obligations to be matched to appropriate and effective remedies when breached ...

Nothing in these Guiding Principles should be read as creating new international law obligations, or as limiting or undermining any legal obligations a State may have undertaken or be subject to under international law with regard to human rights.[49]

This statement is carefully crafted to indicate that the state's 'duty' under Pillar I is intended merely to replicate the existing international legal obligations which states already have under international human rights law.[50] As will be seen in the following chapter, this is a generally accurate statement,

---

[47] Inter-American Court of Human Rights, *Case of the Kaliña and Lokono Peoples v. Suriname*, Judgment of 15 November 2015, paras 223–6, https://iachr.lls.edu/cases/kaliña-and-lokono-peoples-v-suriname.
[48] *Urbaser v. Argentina*, para. 1196— discussed in Chapter 2.
[49] General Principles (Preamble) to UNGPs, 1 (emphasis added).
[50] This confirmed by John Ruggie in Ruggie, *Just Business*, note 8, 84.

though some have argued that the UNGPs could have been more expansive in their terminology to reflect current legal obligations of states under international human rights law.[51]

The aspects of the UNGPs which deal with business responsibilities are, as set out in the quotation above, specifically not intended to be legally binding on business. There is, nevertheless, an argument that setting out business responsibilities, in the way that the UNGPs do, clarifies international law and could be considered to codify the position under international human rights law.[52] Indeed, the SRSG seemed to be aware of this when he wrote:

> The endorsement by states of the corporate responsibility to respect human rights and how to discharge it gives official recognition to a norm that was previously only grounded in the realm of social expectations.[53]

The terminology of a 'norm' used in this context does not automatically equate it to being a legally binding matter of international law. Indeed, Ruggie, as a political scientist, could be using the term 'norm' in a social rather than legal sense,[54] as part of his approach to 'polycentric governance', which is intended to bring together public governance, civil governance, and corporate governance.[55] Nevertheless, the use of the term 'norm' does indicate that the responsibilities on business set out in the UNGPs could be more than mere voluntary expectations.[56]

The term often used about the UNGPs is that they are 'soft law'.[57] This aims to distinguish them from legal binding international law such as

---

[51] De Schutter, note 10, 45.

[52] A similar argument has been made in relation to the work of the International Law Commission: see Danae Azaria, The International Law Commission's Return to the Law of Sources of International Law (2019) 13 *FIU Law Review* 989.

[53] Ruggie, *Just Business*, note 8, 125.

[54] Ibid., 91. Also John Ruggie, 'The Social Construction of the UN Guiding Principles on Business and Human Rights' in Surya Deva and David Birchall (eds), *Research Handbook on Business and Human Rights* (Edward Elgar, 2020), 63.

[55] John Ruggie 'Global Governance and "New Governance Theory": Lessons from Business and Human Rights' (2014) 20 *Global Governance* 8.

[56] Enrico Partiti, 'Polycentricity and Polyphony in International Law: Interpreting the Corporate Responsibility to Respect Human Rights' (2021) 70 *International and Comparative Law Quarterly* 133 and Mark Taylor, 'The Ruggie Framework: Polycentric Regulation and the Implications for Corporate Social Responsibility' (2011) 5 *Nordic Journal of Applied Ethics* 9.

[57] See generally the 'Symposium on Soft and Hard Law on Business and Human Rights' in (2020) *AJIL Unbound*..

treaties (which could be considered as 'hard law'). However, as Alan Boyle and Christine Chinkin note:

> Perhaps the most important point to make at the outset is that some of the forms of 'soft law' under consideration here are potentially law-making in much the same way that multilateral treaties are potentially law-making. The proposition is not that non-binding declarations or resolutions of the General Assembly or any other soft law instrument are invariably law *per se*, but that they may be evidence of existing law, or formative of the *opinio juris* or state practice that generates new law ... Moreover, widespread acceptance of soft law instruments will tend to legitimise conduct and make it harder to sustain the legality of opposing positions.[58]

Thus, Boyle and Chinkin argue that an international instrument may have a normative quality, and so become legally binding for the participants in the international legal system, no matter what it is called. Further, writers have argued that there is no strict binary relationship of 'law or no law' or 'hard law or soft law', as the reality is that the normative nature of law is a matter of degree, with there being a spectrum or sliding scale in which increasing degrees of legally binding obligations arise.[59] Laurence Boisson de Chazournes has noted:

> To conceive the distinction between binding law and non-binding law in the 'Big Bang way' – i.e. that what is not binding has no legal effect— is highly simplistic ... [T]here are ... cases where soft law instruments can be final products and not just intermediate steps. The best-known case is where a soft law instrument aspires to serve as a model for other instruments. In these cases, it has all the characteristics of a hard law instrument, except that it is not binding ... [S]oft law instruments blur the limits of the threshold of what constitutes law since the absence of a

---

[58] Alan Boyle and Christine Chinkin, *The Making of International Law* (OUP, 2007), 211–12.

[59] Dinah Shelton, 'International Law and Relative Normativity' in Malcolm Evans (ed.), *International Law* (OUP, 4th ed., 2014), 137, 141 notes: '[n]ew topics of regulation also require innovative means of rule-making with respect to non-State actors, who generally are not parties to treaties or involved in the creation of customary international law. The emergence of codes of conduct and other "soft law" reflects this development.'

binding character does not exclude the existence of legal effects. There is therefore a normative gradation.⁶⁰

Certainly, the decision in *Milieudefensie v. Royal Dutch Shell*, discussed in Chapter 8, is indicative of an approach which uses an international document—in that instance the UNGPs—to help form a legally binding decision in a case in domestic law.

Perhaps the position is that the UNGPs are, to use the idea in the quotation above, 'a soft law instrument [which] aspires to serve as a model for other instruments' and legitimises conduct consistent with it. The clearest statement about the nature of the UNGPs is from a UN High Commissioner for Human Rights, Zeid Ra'ad Al Hussein, who described the UNGPs as 'the global authoritative standard, providing a blueprint for the steps all states and businesses should take to uphold human rights'.⁶¹

There is also some further embedding of the 'global authoritative standards' of the UNGPs in their influence on other international regulation. For example, while states make a binding commitment to implement the OECD Guidelines, that is not the situation for businesses in those states. For example, the Foreword to the current OECD Guidelines states:

> The OECD Guidelines for Multinational Enterprises are recommendations addressed by governments to multinational enterprises operating in or from adhering countries. They provide non-binding principles and standards for responsible business conduct in a global context consistent with applicable laws and internationally recognised standards. The Guidelines are the only multilaterally agreed and comprehensive code of responsible business conduct that governments have committed to promoting.

Therefore, while these OECD Guidelines are not legally binding for business, they have a strong influential effect, not least through the commitment to them by OECD member states. This is reinforced by the fact that many provisions of the OECD Guidelines directly refer to the actions by

---

⁶⁰ Laurence Boisson de Chazournes, 'The International Law Commission in a Mirror—Forms, Impact and Authority' in United Nations, *Seventy Years of the International Law Commission* (UN, 2020), 133, 136.

⁶¹ Zeid Ra'ad Al Hussein, 'Ethical Pursuit of Prosperity' The Law Society Gazette (23 March 2015))..

businesses in clear terms, such as 'enterprises should' take certain actions.[62] This includes that 'enterprises should ... co-operate through legitimate processes in the remediation of adverse human rights impacts'.[63]

In contrast, the ILO Multinational Enterprises Declaration is a legal document which is binding on governments, employers, and workers, even though it has limited direct legal impact on the latter two groups. It is valuable as a method by which the ILO can work with states and with other international organizations to make change.[64] For example, the ILO has worked with multilateral development banks in the monitoring of labour issues.[65]

In addition, there are an increasing number of business associations and individual businesses which are applying the UNGPs in their standards. For example, the International Council of Mining and Metals (ICMM) expresses the expectations on its members (which include some of the largest extractive businesses) in these terms:

> [To] support the UN Guiding Principles on Business and Human Rights by developing a policy commitment to respect human rights, undertaking human rights due diligence and providing for or cooperating in processes to enable the remediation of adverse human rights impacts that members have caused or contributed to.[66]

Many other sectors have similar guidance for their members' businesses, such as the International Code of Conduct for private security businesses[67]

---

[62] For example, OECD Guidelines, Part I (on General Policies): 'Enterprises should: 1. Contribute to economic, environmental and social progress with a view to achieving sustainable development. 2. Respect the internationally recognised human rights of those affected by their activities...'

[63] OECD Guidelines, Part IV, para. 6.

[64] Virginia Mantouvalou, 'Legal Construction of Structures of Exploitation' in Hugh Collins, Gillian Lester, and Virginia Mantouvalou (eds), *Philosophical Foundations of Labour Law* (OUP, 2018), 188.

[65] For example, World Bank, 'ILO Report Says Uzbekistan Making Progress on Labor Reforms, Organized Child Labor Phased-Out' (1 February 2017), www.worldbank.org/en/news/press-release/2017/01/31/ilo-report-says-uzbekistan-making-progress-on-labor-refo rms-organized-child-labor-phased-out. It has been well analysed that all international organizations, including those involved in international development and finance, have potential and actual adverse human rights impacts and should be expected to implement their obligations consistently with the UNGPs: WGBHR, 'Development Finance Institutions and Human Rights' UN Doc. A/HRC/53/24/Add.4 (12 June 2023).

[66] ICMM, Mining Principles, section 3.1, https://www.icmm.com/en-gb/our-principles/mining-principles/principle-3.

[67] International Code of Conduct Association, https://icoca.ch.

and the Dutch banking sector.[68] Some individual businesses across the world also state their aim to comply with the UNGPs in their public statements, as noted in Chapter 2, and this is confirmed by empirical research.[69]

Therefore, the UNGPs, combined with their influence on other international instruments, do reinforce their development as having some legal effects and as going beyond being merely voluntary for businesses. There is now a breadth of global standards that builds a structure towards the creation of binding international law.

6. Conclusions

There have been almost 50 years of attempts to create international regulation of business activities which adversely affect human rights. These have been fraught with disagreements over the scope, extent, and legal nature of this regulation. With the advent of the UNGPs in 2011, a new way forward was created and generally accepted.[70]

The UNGPs have had a direct influence on existing international regulation in this area. This includes a wide sweep of regulation, including on financial and labour issues, and in the work of international organizations and states. International regulation in this area has become coherent and consistent, which is a significant advance from where it was before the UNGPs were adopted. It is also having a direct influence on national legislation and some national cases. The UNGPs are clearly now the 'global authoritative standard' and the starting point to consider all issues concerning business and human rights. An analysis of the three pillars of the UNGPs will be undertaken in the next three chapters.

---

[68] Dutch Banking Sector Agreement on international responsible business conduct regarding human rights, https://www.imvoconvenanten.nl/en/banking.
[69] For example, Robert McCorquodale, Lise Smit, Stuart Neely, and Robin Brooks, 'Human Rights Due Diligence in Law and Practice: Good Practices and Challenges of Business Enterprises' (2017) 2 *Business and Human Rights Journal* 195.
[70] See generally the series of articles reviewing the UNGPs after 10 years in (2021) 6 *Business and Human Rights Journal* 179–351.

4
State Obligations Concerning Business and Human Rights

1. Context

In 1996, the Social and Economic Rights Action Center (SERAC), a Nigerian-based civil society organization, and the Economic and Social Rights Action Center (ESRAC), a New York-based civil society organization, brought a complaint (known as a 'communication') to the African Commission on Human and People's Rights on behalf of the Ogoni people living in the Niger Delta region of Nigeria. This was an allegation against the Nigerian government under the provisions of the African Charter on Human and Peoples' Rights (ACHPR), which is a treaty currently ratified by 55 states which are members of the African Union (the successor to the Organization of African Unity). The African Commission summarized the allegations as follows:

> The Communication alleges that the oil consortium [including Shell Petroleum Development Corporation and the Nigerian state oil company] has exploited oil reserves in Ogoniland with no regard for the health or environment of the local communities, disposing toxic wastes into the environment and local waterways in violation of applicable international environmental standards. The consortium also neglected and/or failed to maintain its facilities causing numerous avoidable spills in the proximity of villages. The resulting contamination of water, soil and air has had serious short and long-term health impacts, including skin infections, gastrointestinal and respiratory ailments, and increased risk of cancers, and neurological and reproductive problems .... [T]he Nigerian Government has condoned and facilitated these violations by placing the legal and military powers of the State at the disposal of the oil companies.[1]

---

[1] *Social and Economic Rights Action Center and the Economic and Social Rights Action Center v. Nigeria*, African Commission, Communication No. 155/96 (2001–02) 1985–84, paras 2–3 [*SERAC v. Nigeria*].

It was, therefore, an allegation of actions and omissions by oil companies on the basis of which the Nigerian government had breached the human rights of the Ogoni people under the ACHPR.

The complaint alleged violations of a number of human rights in the ACHPR, being the right to non-discrimination, right to life, right to property, right to health, right to family life, right to dispose of their natural resources, and right to the environment.[2] The African Commission eventually found (after five years) that Nigeria had breached every one of these human rights. Their finding included the following statement:

> The Commission notes that in the present case, despite its obligation to protect persons against interferences in the enjoyment of their rights, the Government of Nigeria facilitated the destruction of Ogoniland. Contrary to its Charter obligations and despite such internationally established principles, the Nigerian Government has given the green light to private actors, and the oil Companies in particular, to devastatingly affect the well-being of the Ogonis. By any measure of standards, its practice falls short of the minimum conduct expected of governments.[3]

As a consequence, the African Commission found that the Nigerian government was in breach of the ACHPR. This was despite the fact that many of the actions which formed the basis of the complaint were committed by the oil companies as private businesses. Indeed, the African Commission noted that these actions by the oil companies had occurred 'following [the Nigerian government's] clear blessing or not'.[4]

Even though some of the actions by the oil companies had evidently abused human rights, including when acting without the Nigerian government's consent, those businesses were not found to have breached the ACHPR. Only the government of Nigeria was in breach. This is because *only states* have legal obligations under the ACHPR. It is the same position under all international human rights treaties: only states have international legal obligations under human rights treaties.

---

[2] ACHPR, Arts 2, 4, 14, 16, 18(1), 21, and 24.
[3] *SERAC v. Nigeria*, note 1, para. 58.
[4] Ibid., para. 67. Case commentary by Gina Bekker, 'The Social and Economic Rights Action Center and the Center for Economic and Social Rights/Nigeria' (2003) 47 *Journal of African Law* 126.

The focus of this chapter is to examine the existence and extent of the obligations on states in relation to the activities of businesses which adversely impact human rights. This is because the state is the main duty holder in relation to international human rights treaty law. The chapter approaches this in the context of Pillar I of the UNGPs, with the first two Guiding Principles (called 'foundational principles') providing:

1. States must protect against human rights abuse within their territory and/or jurisdiction by third parties, including business enterprises. This requires taking appropriate steps to prevent, investigate, punish and redress such abuse through effective policies, legislation, regulations and adjudication.
2. States should set out clearly the expectation that all business enterprises domiciled in their territory and/or jurisdiction respect human rights throughout their operations.

These two fundamental principles will be explored within the chapter. It will, though, initially clarify the relevant legal principles under the international law of state responsibility,[5] within which these human rights obligations of states are relevant.

2. State Responsibility

The scope of the international law of state responsibility, introduced in Chapter 2, has been clarified by the International Law Commission (ILC), the body of eminent international lawyers tasked with clarifying international law.[6] Its final document on state responsibility was published in 2001 as the Articles on the Responsibility of States for Internationally Wrongful Acts (ARSIWA),[7] much of which is now considered to be

---

[5] Some of the following section is based on Robert McCorquodale and Penelope Simons, 'Responsibility Beyond Borders: State Responsibility for Extraterritorial Violations by Corporations of International Human Rights Law' (2007) 70 *Modern Law Review* 598.
[6] For a consideration of the role of the ILC, see United Nations, *Seventy Years of the International Law Commission* (UN, 2020).
[7] ILC, *Articles on the Responsibility of States for Internationally Wrongful Acts*, Report of the International Law Commission on the Work of its 53rd session, A/56/10, August 2001, UN GAOR, 56th Sess. Supp. No. 10, UN Doc. A/56/10(SUPP) (2001).

customary international law.⁸ The core element of the international law of state responsibility is summarized by the final Special Rapporteur of ARSIWA, James Crawford, as follows:

> It is a general principle of international law that a breach of an international obligation entails the responsibility of the state concerned. Shortly, the law of responsibility is concerned with the incidence and consequences of unlawful acts, and particularly the form of reparation for loss caused.⁹

Accordingly, the first two Articles of ARSIWA are:

> Article 1: Every internationally wrongful act of a State entails the international responsibility of that State.
>
> Article 2: There is an internationally wrongful act of a State when conduct consisting of an action or omission:
> (a) is attributable to the State under international law; and
> (b) constitutes a breach of an international obligation of the State.

These two international legal principles are applicable to international human rights law, as the ILC makes clear.¹⁰ This is confirmed by human rights treaty bodies, which have applied the general law of state responsibility to the human rights issues before them,¹¹ as have national and international courts more generally.¹² This has included situations involving

---

⁸ Not all of ARSIWA can be considered to be customary international law, though most of the Articles—including those relevant to this book—have been adopted by international tribunals as reflective of customary international law: Arman Savarian, 'The Ossified Debate on a UN Convention on State Responsibility' (2021) 70 *International and Comparative Law Quarterly* 769 and Riccardo Pisillo Mazzechi, 'The Marginal Role of the Individual in the ILC's Articles on State Responsibility' (2004) 14 *Italian Yearbook of International Law* 39.

⁹ James Crawford, *Brownlie's Principles of Public International Law* (OUP, 8th ed., 2012), 540.

¹⁰ James Crawford, *The International Law Commission's Articles on State Responsibility: Introduction, Text and Commentaries* (CUP, 2002) [ILC Commentaries], 76 and 129. Note that the rules set out in ARSIWA are considered by the ILC to be secondary rules of international law (p. 74).

¹¹ For example, the Inter-American Court of Human Rights in *The Mayagna (Sumo) Awas Tingni Community v. Nicaragua*, Inter-American Court of Human Rights, Series C, No. 79 (31 August 2001), para. 153, quoted in Chapter 2. . Also Robert McCorquodale, 'Impact on State Responsibility' in Menno Kamminga and Martin Scheinin (eds), *The Impact of Human Rights Law on General International Law* (OUP, 2009), 235.

¹² Report of the UN Secretary-General to the UN General Assembly, 'Responsibility of States for Internationally Wrongful Acts: Compilation of Decisions of International Courts, Tribunals and Other Bodies' UN Doc. A/77/74 (29 April 2022).

abuses of human rights concerning the actions and omissions of state organs and officials, such as police, military, immigration, and similar officials,[13] even when acting outside their official authority.[14] So if an act or omission can be attributed to a state and there has been a breach of an international legal obligation (under a treaty or customary international law) by that act or omission, then the state is responsible under international law.

However, the acts of non-state actors, such as businesses, are not generally attributable to the state under international law.[15] Nevertheless, there are four situations in which the acts of non-state actors can be attributed to the state, for which the state may incur international responsibility.[16] These are set out below, including examples of their application in relation to business activities.

a. Attribution by Elements of Government Authority

A state would be responsible for the acts of a business when the business has been exercising elements of governmental activity. This is provided for under Article 5 of ARSIWA:

> The conduct of a person or entity which is not an organ of the State...but which is empowered by the law of that State to exercise elements of the governmental authority shall be considered an act of the State under international law, provided the person or entity is acting in that capacity in the particular instance.

For there to be attribution to the state, the conduct by the business must relate to 'governmental activity and not [to] other private or commercial activity'.[17] The ILC Commentaries to ARSIWA make clear that the key factor

---

[13] ARSIWA, Art. 4. Also *Immunity of Special Rapporteur of the Commission on Human Rights* [1999] ICJ Rep. 62, where the ICJ states that this represents a rule of customary international law.
[14] *Caire Claim (France v. Mexico)* 5 RIAA 516 (1929).
[15] ILC Commentaries, note 10, 91 and 121.
[16] The ILC expressly deleted a draft Article (Art. 11) that had stated that actions by non-state actors could not be attributed to the state: Nicola Jägers, *Corporate Human Rights Obligations: In Search of Accountability* (Intersentia, 2002), 143–5.
[17] ILC Commentaries, note 10, 101.

for attribution is the empowerment to exercise governmental authority and not the degree of ownership of the business by the state.[18]

Examples of the type of governmental authority for which attribution of business activities might arise would cover a wide variety of public functions, including where state functions have been privatized.[19] This would include privatization of prisons and detention, and facilities, as well as immigration services.[20] It may even extend to the privatization of natural monopolies, such as water, and to business activity in regulated markets for housing and food.[21]

b. Attribution by Acting under the Instructions, Direction, or Control

A state would be responsible for the actions of a business that was acting under the instructions or direction or control of that state. This is set out in Article 8 of ARSIWA:

> The conduct of a person or group of persons shall be considered an act of a State under international law if the person or group of persons is

---

[18] Ibid.

[19] Aoife Nolan, 'Privatization and Economic and Social Rights' (2018) 40 *Human Rights Quarterly* 815 and Adam McBeth, 'Privatising Human Rights: What Happens to the State's Human Rights Duties when Services are Privatised?' (2004) 5 *Melbourne Journal of International Law* 133. Nolan defines privatization (p. 818) as 'a shift towards provision by nongovernmental or nonstate actors of certain classes of goods and services … for the provision or performance of which, individuals have been accustomed to relying exclusively or mainly on state offices and agencies'.

[20] Koen De Feyter and Felipe Gómez Isa (eds), *Privatisation and Human Rights in the Age of Globalisation* (Intersentia, 2005).

[21] David Birchall, 'Reconstructing State Obligations to Protect and Fulfil Socio-Economic Rights in an Era of Marketisation' (2022) 71 *International and Comparative Law Quarterly* 227. Another example is the activity of AWB Ltd, which had an Australian government-created monopoly on Australian wheat exports, and was involved in illegal payments during the provision of UN food and humanitarian aid to be delivered in Iraq while sanctions were in place from 1996 to 2003; Final Report ('Manipulation of the Oil-for-Food Programme by the Iraqi Regime') of the Independent Inquiry Committee into the United Nations Oil-for-Food Programme, 262, https://web.archive.org/web/20070612181445/http://www.iic-offp.org/documents/Final%20Report%2027Oct05/IIC%20Final%20Report%20-%20Chapter%20Three.pdf and Gonzalo Villalta Puig, 'Unethical Conduct in the Performance of International Government Contracts: AWB Ltd and the United Nations Oil-For-Food Programme' (2007) 37 *Public Contract Law Journal* 59.

in fact acting on the instructions of, or under the direction or control of, that State in carrying out the conduct.

There have been a series of cases before international courts and tribunals which have attempted to determine what is needed for a non-state entity to be under the control—or the effective control—of a state. The most authoritative clarification is that of the ICJ in the *Bosnian Genocide Case*,[22] where it held:

> [P]ersons, groups of persons or entities may, for the purposes of international responsibility, be equated with State organs even if that status would not follow from internal law, provided that in fact the persons, groups or entities act in 'complete dependence' on the State, of which they are ultimately merely the instrument. In such a case, it is appropriate to look beyond legal status alone, in order to grasp the reality of the relationship between the person taking action, and the State to which he is so closely attached as to appear to be nothing more than its agent: any other solution would allow States to escape their international responsibility by choosing to act through persons or entities which supposed independence would be purely fictitious.[23]

By taking this approach of looking at the reality of the instruction, direction, and control by states, international courts and tribunals have found that the actions of individuals and businesses can be attributable to a state.

An example of attribution to the state under these conditions can be seen in the actions of some private business contractors under contract for government military services. For example, during the military operations in Iraq in 2004, pictures emerged of Iraqi prisoners being stripped naked, forced to engage in humiliating sexual acts, and subjected to fear and intimidation tactics by US military personnel.[24] A report by a medical civil society organization concluded that 'all detainees suffered severe physical and mental pain as a result of the assaults [and that] they all experienced

---

[22] *Application of the Genocide Convention (Bosnia-Herzegovina v. Serbia and Montenegro)* [2007] ICJ Rep 191.
[23] Ibid., para. 392.
[24] Steven Schooner, 'Contractor Atrocities at Abu Ghraib: Compromised Accountability in a Streamlined, Outsourced Government' (2005) 16 *Stanford Law and Policy Review* 549.

terror'.²⁵ It became evident that a significant number of those who were committing these acts (which were breaches of human rights) were people employed by businesses which has been contracted by the US government to undertake various military activities.²⁶

The UN Working Group on Human Rights and Mercenaries has noted that the 'growing reliance on private military and security companies by humanitarian actors has brought about significant challenges with regard to protection of civilians, and to human rights and international humanitarian law violations'.²⁷ It concluded:

> In the case of States and international organizations, responsibility for human rights violations revolves around attribution of responsibility for the conduct of private military and security company personnel. States and international organizations have due diligence obligations towards local populations under human rights and international humanitarian law instruments, which may include State obligations to investigate and prosecute perpetrators, the putting in place of preventative measures, and the provision of avenues for redress for harm caused by human rights violations, including by non-State actors ... However, the more unclear the layers of responsibility are, the more difficult it is to pursue accountability.²⁸

The final sentence of this quotation shows why, even if there is attribution to the state through its direction or control of a business, it may still be difficult to ensure accountability for the actions of private military businesses.²⁹

---

[25] Physicians for Human Rights, *Broken Laws, Broken Lives—Medical Evidence of Torture by US Personnel and its Impact* (2008) BrokenLaws_ExecSummary14.pdf (phr.org).

[26] General Fay, *Investigation of the Abu Ghraib Detention Facility and 205ᵗʰ Military Intelligence Brigade 52* (2004), which concludes that '[c]ontracting-related issues contributed to the problems at Abu Ghraib prison'.

[27] Report of the Working Group on the Use of Mercenaries as a Means of Violating Human Rights, 'Impact of the Use of Private Military and Security Services in Humanitarian Action' UN Doc. A/HRC/48/51 (2 July 2021), para. 14.

[28] Ibid., para. 62.

[29] Stuart Wallace, 'Private Security Companies and Human Rights: Are Non-Judicial Remedies Effective' (2016) 35 *Boston University International Law Journal* 69. Though in *Ilascu v. Moldova and Russia* (App. No. 48787/99) (2004) ECHR, 8 July 2004, the actions of a military separatist group seeking to create the Moldavian Republic of Transdniestria were attributed to the state of Russia.

c. Attribution by Adoption of Actions

A state would be internationally legally responsible if it adopts the actions of the business, as is set out in Article 11 of ARSIWA:

> The conduct of a person or group of persons shall be considered an act of a State under international law if the person or group of persons is in fact acting on the instructions of, or under the direction or control of, that State in carrying out the conduct.

An example of this situation in relation to non-state actors was seen in the *Tehran Hostages Case*,[30] where the ICJ found the state of Iran to be responsible for the acts of private groups who seized control of the US Embassy in Tehran and took the diplomatic and consular staff as hostages. The acts were attributable to the Iranian government since the Iranian authorities took no steps to try to prevent the seizure and they subsequently endorsed the actions of the private groups.[31]

An example in relation to businesses can be seen historically in the actions of the UK government in adopting the activities of the East India Company in India to enable the UK state to make a claim to that territory.[32] More recently, there have been reports of Chinese companies purchasing islands for the benefit of the government of China.[33]

d. Complicity

The fourth situation of attribution to the state from the actions of a non-state actor concerns complicity. Article 16 of the ILC Articles provides:

> A State which aids or assists another State in the commission of an internationally wrongful act by the latter is internationally responsible for doing so if:

---

[30] *Case Concerning United States Diplomatic and Consular Staff in Tehran (United States of America v. Iran)* [1980] ICJ Rep. 3.
[31] Ibid., paras 57, 69–71.
[32] William Dalrymple, *The Anarchy: The Relentless Rise of the East India Company* (Bloomsbury, 2019), 310.
[33] 'The Chinese Companies Trying to Buy Strategic Islands' *The Financial Times* (14 April 2022).

(a) that State does so with knowledge of the circumstances of the internationally wrongful act; and
(b) the act would be internationally wrongful if committed by that State.

According to the ILC, a state would be responsible for aiding and abetting, including 'knowingly providing an essential facility or financing the activity in question … facilitating the abduction of persons on foreign soil, or assisting in the destruction of property belonging to nationals of a third country'.[34] In each instance, the assisting state must be aware that it is aiding or assisting in the commission of an internationally unlawful act, it must provide such aid or assistance in order to facilitate the act in question, and the act must constitute an internationally wrongful act if committed by the assisting state.[35]

An example of this situation in relation to businesses can be seen in the role of export credit agencies in some states. Export credit agencies provide services to those businesses which are incorporated in that state, with the purpose of assisting those businesses to export their product or service to another state. It does this by, for example, the provision of loans, guarantees, and risk insurance, to help businesses develop essential contacts and trade in other states.[36] There are usually three types of institutional structure of export credit agencies: as state agencies or departments; as state-owned businesses that are operated independently but have government oversight; and as consortia of public/private businesses that may be controlled by a government through funding or regulation.[37] While those export credit agencies that are state agencies or form part of a government department will have their actions attributable to the state in the normal way, as being state agents, that is not the situation with those export credit agencies which have a private business structure.

In a 2018 report, the UN Working Group on Business and Human Rights explored some of the human rights impacts of export credit agencies.[38]

---

[34] ILC Commentaries, note 10, 148.
[35] Ibid., 149.
[36] Sara Seck and Özgür Can, 'The Legal Obligations with Respect to Human Rights and Export Credit Agencies' (2006) Schulich Law Scholars, The Legal Obligations with Respect to Human Rights and Export Credit Agencies (dal.ca).
[37] WGBHR, Report to the UN General Assembly on the State as an Economic Actor, UN Doc. A/HEC/38/48 (2 May 2018), https://documents-dds-ny.un.org/doc/UNDOC/GEN/G18/123/33/PDF/G1812333.pdf?OpenElement, para. 40.
[38] Ibid.

They found a range of situations of adverse human rights impacts by export credit agencies, including those providing funding for businesses to build dams or pipelines in other states, where there were human rights impacts through population resettlement and the destruction of cultural heritage.[39] Another example was an expert credit agency's support for surveillance products in other states leading to adverse impacts on the right to life, right to arbitrary detention, freedom from torture, and potential violations of other civil and political rights.[40]

In each of these situations, the actions of the export credit agency would be attributable to the state, even though it was acting outside the territory of the state (as is discussed further in Section 4 below). Thus, the states that have provided financial backing for projects in other states through their privatized export credit agency, even if it is to businesses and not directly to those other states, may be found to be complicit in a host state's internationally wrongful act (i.e. a violation of its human rights obligations) in relation to protecting the international human rights of persons affected by the activities of business.

Under international law, in order for the state to be held responsible for complicity in these situations, it must be shown that the state knew that it was aiding or assisting in the commission of the wrongful act.' Yet, where the assistance is provided by an export credit agency, constructive knowledge could be assumed where the agency maintains that it takes the human rights or social impact of a project into account in its decision-making or it is normally required to undertake assessments of, or investigations into, the human rights impacts of a particular project.[41] In addition, as the ICJ indicated in the *Bosnian Genocide Case*,[42]

---

[39] For example, the Baku-Ceyhan pipeline, where the major lenders included the International Finance Corporation, the European Bank for Reconstruction and Development, and ECAs from the UK, US, Japan, France, Italy and Germany: https://www.bp.com/en_az/azerbaijan/home/who-we-are/operationsprojects/pipelines/btc.html and https://risingtide.org.uk/content/baku-ceyhan-pipeline-campaign.

[40] WGBHR, Report to the UN General Assembly on the State as an Economic Actor, note 37, para. 44.

[41] Seck and Can, note 36, 9, who raise the issue that '[t]he social and environmental impact assessments that ECAs [export credit agencies] conduct of TNC activities and the resulting conditions that are applied in the loan agreements may represent an implicit acknowledgement of the ECA's due diligence obligations'.

[42] *Application of the Genocide Convention (Bosnia-Herzegovina v. Serbia and Montenegro)*, note 22, para. 420: 'The Court sees no reason to make any distinction of substance between "complicity in genocide", within the meaning of Article III, paragraph (e), of the [Genocide] Convention, and the "aid or assistance" of a State in the commission of a wrongful act by another State within the meaning of the aforementioned Article 16.'

the wrongful act may include international crimes. While litigation is unusual, it is not that uncommon.[43]

3. State Obligations and Human Rights

Other than through attribution, a state may incur international responsibility for a breach of an obligation where it fails to exercise due diligence to prevent the effects of actions by businesses.[44] While due diligence is a concept found across many areas of international law,[45] it was initially applied to international human rights law by the Inter-American Court of Human Rights in *Vélásquez Rodriguez v. Honduras*.[46] There the Court decided that a state may be held liable for human rights violations caused by a non-state actor (in that case, it was an armed group) where the state has failed to exercise due diligence to prevent the violation or to respond by investigating the violation. This has been confirmed and applied by other international human rights bodies.[47]

The legal foundation for this series of decisions is that the state has an international obligation to take measures domestically to ensure compliance with its international human rights obligations towards all persons within the state's jurisdiction, including to prevent human rights violations.[48] This obligation of due diligence within the international law of state responsibility is a positive obligation on a state, demanding considerable

---

[43] *R (on the Application of Friends of the Earth Limited) v. The Secretary of State for International Trade and Export Credits Guarantee Department (UK Export Finance)* [2022] EWHC 568, 15 March 2022 (UK court).

[44] The concept of 'human rights due diligence' as part of a business's own responsibilities is discussed in the next chapter. Human rights due diligence, as explained in Chapter 5, is not the same as a state's due diligence discussed here.

[45] International Law Association, Study Group on Due Diligence in International Law, Second Report (July 2016) 1, ttps://www.ila-hq.org/en_GB/documents/draft-study-group-report-johannesburg-2016, Neil McDonald, 'The Role of Due Diligence in International Law' (2019) 68 *International and Comparative Law Quarterly* 1041, and Jan Hessbruegge, 'The Historical Development of the Doctrines of Attribution and Due Diligence in International Law' (2004) 36 *International Law and Politics* 265.

[46] *Vélásquez Rodriguez v. Honduras* (1989) 28 *International Legal Materials* 294.

[47] For example, *Herrera Rubio v. Colombia*, Communication No. 161/1983, (1988) HRC Report, UN GAOR, 43rd Sess. Supp. No. 40, 190 [11]; *Ergi v. Turkey* (App. No. 23818/94) (1998) 32 EHRR 388; *Timurtas v. Turkey* (App. No. 23531/94) (2000) ECHR, 13 June 2000; and *A v. UK* (App. No. 25599/94) (1999) 27 EHRR 611.

[48] Andrew Clapham, *Human Rights in the Private Sphere* (OUP, 1993) and Andrew Clapham, 'Revisiting *Human Rights in the Private Sphere*: Using the ECHR to Protect the Right of Access to the Civil Court' in Craig Scott (ed.), *Torture as Tort* (Hart, 2001), 513.

state resources, such as to pass legislation, undertake fact-finding, launch a criminal investigation and, perhaps, undertake prosecution in a transparent, 'accessible and effective manner'.[49] The UN Human Rights Committee (HRC) has expressed these obligations on the state in this way:

> [T]he positive obligations on States Parties to ensure Covenant [International Covenant on Civil and Political Rights] rights will only be fully discharged if individuals are protected by the State, not just against violations of Covenant rights by its agents, but also against acts committed by private persons or entities that would impair the enjoyment of Covenant rights in so far as they are amenable to application between private persons or entities. There may be circumstances in which a failure to ensure Covenant rights ... would give rise to violations by States Parties of those rights, as a result of States Parties' permitting or failing to take appropriate measures or to exercise due diligence to prevent, punish, investigate or redress the harm caused by such acts by private persons or entities.[50]

This means that, while the conduct of private actors is not attributable to the state in this type of situation—in contrast to the situations given in the previous section—the state is nevertheless under an ongoing obligation to satisfy a certain standard of conduct—that of due diligence—in preventing and responding to the conduct of businesses.[51] Thus, states have ongoing obligations under international human rights law to exercise due diligence in relation to the activities of businesses within their territory or jurisdiction.

This position is confirmed by GP 1 of the UNGPs, which articulates the state's responsibility to protect people from human rights abuse by businesses by using the same five words as in the final sentence of the HRC's

---

[49] *Jordan v. UK* (App. No. 24746/94) ECHR, 4 May 2001 [143], where the ECtHR considered that the conduct of the investigation, the coroner's inquest, delay, the lack of both legal aid for the victim's family, and the lack of public scrutiny of the reasons of the Director of Public Prosecutions not to prosecute, amounted to a violation of Art. 2 of the ECHR. Also Naomi Roht-Arriaza, 'State Responsibility to Investigate and Prosecute Grave Human Rights Violations in International Law' (1990) 78 *California Law Review* 449.

[50] HRC, General Comment No. 31, Nature of the General Legal Obligation Imposed on States Parties to the Covenant, UN Doc. CCPR/C/21/Rev.1/Add.13 (29 March 2004), para. 8.

[51] Timo Koivurova, 'Due Diligence' in Rüdiger Wolfrum (ed.), *Max Planck Encyclopedia of Public International Law* (OUP, 2008), para. 3: 'A breach of these obligations [to exercise due diligence] consists not of failing to achieve the desired result but failing to take the necessary, diligent steps towards that end.'

General Comment quoted above, i.e. that states must take 'appropriate steps to *prevent, investigate, punish and redress* human rights abuse by third parties'. Accordingly, states have been found by human rights treaty bodies to be in breach of their human rights obligations in situations of business activities where, for example, employees have been dismissed or victimized for joining a trade union,[52] the activities of businesses have polluted the air or land,[53] and there have been failures by the state to protect Indigenous peoples' land from harm caused by business activities.[54]

Further, in *RAID v. Democratic Republic of Congo*,[55] the African Commission on Human and People's Rights found a range of violations of human rights by the government of the Democratic Republic of Congo (DRC) for its action in the killing of over 70 people in the Kilwa district and ordered the DRC to pay $US2.5m to the victims as compensation. In addition, the Commission requested that the DRC 'take all diligent measures to prosecute and punish State's agents and Anvil Mining Company staff who were involved in the violations',[56] including recommending that the DRC undertake a criminal investigation of that business. This issue arose due to the role of the Australian-Canadian mining business, Anvil Mining Company, in which it allegedly provided logistical support to the DRC soldiers to enable them to undertake these human rights violations.[57] However, the business itself could not be found to have violated the ACHPR—for the reasons examined in *SERAC v. Nigeria* at the beginning of this chapter—even if the Commission had found that the business was clearly complicit in the violations of human rights by the state.

A 2021 case before the Inter-American Court of Human Rights illustrates this situation. In the *Case of the Miskito Divers (Lemoth Morris et al.) v. Honduras*,[58] there was a complaint by a group of divers of the Miskito

---

[52] *Young, James and Webster v. UK* (App. No. 7601/76) (1982) 4 EHRR 38.
[53] *Lopez Ostra v. Spain* (App. No. 16798/90) (1994) 20 EHRR 277 and *Guerra v. Italy* (App. no. 00014967/89) (1998) 26 EHRR 357.
[54] *Yanomani v. Brazil*, Inter-American Court of Human Rights Res. No. 12/85 Annual Rep Inter-American Commission on Human Rights 1985–84; *The Mayagna (Sumo) Awas Tingni Community v. Nicaragua*, Inter-American Court of Human Rights, Series C, No. 79 (31 August 2001); and *Hopu and Bessert v. France*, HRC, UN Doc. CCPR/C/60/D/549/1993/Rev.1 (1997).
[55] *Institute for Human Rights and Development and Others v. Democratic Republic of Congo*, Communication No. 393/10, ESCR-Net, 18 June 2016.
[56] Ibid., para. 154(i).
[57] Business & Human Rights Resource Centre, 'NGOs Coalition Welcomes African Commission's Landmark USD2.5 Million Award to DR Congo Massacre Victims', business-humanrights.org.
[58] *Case of the Miskito Divers (Lemoth Morris et al.) v. Honduras*, [2021] IACHR (Case No. 12.738, Judgment of 31 August 2021.

people, who are an Indigenous people who share the border territories of Honduras and Nicaragua. Their complaint was that the state of Honduras had caused deaths and injuries due to the state's omissions and indifference to the problem of labour exploitation by fishing businesses and in allowing diving activities in dangerous conditions. In finding in favour of the Miskito divers, the Court specifically referred to the UNGPs and confirmed that 'States have a duty to prevent human rights violations by private companies, and therefore must adopt legislative and other measures to prevent such violations, and to investigate, punish and provide reparation when they occur'.[59] The Court then held:

> [T]his Court considers that ... States should adopt measures to ensure that business enterprises have: a) appropriate policies for the protection of human rights; b) due diligence processes for the identification, prevention and correction of human rights violations, as well as to ensure decent and dignified work; and c) processes that allow businesses to remedy human rights violations that result from their activities, especially when these affect people living in poverty or belonging to vulnerable groups. The Court considers that, in this context, States should actively encourage businesses to adopt good corporate governance practices that focus on stakeholders and actions aimed at orienting business activity towards compliance with human rights and standards, including and promoting the participation and commitment of all the stakeholders involved, and the redress of affected persons.[60]

These are strong statements by the Court as to the responsibility of the state for business activities that adversely impact on human rights.

In all these examples, the state was in breach of its obligations under the relevant human rights treaty because its acts or omissions enabled the businesses to act as they did. Thus, in the context of international human rights law, the concept of a state's due diligence is primarily relevant in defining the extent of a state's international legal obligations in relation to the conduct of businesses in situations where the business conduct is not attributable to the state.

---

[59] Ibid., para. 48.
[60] Ibid., para. 49.

4. Actions Beyond a State's Territory

A key issue of debate concerning the UNGPs has been the extent of the state's international obligations beyond its territory. GP 1 provides that 'States must protect against human rights abuse within their *territory and/ or jurisdiction* by [business enterprises]'.[61] This provision acknowledges that, under international human rights law, states have obligations in relation to both their territory and their jurisdiction, as is confirmed in most international human rights treaties.[62] This is because a state may have powers—and hence legal obligations—beyond its land and maritime territory. However, the exercise by states of powers beyond their territory can be controversial due to state sovereignty, whereby each state should be able to regulate activities within its own territory in accordance with its own policies and priorities, and without interference by other states.[63]

The difference between 'territory' and 'jurisdiction' was clarified by the Inter-American Commission on Human Rights:

> [The Commission] does not believe ... that the term 'jurisdiction' in the sense of Article 1(1) is limited to or merely coextensive with national territory. Rather, the Commission is of the view that a state party to the American Convention may be responsible under certain circumstances for the acts and omissions of its agents which produce effects or are undertaken outside that state's territory.[64]

---

[61] Emphasis added.

[62] For example, this is the position under the American Convention on Human Rights 1969 (ACHR), Art. 1(1); the European Convention on Human Rights 1950 (ECHR), Art. 1; and the International Covenant on Civil and Political Rights (ICCPR), Art. 2(1). The International Covenant on Economic, Social and Cultural Rights (ICESCR) and ACHPR have no such express jurisdictional clause, though it is assumed that they would also apply to a state's jurisdiction: see the Committee on Economic Social and Cultural Rights (CESCR) General Comment No. 8, The Relationship between Economic Sanctions and Respect for Economic, Social and Cultural Rights, UN Doc. E/C.12/1997/8 (12 December 1997), para. 7.

[63] Some commentators have stated that the exercise of powers beyond a state's territory also raises issues of imperialism and neocolonial assertion of jurisdiction on the part of the Global North states: Ugo Mattei and Jeffrey Lena, 'US Jurisdiction over Conflicts Arising outside of the United States: Some Hegemonic Implications' (2000) 24 *Hastings International & Comparative Law Review* 381.

[64] *Saldaño v. Argentina* (Report No. 38/99) Inter-American Commission on Human Rights (11 March 1999), para. 17. The Commission made clear that this applied in relation to the application of both the ACHR and the American Declaration of the Rights and Duties of Man.

The HRC and the European Court of Human Rights (ECtHR) have taken similar approaches, with the former stating:

> A State party must respect and ensure the rights laid down in the Covenant to anyone within the power and effective control of that State Party, even if not situated within the territory of the State Party ... regardless of the circumstances in which such power or effective control was obtained.[65]

In *Loizidou v. Turkey*,[66] before the ECtHR, the issue concerned whether Turkey could be responsible under the ECHR for the illegal seizure of property by the authorities in the non-recognized entity of the Turkish Republic of Northern Cyprus. The ECtHR decided:

> The responsibility of Contracting Parties can be involved because of acts of their authorities, *whether performed within or outside national boundaries, which produce effects outside their own territory.* Bearing in mind the object and purpose of the Convention, the responsibility of a Contracting Party may also arise when as a consequence of military action—whether lawful or unlawful—it exercises effective control of an area outside its national territory. The obligation to secure, in such an area, the rights and freedoms set out in the Convention, derives from the fact of such control whether it be exercised directly, through its armed forces, or through a subordinate local administration.[67]

As a consequence, the Court held that the complainant fell within the jurisdiction of Turkey and so Turkey was internationally responsible for violations of human rights in the non-recognized entity of the Turkish Republic of Northern Cyprus.[68]

---

[65] Whilst Art. 2(1) of the ICCPR refers to both territory and jurisdiction, the HRC has clarified that the state's obligation extends to both individuals within a state's territory as well as to those who are not within the state's territory but who are subject to its jurisdiction: HRC, General Comment No. 31(80), Nature of the General Legal Obligation Imposed on States Parties to the Covenant, UN Doc. CCPR/C/21/Rev.1/Add.13 (26 May 2004) [HRC GC 31], para. 10.

[66] *Loizidou v. Turkey* (Preliminary Objections) (App. No. 15318/89) (1995) 20 EHRR 99. Also *Drozd and Janousek v. France and Spain* (App. No. 12747/8) (1992) 14 EHRR 745, para. 91. Under the ECHR, states can also choose to extend the obligations under the ECHR to their colonies or other overseas territories.

[67] *Loizidou v. Turkey*, note 66, para. 62 (emphasis added).

[68] *Loizidou v. Turkey* (Merits) (App. No. 15318/89) (1997) 23 EHRR 513, para. 56. Contrast with *Banković v. Belgium* (App. No. 52207/99) (2002) 41 ILM 517, para. 59; Rick Lawson, 'The

This conclusion is supported by decisions of the ICJ. In its *Advisory Opinion on the Wall* it stated that Israel had obligations under the International Covenant on Civil and Political Rights (ICCPR), the International Covenant on Economic, Social and Cultural Rights (ICESCR), and the Convention on the Rights of the Child (CRC) in relation to the Occupied Palestinian Territories (OPT), and that the ICCPR was 'applicable in respect of acts done by a State in the exercise of its jurisdiction outside its own territory'.[69] This position was confirmed by the ICJ in its decision in *Democratic Republic of Congo v. Uganda*, in finding that the ICCPR, the CRC, and the ACHPR all applied in relation to Uganda's actions within the territory of the DRC. Indeed, in this latter case the ICJ went further in stating that 'international human rights instruments are applicable in respect of acts done by a state in the exercise of its jurisdiction outside its own territory, particularly in occupied territories'.[70]

The extent to which these general obligations apply to states in relation to businesses was considered in the UNGPs. The Commentary to GP 2 provides:

> At present States are not generally required under international human rights law to regulate the extraterritorial activities of businesses domiciled in their territory and/or jurisdiction. Nor are they generally prohibited from doing so, provided there is a recognized jurisdictional basis. Within these parameters some human rights treaty bodies recommend that home States take steps to prevent abuse abroad by business enterprises within their jurisdiction.

This Commentary, indicating that states are not generally required to regulate their businesses operating in another state, was justified by John Ruggie as follows:

> The UN treaty bodies traditionally paid relatively little attention to business-related issues. Their general guidance suggested that treaties

---

Concept of Jurisdiction in the European Convention on Human Rights' in Pieter Slot and Meille Bulterman (eds), *Globalisation and Jurisdiction* (Kluwer Law International, 2004), 201.

[69] *Advisory Opinion on the Legal Consequences on the Construction of a Wall in the Occupied Palestinian Territory* (2004) 43 ILM 1009, paras 107–13.
[70] *Case Concerning Armed Activities on the Territory of the Congo (Democratic Republic of the Congo v. Uganda)* [2015] ICJ Rep 116, para. 216.

do not require states to exercise extraterritorial jurisdiction over business abuse, but that they are not generally prohibited from doing so either, provided there is a recognised jurisdictional basis: for example, where the actor or victim is a national, where the acts have substantial adverse effects on the state, or where specific international crimes are involved.[71]

This statement and its reasoning have been extensively criticized by many commentators.[72] The criticism is primarily based on two aspects: the Commentary to GP 2 on this issue is inconsistent with the statements by the human rights treaty bodies, as set out above (and noted by John Ruggie), and it is inconsistent with state practice.[73] Each will be considered in turn.

Subsequent to the adoption of the UNGPs, two treaty bodies have expressed their views on transnational jurisdiction in relation to a state's obligations with respect to business activities.[74] In 2013, the Committee on the Rights of the Child recommended that states afford jurisdictional remedies 'for children and their families whose rights have been violated by business enterprises extraterritorially when there is a reasonable link between the State and the conduct concerned'.[75] In 2017, the Committee on Economic Social and Cultural Rights (CESCR) published General Comment No. 24 on state obligations under the ICESCR in the context

---

[71] John Ruggie, *Just Business* (Norton, 2013), 45. Also Claire Methven O'Brien, 'The Home State Duty to Regulate the Human Rights Impacts of TNCs Abroad: A Rebuttal' (2018) 3 *Business and Human Rights Journal*, 47.

[72] For example, Nadia Bernaz, 'Enhancing Corporate Accountability for Human Rights Violations: Is Extraterritoriality the Magic Potion?' (2013) 117 *Journal of Business Ethics* 493 and Anita Halvorssen and Karin Buhmann, 'Extraterritorial Regulation of Companies and the UN Guiding Principles on Human Rights and Business' in M.K. Sinha (ed.), *Business and Human Rights* (Sage, 2013).

[73] Gamze Erdem Turkelli, Mark Gibney, Markus Krajewski, and Wouter Vandenhole (eds), *Routledge Handbook on Extraterritorial Human Rights Obligations* (Routledge, 2021), as well as ESCR-Net, *Global Economy, Global Rights: A Practitioner's Guide for Interpreting Human Rights Obligations in the Global Economy* (2014), Global Economy Global Rights.pdf (escr-net.org).

[74] The Maastricht Principles on Extraterritorial Obligations of States in the Area of Economic, Social and Cultural Rights 2013, which were drafted by a group of international human rights law experts and draw on international law in order to clarify the content of extraterritorial state obligations https://www.icj.org/wp-content/uploads/2012/12/Maastricht-ETO-Principles-ENG-booklet.pdf.

[75] Committee on the Rights of the Child, General Comment No. 16, UN Doc. CRC/C/GC/16 (17 April 2013), para. 44.

of business activities.[76] In General Comment No. 24, the CESCR made clear that states do have international legal obligations to respect, protect, and fulfil economic, social, and cultural rights in relation to the actions of businesses. In relation to the responsibility to protect, it stated:

> 30. The extraterritorial obligation to protect requires States parties to take steps to prevent and redress infringements of Covenant rights that *occur outside their territories due to the activities of business entities over which they can exercise control*, especially in cases where the remedies available to victims before the domestic courts of the State where the harm occurs are unavailable or ineffective.
>
> 31. ... [A] State party would be in breach of its obligations under the Covenant where the violation reveals a failure by the State to take reasonable measures that could have prevented the occurrence of the event. The responsibility of the State can be engaged in such circumstances even if other causes have also contributed to the occurrence of the violation, and even if the State had not foreseen that a violation would occur, provided such a violation was reasonably foreseeable...
>
> 33. In discharging their duty to protect, States parties should also require corporations to deploy their best efforts to ensure that entities whose conduct those corporations may influence, such as subsidiaries (including all business entities in which they have invested, whether registered under the State party's laws or under the laws of another State) or business partners (including suppliers, franchisees and subcontractors), respect Covenant rights. Corporations domiciled in the territory and/or jurisdiction of States parties should be required to act with due diligence to identify, prevent and address abuses to Covenant rights by such subsidiaries and business partners, wherever they may be located. The Committee underlines that, *although the imposition of such due diligence obligations does have impacts on situations located outside these States' national territories since potential violations of Covenant rights in global supply chains or in multinational groups of companies should be*

---

[76] CESCR, General Comment No. 24, State Obligations under the International Covenant on Economic, Social and Cultural Rights in the Context of Business Activities, UN Doc. E/C.12/GC/24 (10 August 2017). See also commentary by Tara Van Ho, 'General Comment No. 24 (2017) on State Obligations Under the International Covenant on Economic, Social and Cultural Rights in the Context of Business Activities (CESCR)' (2019) 58 *International Legal Materials* 872.

prevented or addressed, this does not imply the exercise of extraterritorial jurisdiction by the States concerned.[77]

This detailed General Comment seeks to clarify a number of elements of a state's transnational obligations in relation to business activities. First, that the state's obligations include those to prevent and redress abuses by businesses domiciled in their territory, even if the abuse occurred in another state.[78] Second, that a state has an obligation for both its acts and omissions if it fails to take reasonable measures, including where abuses are foreseeable. Third, that a state's obligations extend to undertaking its best efforts in relation to the subsidiaries and business partners of a business. Further, while the CESCR uses the term 'extraterritorial' to describe these jurisdictional powers, there is a strong view that 'transnational' jurisdiction is the better term when dealing with the activities of transnational corporations crossing many boundaries.[79]

Finally, in relation to a state's human rights obligations, the ICJ held in *Pulp Mills on the River Uruguay (Argentine v. Uruguay)*:[80]

> A State is thus obliged to use all means at its disposal in order to avoid activities which take place in its territory, or in any area under its jurisdiction, causing significant damage to the environment of another State ... [The State's duty of due diligence includes] a certain level of vigilance in their enforcement and the exercise of administrative control applicable to public and private operators ... to safeguard the rights of the other party.[81]

Nevertheless, issues of infringement of state sovereignty can arise due to the exercise of powers beyond a state's territory, especially in light of the increasing globalization of business activities.

In relation to the criticism of the UNGPs' approach to transnational jurisdiction being contrary to state practice, research has shown that states

---

[77] CESCR, General Comment No. 24, note 76 (emphasis added).
[78] The term 'domicile' is considered in the next section.
[79] Douglass Cassel, 'State Jurisdiction over Transnational Business Activity affecting Human Rights' in Surya Deva and David Birchall (eds), *Research Handbook on Business and Human Rights* (Edward Elgar, 2020) 198 at 200.
[80] *Pulp Mills on the River Uruguay (Argentine v. Uruguay)* [2010] ICJ Rep. 14.
[81] Ibid., paras 101 and 197.

are—in reality—already taking a range of measures which have transnational implications and effects. Jennifer Zerk's research has indicated this:

> States have made use of domestic measures with [indirect] extraterritorial implications to help influence the behavior of private actors abroad without the direct use of extraterritorial jurisdiction ... [In addition] States are increasingly prepared to use direct extraterritorial jurisdiction in relation to criminal activity such as terrorism, money laundering, corruption, grave human rights breaches and 'sex tourism.' In competition law and securities law, too, states have made more extensive jurisdictional claims over foreign companies and conduct based on previously contested legal theories ... When exercised with other states' concerns in mind, the use of direct extraterritorial jurisdiction has been recognised as useful in closing regulatory and accountability gaps and delivering justice.[82]

This research highlights the difference between direct and indirect transnational jurisdiction, with the former being where the state exercises power in another jurisdiction in relation to a business's activities outside the state, and indirect transnational jurisdiction, where the state exercises power within its own jurisdiction in relation to businesses domiciled within its territory in relation to that business's activities outside the state, such as its subsidiaries domiciled in another state. The latter jurisdiction is much more common and often considered as involving domestic measures with transnational effects.

As the Commentary to GP 2 notes, examples of domestic measures with transnational effects 'include requirements on "parent" companies to report on the global operations of the entire enterprise; multilateral soft-law instruments such as the Guidelines for Multinational Enterprises of the Organisation for Economic Co-operation and Development; and performance standards required by institutions that support overseas investments'. Such state action is now increasing due to legislation subsequent to the UNGPs, such as France's Duty of Vigilance Act, discussed in Chapter 7. There is also the broader argument made by Surya Deva:

---

[82] Jennifer Zerk, 'Extraterritorial Jurisdiction: Lessons for the Business and Human Rights Sphere from Six Regulatory Areas' (2010) www.hks.harvard.edu/m-rcbg/CSRI/publications/workingpaper_59_zerk.pdf.

For international human rights to remain relevant in the twenty-first century, it should evolve as per the changing needs to protect human rights outside territorial boundaries in appropriate situations. Failure to recognize extraterritorial obligations on the part of states would have serious consequences because actions (or omissions) originating in one's territory could have serious consequences on the human rights of people outside the territory.[83]

There may, therefore, be good evidence of a move towards accepting that there are transnational obligations on states in relation to business activities which adversely impact human rights.

5. Domicile of a Business

GP 2 makes clear that the state's obligations are in relation to 'all business enterprises domiciled' in that state. This use of the term 'domiciled' requires clarification, as it affects a state's obligations. Traditionally, a business was only a national of a state if it was incorporated (registered) in that state, and thus the state had jurisdiction over it only in those instances.[84] Over time, this has changed, largely due to European Union (EU) private international law legislation. Under the Brussels I Regulation (Brussels I—now Brussels 1 Recast) the national courts within the EU Member States have jurisdiction over all legal persons who are 'domiciled' in their jurisdiction.[85] In relation to the legal personality of a business, Brussels I defines 'domicile' as the location of a business's statutory seat (i.e. where it is incorporated/registered), the central administration, or its principal place of business.[86] This definition applies to all EU-domiciled businesses, and so the courts of EU Member States are obligated to accept jurisdiction over claims against

---

[83] Surya Deva, 'Business and Human Rights: Alternative Approaches to Transnational Regulation' (2021) 17 *Annual Review of Law and Social Science* 9.1, 9.7.

[84] *Barcelona Traction, Light and Power Company Limited Case* (*Belgium v. Spain*) (*Second Phase*) [1970] ICJ Rep. 3 and F.A. Mann, 'The Doctrine of International Jurisdiction Revisited After Twenty Years' (1984) III Hague Recueil des Cours 56.

[85] Council Regulation (EC) No. 44/2001 of 22 December 2000 on Jurisdiction and the Recognition and Enforcement of Judgments in Civil and Commercial Matters [2001] OJ L12/1–23, 16.1.2001 (Brussels I), Art. 2(1); now Regulation (EU) No. 1215/2012 of 12 December 2012 of the European Parliament and of the Council of 12 December 2012 on Jurisdiction and the Recognition and Enforcement of Judgments in Civil and Commercial Matters [2012] OJ L351/1–32, 20.12.2012 (Recast Brussels Regulation), Art. 4.1.

[86] Recast Brussels Regulation, note 85, Art 4.1.

businesses domiciled in their state for violations committed entirely or partly outside Europe.

The global influence of these EU developments is seen in, for example, General Comment No. 24 by the CESCR, referred to above, where it is stated:

> Consistent with the admissible scope of jurisdiction under general international law, States may seek to regulate corporations that are domiciled in their territory and/or jurisdiction: this includes corporations incorporated under their laws, or which have their statutory seat, central administration or principal place of business on their national territory.[87]

Hence, the use of the term 'domicile' in GP 2 indicates a wider understanding about those businesses over which a state will have legal obligations, rather than simply considering only where a business may be registered. This means, for example, that a business may be registered in one state but have its principal place of business in another state, in which case both states have obligations in relation to it, and each can exercise territorial and transnational jurisdiction in relation to it.

6. Other Aspects of State Obligations

The UNGP set out a number of specific 'operational principles' in relation to the legal obligations on states. These will be considered here.

a. Regulation

The UNGPs make a strong statement that 'States should not assume that businesses invariably prefer, or benefit from, State inaction'.[88] Hence GP 3 sets out a range of measures which states can undertake to ensure business respect for human rights:

---

[87] CESCR, General Comment No. 24, note 76, para. 31.
[88] Commentary to GP 3.

In meeting their duty to protect, States should:
(a) Enforce laws that are aimed at, or have the effect of, requiring business enterprises to respect human rights, and periodically to assess the adequacy of such laws and address any gaps;
(b) Ensure that other laws and policies governing the creation and ongoing operation of business enterprises, such as corporate law, do not constrain but enable business respect for human rights;
(c) Provide effective guidance to business enterprises on how to respect human rights throughout their operations;
(d) Encourage, and where appropriate require, business enterprises to communicate how they address their human rights impacts.

Each of these obligations is expected of states. However, the lack of action by states on regulation was one of the main reasons for the movement towards a treaty on business and human rights, so as to place these operational principles into international legal obligations,[89] which is discussed in Chapter 8.

GP 3(b) includes reference to corporate law, since that is often a barrier both to enabling businesses to respect human rights and for victims to access remedies.[90] Research has shown that current national legislation on corporate law, such as that relating to the separate legal personality of businesses, including the distinction between a parent company and its wholly owned subsidiary, and the limited regulation of director's duties, can restrict both respect for human rights and access to remedies.[91]

There is a specific consideration of a state's legal obligations in relation to businesses operating in conflict areas in GP 7. This is '[b]ecause the risk of gross human rights abuses is heightened in conflict-affected areas, [thus] States should help ensure that business enterprises operating in those contexts are not involved with such abuses'.[92] The Working Group on Business and Human Rights (WGBHR) has provided a detailed clarification of the

---

[89] HuffPost UK Politics, Statement by Ecuador's Minister for Foreign Affairs, Transnational Misconduct Must End, https://www.huffingtonpost.co.uk/ricardo-patino/ecuador-ricardo-patino_b_6040920.html,, 20 October 2014).
[90] Jennifer Zerk, 'Corporate Liability for Gross Human Rights Abuses' (2014) Report for the Office of the UN High Commissioner for Human Rights, www.ohchr.org/Documents/Issues/Business/DomesticLawRemedies/StudyDomesticLawRemedies.pdf.
[91] Ibid., 37 and Robert McCorquodale and Stuart Neely, 'Director's Duties and Human Rights: A Comparative Approach' [2022] *Journal of Corporate Legal Studies* 1.
[92] GP 7.

need for 'heightened' human rights due diligence in situations of conflict-affected regions.[93]

There is an express reference in GP 7 to the concerns over gender-based and sexual violence in conflict-affected areas, and that the host state may not be able to protect human rights adequately. In these areas, there is an increased expectation that states, especially home states, will act to assist businesses, as well as to 'attach appropriate consequences to any failure by enterprises to cooperate in these contexts, including by denying or withdrawing existing public support or services, or where that is not possible, denying their future provision'.[94] The particular concerns about businesses operating in conflict-areas are reflected in GPs 12 and 23, which are discussed in the next chapter.

b. Policies and Oversight

GPs 8 and 9 set out that states should have policy coherence across all their domestic organs and in their international relations. The former enables the activities of state departments, agencies, and other organs to operate cohesively in this area. This approach, combined with GP 6 concerning state contracts with businesses, should enable the use of public procurement processes to provide incentives for businesses to respect human rights while restricting access to those businesses that do not.[95] GP 5 deals with privatization, as discussed above, with requirements of monitoring, and the reminder that 'States do not relinquish their international human rights law obligations when they privatize the delivery of services that may impact upon the enjoyment of human rights'.[96]

GP 9 specifically refers to investment treaties and contracts, as well as trade agreements, with the Commentary to GP 9 pointing out:

---

[93] WGBHR, Report on Conflict-Affected Regions, 21 July 2020, https://undocs.org/en/A/75/212.

[94] Commentary to GP 10.

[95] Claire Methven O'Brien and Olga Marin-Ortega, 'Human Rights and Public Procurement of Goods and Services' in Deva and Birchall, BHR, note 79, 245 and Sope Williams-Elegbe, 'Public Procurement as an Instrument to pursue Human Rights Protection' in Axel Marx, Geert Van Calster, and Jan Wouters (eds), *Global Governance, Business and Human Rights* (Edward Elgar, 2022), 143.

[96] Commentary to GP 5.

Economic agreements concluded by States, either with other States or with business enterprises—such as bilateral investment treaties, free-trade agreements or contracts for investment projects—create economic opportunities for States. But they can also affect the domestic policy space of Governments. For example, the terms of international investment agreements may constrain States from fully implementing new human rights legislation, or put them at risk of binding international arbitration if they do so. Therefore, States should ensure that they retain adequate policy and regulatory ability to protect human rights under the terms of such agreements, while providing the necessary investor protection.

This aspect of international investment and trade law is a major issue in relation to potential conflicts with business and human rights matters, as these types of international economic arrangements 'may limit the policy choices of governments when protecting and fulfilling human rights'.[97] While bilateral investment treaties and some trade agreements are designed to protect business and enhance their opportunities globally, they can restrict the abilities of states to protect human rights, as was seen in the example of *Urbaser v. Argentina*[98] discussed in Chapter 2. They can also limit the incentives for businesses to undertake actions to protect communities.[99]

There has been considerable debate over this matter, with some writers raising issues of conflicting obligations on states and others concerned about the ability of states to regulate business in relation to human rights where there are relevant bilateral investments in operation.[100] The CESCR in General Comment No. 24 noted:

---

[97] Markus Krajewski, 'Framing the Broader Context of Business and Human Rights: The Impact of Trade Agreements on Human Rights' in Deva and Birchall, BHR, note 79, 269, 288.
[98] *Urbaser v. Argentina*, ICSID Case No. ARB/07/26, decided 8 December 2016.
[99] For example, the arbitral decision in *Bear Creek Mining Corporation v. Republic of Peru*, ICSID Case No. ARB/14/2, Award, decided 30 November 2017, where the business had not engaged fully with the affected local communities and had not undertaken an environmental impact assessment, and yet it succeeded in the case: Jesse Coleman, Kaitlin Cordes, and Lise Johnson, 'Human Rights Law and the Investment Treaty Regime' in Deva and Birchall, BHR, note 79, 290.
[100] Susan Karamanian, 'Human Rights Dimensions of Investment Law' in Erica De Wet and Jure Vidmar (eds), *Hierarchy in International Law* (OUP, 2012), 236 and Zoe Williams, 'Investor-State Arbitration in Domestic Mining Conflicts' (2016) 16 *Global Environmental Politics* 32.

States parties should identify any potential conflict between their obligations under the Covenant and under trade or investment treaties, and refrain from entering into such treaties where such conflicts are found to exist ... Such impacts on human rights of the implementation of the agreements should be regularly assessed ... [and the] interpretation of trade and investment treaties currently in force should take into account the human rights obligations of the State ... States parties cannot derogate from the obligations under the Covenant in trade and investment treaties that they may conclude. They are encouraged to insert, in future treaties, a provision explicitly referring to their human rights obligations, and to ensure that mechanisms for the settlement of investor-State disputes take human rights into account in the interpretation of investment treaties or of investment chapters in trade agreements.[101]

One consequence of this debate has been that there have been proposals for limiting the scope of trade and investment treaties in relation to human rights issues in the drafts of the business and human rights treaty (discussed in Chapter 8).

Related to international policy coherence is GP 10, which deals with a state's engagement with international organizations of which they are a member. It provides that in these contexts, states should:

(a) Seek to ensure that those institutions neither restrain the ability of their member States to meet their duty to protect nor hinder business enterprises from respecting human rights;
(b) Encourage those institutions, within their respective mandates and capacities, to promote business respect for human rights and, where requested, to help States meet their duty to protect against human rights abuse by business enterprises, including through technical assistance, capacity-building and awareness-raising;
(c) Draw on these Guiding Principles to promote shared understanding and advance international cooperation in the management of business and human rights challenges.

The Commentary to GP 10 refers expressly to international trade and financial institutions having a distinct responsibility in this area:

---

[101] CESCR, General Comment No. 24, note 76, para. 13.

Capacity-building and awareness-raising through such [international trade and financial] institutions can play a vital role in helping all States to fulfil their duty to protect, including by enabling the sharing of information about challenges and best practices, thus promoting more consistent approaches.[102]

Thus, there is, at the very least, an expectation that these international organizations will comply with business and human rights regulation, as doing so would mean that they are not acting to prevent or restrain their member states from complying with the state's own obligations.[103] This would be consistent with the position that a state cannot give an international organization a competence that the state does not itself possess.[104]

c. State-Owned Entities

GP 4 contains a specific provision about state-owned entities:

States should take additional steps to protect against human rights abuses by business enterprises that are owned or controlled by the State, or that receive substantial support and services from State agencies such as export credit agencies and official investment insurance or guarantee agencies, including, where appropriate, by requiring human rights due diligence.

The rationale given for this specific provision is by reference to the rules on attribution to the state, as discussed above.[105] In addition, it is stated that '[w]here States own or control business enterprises, they have greatest means within their powers to ensure that relevant policies, legislation and regulations regarding respect for human rights are implemented'.[106] There is also the reality that in some sectors, such as the extractive sector, many of

---

[102] Commentary to GP 10.
[103] Mac Darrow and Louise Arbour, 'The Pillar of Glass: Human Rights in the Development Operations of the United Nations' (2009) 103 *American Journal of International Law* 446.
[104] *Waite and Kennedy v. Germany*, ECtHR [GC] No. 26083/94 ECHR 1999-1, especially para. 67, and *Bosphorus v. Ireland*, ECtHR [GC] No. 45036/98 ECHR, 2005-VI, especially pp. 157–8. Also ILC, Articles on the Responsibilities of International Organisations 2011, Arts 58–63.
[105] Commentary to GP 4.
[106] Ibid.

the largest businesses are state-owned entities, and that contracts across different value chains may include those with a state-owned entity.[107] Also, as discussed above, the WGBHR has criticized the role of those export credit agencies which are state-owned entities, for not taking enough account of human rights matters in their provision of financial support to businesses.

There is, though, no agreed definition of state-owned entities.[108] The OECD Guidelines on Corporate Governance of State-Owned Enterprises (SOEs) define state-owned entities as:

> [A]ny corporate entity recognised by national law as an enterprise, and in which the state exercises ownership ... if their purpose and activities, or parts of their activities, are of a largely economic nature.[109]

This is a narrow definition, which may make it difficult to apply to some non-capitalist states, such as China.[110] This definition does not, however, make the determination of state-owned entities solely about ownership but, instead, about effective control. This is consistent with the Commentary to GP 4, as it notes that, in a state-owned entity, '[s]enior management typically reports to State agencies, and associated government departments have greater scope for scrutiny and oversight, including ensuring that effective human rights due diligence is implemented'.[111]

The requirement under GP 4 is that the state should take 'additional steps' without making clear what these steps are. The WGBHR, in its report on state-owned entities,[112] considered that the necessary additional steps are 'measures in addition to those outlined in Principles 1 to 3, which are applicable to all companies'.[113] It acknowledges that while 'the call to take additional steps applies to all States equally, its precise implications will be

---

[107] Daniela Chimisso dos Santos and Sara Seck, 'Human Rights Due Diligence and Extractive Industries' in Deva and Birchall, BHR note 79, 151.

[108] For a full discussion on the definitions of SOEs and the subject area generally, see Mihaela Maria Barnes, *State-Owned Entities and Human Rights: The Role of International Law* (CUP, 2022).

[109] OECD Guidelines on Corporate Governance of State-Owned Enterprises (OECD, 2015), 14.

[110] Larry Catá Backer, 'Human Rights Responsibilities of State-Owned Enterprises' in Deva and Birchall, BHR, note 79, 223, 230–8.

[111] Commentary to GP 4.

[112] WGBHR, Report on State-Owned Entities, UN Doc. A/HRC/32/45 (4 May 2016). It states at para. 33: '[w]hat matters is whether the business entity is completely dependent on the State, is empowered by law to exercise elements of government function and acts under those powers, or acts under the instructions, direction or control of the State.'

[113] Ibid., para. 23.

context- and company-specific'.[114] The recommendations by the WGBHR for what this means in practice include the following: state-owned entities should be required by the state to take the steps necessary to ensure that they respect human rights, with explicit human rights targets, and conduct human rights due diligence, all of which should be monitored by their boards; state-owned entities should report on environmental, social, and human rights performance; and state-owned entities should cooperate fully with judicial and non-judicial grievance mechanisms and provide remediation for human rights abuses that they may be causing or to which they contribute.[115] In doing this, the WGBHR expects that the state-owned entities should lead by example in this field.[116]

This guidance may also affect the scope of a state-owned entity's responsibility as a business enterprise. This is because, unlike most of the state's obligations under Pillar I of the UNGPs, state-owned entities are expressly stated to have responsibilities under Pillar II as well.[117] This creates an unusual form of obligation and responsibility on state-owned entities and 'raises the difficult issue of the disjunction between the scope of the enterprise's responsibility to respect human rights and the limits of a state's legal duty under international law applied within its domestic legal order with respect to those human rights norms and instruments domestically legalized'.[118] For example, in current national legislation on business and human rights matters, only the Australian Modern Slavery Act 2018 requires government departments and other government bodies, including state-owned entities, to comply with it.[119]

State-owned entities are also relevant in regard to other international legal principles, such as the immunity of a state entity from the courts of other states, unless (generally) the entity is a commercial enterprise.[120] This can cause issues of access to remedies.[121] Accordingly, it is argued:

---

[114] Ibid., para. 90.
[115] Ibid., paras 58, 61, 67, 77, 80, and 84.
[116] Ibid., para. 52.
[117] Commentary to GP 4 '(These enterprises are also subject to the corporate responsibility to respect human rights, addressed in chapter II)' (brackets in original).
[118] Catá Backer, note 110, 242.
[119] Modern Slavery Act 2018 (Commonwealth of Australia), s. 5 (1)(b) and (c). See further in Chapter 7.
[120] Hazel Fox and Philippa Webb, *The Law of State Immunity* (OUP, 3rd ed., 2015).
[121] Mark Weidemaier and Matt Gauthier, 'Venezuela as a Case Study in Limited (Sovereign) Liability' (2017) 12 *Capital Markets Law Journal* 215. See further in Chapter 6.

The UNGP mirrors the conceptual division between the law-based system of sovereign immunities, and the markets-based systems of governance norms, while attempting to cover the governance gaps that this tension produces. Yet it may also move a step closer to the vision of creating directly applicable human rights obligations of enterprises under international law.[122]

This difference between an internationally legally binding state obligation under Pillar I and the corporate responsibility under Pillar II will be considered in the next chapter.

7. Conclusions

This chapter began by acknowledging that states alone have explicit international legal obligations under international human rights law and that states can be liable for actions of business in some circumstances. It showed how the law of state responsibility does include responsibility on states for the actions of businesses, although this is in limited circumstances where those actions can be attributed to the state. Developments in international human rights law have extended the obligations on states to actions of businesses, in a range of situations, with states having an obligation of due diligence to investigate and respond to activities by businesses which abuse the human rights of those within that state's jurisdiction. The UNGPs restate this international legal position.

There is debate as to whether states have transnational jurisdiction over the actions of businesses. Where a state does exercise this jurisdiction, it is usually by regulation of those businesses which are domiciled in the state to include the actions of their subsidiaries and possibly their business partners in other states. Occasionally, it can be through direct jurisdiction in another state, though that raises issues of possible infringements of state sovereignty.

Finally, in a sharp contrast with the case with which this chapter began, the Inter-American Court of Human Rights held in the *Case of the Miskito Divers* (which was discussed above):

---

[122] Catá Backer, note 110, 243.

> This Court considers it pertinent to point out that it is the companies that are primarily responsible for behaving responsibly in the activities they carry out, since their active participation is fundamental for the respect and enforcement of human rights. Businesses should adopt, at their own expense, preventive measures to protect the human rights of their workers, as well as measures aimed at preventing their activities from having a negative impact on the communities in which they operate or on the environment.[123]

Hence, while states have international legal obligations in relation to business activities which violate human rights treaties, it is necessary to examine what responsibilities are placed on those businesses themselves. This is the focus of the next chapter.

---

[123] *Case of the Miskito Divers*, note 58, para. 51.

5
Corporate Responsibilities and Human Rights Due Diligence

1. Context

A core aspect of the corporate responsibility to respect human rights under the United Nations Guiding Principles on Business and Human Rights 2011 (UNGPs) is set out in GP 13:

> The responsibility to respect human rights requires that business enterprises:
> (a) Avoid causing or contributing to adverse human rights impacts through their own activities, and address such impacts when they occur;
> (b) Seek to prevent or mitigate adverse human rights impacts that are directly linked to their operations, products or services by their business relationships, even if they have not contributed to those impacts.

When considering how to implement the UNGPs, a group of financial institutions, known as the Thun Group of Banks (because they met in Thun in Switzerland) adopted two 'Discussion Papers'. In the second one, adopted in 2017, the Thun Group produced a *Discussion Paper on the Implications of UN Guiding Principles 13 & 17 in a Corporate and Investment Banking Context*.[1] In the consideration of each bank's responsibilities under GP 13, the Discussion Paper stated:

---

[1] Thun Group of Banks, *Discussion Paper on the Implications of UN Guiding Principles 13 & 17 in a Corporate And Investment Banking Context* (2017), https://www.business-humanrights.org/en/latest-news/thun-group-paper-on-the-implications-of-un-guiding-principle-13b-17-in-a-corporate-and-investment-banking-context/. There is an earlier *Discussion Paper for Banks on Implications of Principles 16–21* (2013) Discussion Paper 2013.

While the provision of wholesale financial products and services may under specific circumstances reach the level of contribution [under GP 13a], in an investment banking context banks are, with a sound due diligence process in place according to the criteria outlined in the Thun Group's 2013 Discussion Paper, more likely to be directly linked to adverse human rights impacts under UNGP 13b ... For this reason, *the focus of this paper is on direct linkage* according to UNGP 13b.[2]

This approach, of focusing solely on the directly linked aspect of GP 13 and ignoring the possibility of banks causing or contributing to adverse human rights impacts through their loans and other services, was strongly rejected by John Ruggie. He wrote:

> I am deeply troubled by the discussion paper the Thun Group has just recently published. It misconstrues *the* central Guiding Principle regarding the corporate responsibility to respect human rights ... [The] scope of due diligence should depend on the nature of the risk and the bank's connection to it ... not on the type of loan on an a priori basis. For example, providing a general corporate loan to a private prison company that is alleged to engage in severe human rights abuses ought to require a very deep dive by the bank, coupled with the imposition of strict conditions if it decides to go ahead with the loan. If the bank does neither and yet proceeds, then it is squarely in 'contribution' territory [under GP 13a] for any adverse impacts, even though the loan is not asset or project specific.[3]

---

[2] Thun Group of Banks, *Discussion Paper on the Implications of UN Guiding Principles 13 & 17 in a Corporate and Investment Banking Context* (2017), note 1, 6 (emphasis added).

[3] John Ruggie, 'Comments on Thun Group of Banks Discussion Paper on the Implications of UN Guiding Principles 13 & 17 in a Corporate and Investment Banking Context' (21 February 2017), www.banktrack.org/download/comments_on_thun_group_of_banks_discussion_paper/thunfinal.pdf, 1–3 (emphasis in original). Ruggie stated later: 'Putting the word "directly" before "linked" [in the UNGPs] was intended to stress that any abuse must be linked to the company's operations, products or services, not merely to the fact of a relationship itself ... For example, the Thun paper conceives of "contributing" to human rights harm in such a way that banks virtually by definition cannot contribute to harm committed by clients. This is not only inconsistent with the [UN]GPs and the [OECD Guidelines]; it also defies common logic and recent conduct': John Ruggie, Letter to OECD,(6 March 2017), https://www.business-humanrights.org/en/latest-news/john-ruggie-clarifies-key-terms-of-un-guiding-principles-including-cause-contribute-directly-linked/, 2. This response by Ruggie was followed by a similar response to the Thun Group of Banks from the WGBHR: https://media.business-humanrights.org/media/documents/files/documents/20170223_WG_BHR_letter_to_Thun_Group.pdf.

This exchange, in which Ruggie rebuked the Thun Group, was due to the misunderstanding by these financial institutions that they could never cause or contribute to adverse human rights impacts through their lending activities. As Ruggie noted, there are many circumstances in which financial institutions could contribute to adverse human rights impacts in their provisions of loans and investments.

This exchange also shows that there is still a great deal to be done to clarify and implement the corporate responsibility to respect human rights under the UNGPs. This chapter will analyse the main aspects of Pillar II, with a particular focus on the core element of human rights due diligence.

2. Corporate Responsibility

a. Definition

The broad idea of the corporate responsibility to respect human rights is set out in the first of the 'foundational principles' in Pillar II of the UNGPs, being GP 11:

> Business enterprises should respect human rights. This means that they should avoid infringing on the human rights of others and should address adverse human rights impacts with which they are involved.

The basis for the corporate responsibility to respect human rights was set out in the initial Framework Report,[4] which foreshadowed the UNGPs (as discussed in Chapter 3). The Framework stated:

> [The corporate] responsibility to respect is defined by social expectations—as part of what is sometimes called a company's social license to operate ... [and] 'doing no harm' is not merely a passive responsibility for firms but may entail positive steps. To discharge the responsibility to respect requires due diligence. This concept describes the

---

[4] Report of the Special Representative of the Secretary-General on the issue of human rights and transnational corporations and other business enterprises, 'Framework of Protect, Respect and Remedy', UN Human Rights Council, UN Doc. A/HRC/8/5 (7 April 2008) www.reports-and-materials.org/Ruggie-report-7-Apr-2008.pdf [Framework Report].

steps a company must take to become aware of, prevent and address adverse human rights impacts.[5]

As seen in this quotation, the corporate responsibility is called a 'social expectation' as part of a 'social license to operate' in the Framework Report of 2008. In the following year's Report by the Special Rapporteur of the Secretary-General (SRSG) it is called a 'social norm'[6] and in the 2010 Report it is stated as being a 'standard of expected conduct'.[7] These changing ideas of what are variously called social expectations/licences/norms/conduct of a business are considered by some writers as being 'based on the expectation that private companies should no longer base their actions on the needs of their shareholders alone, but rather have obligations towards the society in which the company operates'.[8]

It has been pointed out that there is a real difficulty in determining a social expectation or a social norm of a business, because

> [there is] frequently a gap between citizen's expectations and what they perceive to be the reality of business behaviour. This gap is caused partly by ... an insufficient understanding on the part of some enterprises of fast evolving societal expectations, as well as by an insufficient awareness on the part of citizens of the achievements of enterprises and the constraints under which they operate.[9]

Even if a social expectation can be discerned through empirical evidence, it is not clear which 'society' is the relevant society for determining the expectation. Is it only the industrialized, consumer-active Global North and their shareholders or does it include the rural poor in non-industrialized states? Will it affect those businesses that produce consumer goods (especially to the Global North) more than those that do not produce consumer

---

[5] Ibid., paras 54–61.

[6] Report of Special Rapporteur of the Secretary-General (SRSG), UN Doc. A/HRC/11/13 (22 April 2009), www2.ohchr.org/english/bodies/hrcouncil/docs/11session/A.HRC.11.13.pdf [SRSG Report 2009].

[7] Report, UN Doc. A/HRC/14/27 (9 April 2010), http://198.170.85.29/Ruggie-report-2010.pdf [SRSG Report 2010].

[8] Elisa Morgera, *Corporate Accountability in International Environmental Law* (OUP, 2009), 18. She prefers the use of the term 'corporate accountability', as it implies that businesses are answerable to others for their actions.

[9] European Commission, 'A Renewed EU Strategy 2011–14 for Corporate Social Responsibility' COM (2011) 681 final (25 October 2011), http://eur-lex.europa.eu/LexUriServ/LexUriServ.do?uri=COM:2011:0681:FIN:EN:PDF, para. 4.2.

goods or that only produce goods in the Global South?[10] It has been argued that, if there is such a social licence for a business enterprise to operate, then it is highly unlikely that those who are oppressed and those whose human rights are abused by a business will be in a position to withdraw that social licence.[11] This response is linked with a concern that these social expectations could be defined to serve only some entrenched economic interests or selected social or business partners.[12] Nevertheless, there remains across the business and human rights field an understanding of there being a social licence or purpose to business activities.[13]

b. Respect

'Respect' is defined by GP 11, as being to 'avoid infringing on the human rights of others and (to) ... address adverse human rights impacts with which they are involved'. This idea of 'respecting' human rights arises from the tripartite typology of 'the obligation to respect, the obligation to protect, and the obligation to fulfil' human rights, which was formulated by Henry Shue,[14] and reworked for international human rights law by Asbjørn Eide.[15] It has become a familiar typology to international human rights lawyers. For Eide, this typology was in relation to the obligations on a state:

> The obligation to respect requires the State, and thereby all its organs and agents, to abstain from doing anything that violates the integrity of the individual or infringes on her or his freedom, including the freedom to use the material resources available to that individual in the way she or he finds best to satisfy the basic needs.[16]

---

[10] Surya Deva, *Regulating Corporate Human Rights Violations: Humanising Business* (Routledge, 2014).
[11] Ibid., 109–10.
[12] Michael Porter and Mark Kramer, 'Creating Shared Value' [2011] *Harvard Business Review* www.waterhealth.com/sites/default/files/Harvard_Business_Review_Shared_Value.pdf
[13] For example, British Academy, *Reforming Business for the 21st Century* (British Academy, 2019).
[14] Henry Shue, *Basic Rights: Subsistence, Affluence, and US Foreign Policy* (Princeton University Press, 2nd ed., 1996) 52.
[15] UN Economic and Social Council, 'The New International Economic Order and the Promotion of Human Rights—Report on the Right to Adequate Food as a Human Right Submitted by Mr. Asbjørn Eide, Special Rapporteur' UN Doc. E.CN.4/Sub.2/1987/23 (7 July 1987), para. 66.
[16] Ibid., para. 67.

Under the Framework Report, this approach was used in relation to businesses: '[t]o respect rights essentially means not to infringe on the rights of others—put simply, to do no harm.'[17] John Ruggie clarified this:

> '[R]especting' rights means to not violate them, to not facilitate or otherwise be involved in their violation. And it entails a correlative responsibility to address harms that do arise ... not infringing on human rights is the baseline norm with the widest possible global recognition.[18]

Thus the core sense of respecting human rights by businesses was of acting positively not to do harm. As Mark Taylor has argued, this means that 'a business should be responsible for what it does, including to whom it relates, not for activities in an ill-defined space in which it has some influence'.[19]

c. Distinction from State Obligations

There is a distinction in terminology in the UNGPs between a 'duty' of a state (which is a legal obligation) and a corporate 'responsibility' (which is not a legal obligation). This can be confusing for international lawyers, as the international law principle of state responsibility, which was discussed in Chapter 4, uses the terminology of 'responsibility' to mean a legal obligation on a state. Yet the UNGPs make clear that 'the responsibility of business enterprises to respect human rights is distinct from issues of legal liability and enforcement'.[20] This terminology mismatch is probably because the drafters of the UNGPs did not want to alter the position under the current international human rights law that businesses do not generally have any direct international legal obligations (as discussed in Chapter 2). However,

---

[17] Framework Report, note 4, para. 24.
[18] John Ruggie, *Just Business* (Norton, 2013), 95 [Ruggie, Just Business].
[19] Mark B. Taylor, 'Human Rights Due Diligence in Theory and Practice' in Surya Deva and David Birchall (eds), *Research Handbook on Business and Human Rights* (Edward Elgar, 2020) [Deva and Birchall, BHR], 88, 98.
[20] Commentary to GP 12. This is confirmed by Ruggie, Just Business, 91, *contra* Special Representative of the Secretary-General, 'Report of the Special Representative of the Secretary-General on the Issue of Human Rights and Transnational Corporations and Other Business Enterprises' UN Doc. A/HRC/4/35 (19 February 2007) [SRSG Report 2007], para. 6: '[the corporate responsibility to respect includes] the *legal*, social or moral obligations imposed on companies.' (emphasis added).

it was acknowledged that this business responsibility is not a law-free zone and will be affected by developments in law, especially national law.[21]

The distinction between corporate responsibilities and a state's legal obligations is made clearer in the Commentary to GP 11, which notes that the corporate responsibility to respect human rights 'exists independently of states' abilities and/or willingness to fulfil their own human rights obligations [and] ... over and above compliance with national laws and regulations'.[22] Thus, simply complying with a state's domestic law is insufficient for a business to comply with the UNGPs. This is confirmed in GP 23:

> In all contexts, business enterprises should:
> (a) Comply with all applicable laws and respect internationally recognized human rights, wherever they operate;
> (b) Seek ways to honour the principles of internationally recognized human rights when faced with conflicting requirements;
> (c) Treat the risk of causing or contributing to gross human rights abuses as a legal compliance issue wherever they operate.

The Commentary to GP 23 notes that '[w]here the domestic context renders it impossible to meet this responsibility fully, business enterprises are expected to respect the principles of internationally recognized human rights to the greatest extent possible in the circumstances, and to be able to demonstrate their efforts in this regard'. Thus, the UNGPs indicate that all businesses should respect the 'entire spectrum of internationally recognised human rights' in GP 23(b) and also acknowledge that there can be times when a business may not be able to do so because of the actions of the state in which they operate. This creates a governance gap between business activities and state actions.[23]

The Office of the High Commissioner for Human Rights' (OHCHR) Interpretive Guide on the Corporate Responsibility to Respect Human Rights (Interpretive Guide)[24] elaborates on GP 23. It states that, where there are no national laws to protect human rights or when national laws

---

[21] SRSG Report 2010, note 7, para. 66. See further in Chapter 7.
[22] Commentary to GP 11.
[23] Penelope Simons and Audrey Macklin, *The Governance Gap: Extractive Industries, Human Rights, and the Home State Advantage* (Routledge, 2015).
[24] OHCHR, *An Interpretive Guide* (OHCHR, 2012), www.ohchr.org/Documents/Issues/Business/RtRInterpretativeGuide.pdf [OHCHR, Interpretive Guide].

'offer a level of human rights protection that falls short of internationally recognised human rights standards', businesses are expected to 'operate to the higher standard'.[25] In other situations, the national law or practice may 'require (as against merely allowing for)' businesses to act in ways that contradict their responsibility to respect international human rights.[26] In such situations, GP 23(b) provides that businesses should seek to 'honour' the principles of international human rights when faced with conflicting requirements. This term is also used in the OECD Guidelines, where it makes clear that businesses 'should seek ways to honour such principles and standards to the fullest extent which does not place them in violation of domestic law'.[27]

The use of the term 'honour' is unusual in international law. The term does not appear in any of the international human rights instruments mentioned in the UNGPs.[28] While rare, 'honour' has been used in relation to UN Resolutions, where the International Court of Justice (ICJ) has considered that where an original legal obligation was owed by one entity, other entities can be called upon to honour that obligation as a consequence of the original obligation.[29] Similarly, the word 'honour' is used in the UN Convention on the Law of the Sea, where the '[Seabed] Authority and its organs shall recognise and honour the rights and obligations arising from this resolution and the decisions of the Commission taken pursuant to it'.[30] Thus it has been argued that the term 'honour' used in the UNGPs might indicate that there is a responsibility on businesses, which could be considered to be a moral one with legal effects, that arises from the legal obligations on states under international human rights law.[31]

---

[25] Ibid., 77.
[26] Ibid., 78.
[27] OECD Guidelines, Chapter I, para. 2.
[28] GP 12, discussed below.
[29] ICJ, *Advisory Opinion in the Certain Expenses of the United Nations* [1962] ICJ Rep. 151, 169: '[O]bligations of the [United Nations] Organization may be incurred by the Secretary-General, acting on the authority of the Security Council or of the General Assembly, and the General Assembly has no alternative but to honour these engagements.' Also Divac Oberg, 'The Legal Effects of Resolutions of the Security Council and the General Assembly in the Jurisprudence of the ICJ' (2005) 16 *European Journal of International Law* 879.
[30] Resolution II in Annex I to the UN Convention on the Law of the Sea 1982, 1833 UNTS 397, para. 13.
[31] Arianne Griffith, Lise Smit, and Robert McCorquodale, 'Responsible Business Conduct and State Laws: Addressing Human Rights Conflicts' (2020) 20 *Human Rights Law Review* 641. Much of this section is taken from this article. Those authors set out a typology of different levels of state law and practices, which enable businesses to determine how to respond, using the key concept of human rights due diligence, which is discussed below.

The Canadian National Contact Point (NCP) under the OECD Guidelines (discussed in Chapter 6), has considered the situation of conflicting requirements on a business:

> Where host country requirements differ from the international standards, it is the duty of the company to meet the higher, more rigorous standards.
>
> The Government of Canada also expects Canadian companies to operate in accordance with internationally recognised labour standards in all cases, even where a host country fails to enforce domestic laws or implement international standards or in challenging environments such as a weak governance zone, zones of conflict or an unstable political environment.[32]

This statement indicates that there may be consequences in the home state of a business if a business fails to honour international human rights standards when operating in a host state. While these statements are not legally binding, they do offer clarity on the understanding of these terms by competent bodies. Industry standards are also being developed to assist businesses,[33] with the International Organisation of Employers (IOE) accepting that the UNGPs should be implemented by all their business members.[34]

3. Business Enterprises

The terminology used by the UNGPs for which entities have this responsibility to respect is 'business enterprises'. This term is defined in GP 14 to

---

[32] Final Statement of the Canadian NCP in *Former Employees v. Banro in the DRC* (filed 26 February 2016), para. 7: www.oecdwatch.org/cases/Case_469.

[33] For example, the European Commission, Shift and Institute for Human Rights and Business (IHRB), *ICT Sector Guide on Implementing the UN Guiding Principles on Business and Human Rights; Oil and Gas Sector Guide on Implementing the UN Guiding Principles on Business and Human Rights; Employment and Recruitment Agencies Sector Guide on Implementing the UN Guiding Principles on Business and Human Rights*, www.ec.europa.eu/anti-trafficking/publications/european-commission-sector-guides-implementing-un-guiding-principles-business-and-hum-0_en; and OHCHR, 'Tackling Discrimination Against Lesbian, Gay, Bi, Trans, & Intersex People: Standards of Conduct for Business' (September 2017), www.unfe.org/wp-content/uploads/2017/09/UN-Standards-of-Conduct.pdf.

[34] IOE, 'Input for the Roadmap for the Next Decade—Building Blocks for Realizing UNGPs Implementation toward 2030' (20 September 2021), https://www.ioe-emp.org/news/details/final-ioe-and-biac-statement-on-business-priorities-for-the-ungp-roadmap

include 'all enterprises regardless of their size, sector, operational context, ownership and structure',[35] and to extend 'throughout the business enterprise'.[36] Thus this term is intended to be broad enough to cover the multitude of 'complex organizational forms characteristic of modern business enterprises'.[37] As such, this term is meant to include entities incorporated in states (usually termed 'corporations' or 'companies'), and other registered or unregistered entities, such as partnerships. Similarly, the OECD Guidelines apply to 'multinational enterprises' and are 'addressed to all the entities within the multinational enterprise (parent companies and/or local entities)'.[38] Due to the divergent terminologies used, as stated in Chapter 1, this book generally uses the term 'business' to cover all types of business enterprise, unless the context or quotation is otherwise.

Guiding Principle 14 also states that 'the scale and complexity of the means through which enterprises meet [their corporate] responsibility [to respect human rights] may vary according to these factors [of size, etc.,] and with the severity of the enterprise's adverse human rights impacts'. The Commentary to GP 14 clarifies this:

> [S]ome small and medium-sized enterprises can have severe human rights impacts, which will require corresponding measures regardless of their size. Severity of impacts will be judged by their scale, scope and irremediable character. The means through which a business enterprise meets its responsibility to respect human rights may also vary depending on whether, and the extent to which, it conducts business through a corporate group or individually. However, the responsibility to respect human rights applies fully and equally to all business enterprises.

This Commentary is a reminder that the responsibility to respect human rights applies to all businesses, which is an important aspect of the UNGPs.

---

[35] GP 14.
[36] GP 16 (and also GP 3).
[37] Framework Report, note 4, para. 20.
[38] OECD Guidelines, Part I, para. 4.

4. Human Rights

The scope of human rights for which businesses are responsible is set out in the second 'foundational' principle of the corporate responsibility to respect human rights, being GP 12:

> The responsibility of business enterprises to respect human rights refers to internationally recognized human rights—understood, at a minimum, as those expressed in the International Bill of Human Rights and the principles concerning fundamental rights set out in the International Labour Organization's Declaration on Fundamental Principles and Rights at Work.

This GP establishes one of the key elements of the UNGPs: '[b]ecause business enterprises can have an impact on virtually the entire spectrum of internationally recognized human rights, their responsibility to respect applies to all such rights.'[39] This powerful statement appears to have arisen after a study for the SRSG of hundreds of reports of adverse human rights impacts of businesses showed that 'because [businesses] can affect virtually all internationally recognized rights, they should consider the responsibility to respect in relation to all such rights ... [and] there are few if any internationally recognized rights business cannot impact—or be perceived to impact—in some manner.'[40] A very helpful report on how businesses can affect every human right was produced by Monash University and the OHCHR called *Human Rights Translated*,[41] which provides valuable examples and guidance in this regard.

The list of 'internationally recognized human rights' in GP 12 includes the 'International Bill of Human Rights', which is a shorthand term for three international documents: the Universal Declaration on Human Rights 1948 (UDHR); the International Covenant on Economic, Social and Cultural Rights 1966 (IESCR); and the International Covenant on Civil and Political Rights 1966 (ICCPR). While both of the Covenants are ratified by a large majority of states—there being over 170 state parties to each—some states are not party to either or both of them, yet the UNGPs effectively includes

---

[39] Commentary to GP 12.
[40] Framework Report, note 4, paras 52 and 24.
[41] OHCHR, *Human Rights Translated 2.0: A Business Reference Guide*, (OHCHR, 2017) https://www.ohchr.org/en/publications/special-issue-publications/human-rights-translated-20-business-reference-guide.

these states through the breadth of GP 12. Further, the UDHR is not a treaty but rather a Declaration by the UN General Assembly and so has traditionally been considered not to be legally binding. There is, though, a growing view that some or all of the UDHR is now customary international law.[42] This view is assisted by the fact that the UDHR is one of the documents about which all states must report on their compliance to the UN Human Rights Council in relation to their obligations under the Universal Periodic Review of a state's implementation of human rights, and about which no state has objected.[43]

The other document referred to in GP 12 is the International Labour Organization's Declaration on Fundamental Principles and Rights at Work. This is also not a treaty but is, instead:

> [A]n expression of commitment by governments, employers' and workers' organizations to uphold basic human values—values that are vital to our social and economic lives. It affirms the obligations and commitments that are inherent in membership of the ILO, namely:
> 1. freedom of association and the effective recognition of the right to collective bargaining;
> 2. the elimination of all forms of forced or compulsory labour;
> 3. the effective abolition of child labour;
> 4. the elimination of discrimination in respect of employment and occupation; and
> 5. a safe and healthy working environment.[44]

With so many actual or potential adverse human rights impacts from business activities relating to labour rights,[45] it is a significant statement that this Declaration is expressly included in the UNGPs.

---

[42] Hugh Thirlway, 'Human Rights in Customary Law: An Attempt to Define some of the Issues' (2015) 28 *Leiden Journal of International Law* 495.

[43] UN Human Rights Council Res. 5/1 (2007). Also Françoise Hampson, 'An Overview of the Reform of the UN Human Rights Machinery' [2007] *Human Rights Law Review* 7 and Rhona Smith, '"To See Themselves as Others See Them": The Five Permanent Members of the Security Council and the Human Rights Council's Universal Periodic Review' (2013) 35 *Human Rights Quarterly* 1.

[44] ILO Declaration on Fundamental Principles and Rights at Work.

[45] Anne Trebilcock, 'Due Diligence on Labour Issues—Opportunities and Limits of the UN Guiding Principles on Business and Human Rights' in Adelle Blackett and Anne Trebilcock (eds), *Research Handbook on Transnational Labour Law* (Edward Elgar, 2015).

The phrase 'at a minimum' in GP 12 is also important, as there are other international human rights treaties which are not included in the above list but would nevertheless be commonly understood to constitute 'internationally recognized human rights'. Examples include the Convention on the Rights of the Child (the most widely ratified international human rights treaty), the Convention on the Elimination of all Forms of Discrimination Against Women, the Convention Against All Forms of Racial Discrimination, and the Convention on the Rights of Persons with Disabilities.[46] In addition, the Declaration on the Rights of Indigenous Peoples has had widespread influence, indicating that parts of it might be reflective of customary international law.[47] These international documents are indirectly referred to in the Commentary to GP 12:

> Depending on circumstances, business enterprises may need to consider additional standards. For instance, enterprises should respect the human rights of individuals belonging to specific groups or populations that require particular attention, where they may have adverse human rights impacts on them. In this connection, United Nations instruments have elaborated further on the rights of indigenous peoples; women; national or ethnic, religious and linguistic minorities; children; persons with disabilities; and migrant workers and their families. Moreover, in situations of armed conflict enterprises should respect the standards of international humanitarian law.

However, such a casual indication of there being other major human rights treaties which businesses 'may' consider—in contrast to the previous international documents being 'an authoritative list of the core internationally recognized human rights'[48]—has been strongly criticized as giving a hierarchy of human rights, which is contrary to international human

---

[46] OHCHR, The Core International Human Rights Instruments and their Monitoring Bodies, https://www.ohchr.org/en/core-international-human-rights-instruments-and-their-monitoring-bodies.

[47] For example, the decision of the Inter-American Court of Human Rights in *Kichwa Indigenous People of Sarayaku v. Ecuador*, IACtHR Series C No. 245 (27 June 2012), para. 217 indicates this, and the Belize Supreme Court decided that the property provisions of the Declaration embodied 'general principles of international law' that had the same force as a treaty: *Aurelio Cal and the Maya Village of Santa Cruz v. Attorney General of Belize; and Manuel Coy and Maya Village of Conejo v. Attorney General of Belize* (Consolidated) Claim Nos 171 and 17 (18 October 2007).

[48] Commentary to GP 12.

rights law.[49] Feminist and Third World Approaches to International Law (TWAIL) scholars note a bias in this hierarchy of the UNGPs, as it suggests, for example, that women's human rights and those of other marginalized groups, such as Indigenous people, are not 'equally universal, but ... [are] particular, biased, special interests'.[50]

This of particular concern as, for example, feminist international human rights scholars have long argued that 'the development of international human rights law generally has been partial and androcentric, privileging a masculine world view'.[51] What is noteworthy about this critique is that it highlights that the UNGPs do themselves make specific reference to the need for states and for business to pay special attention to those who are particularly vulnerable or marginalized and the additional risks to women.[52] This has led to an insightful report by the WGBHR on the gender dimensions of the UNGPs, which is discussed in section 7.b.(ii) below.[53]

5. Human Rights Impacts

The UNGPs, and especially Pillar II, focus on 'adverse human rights impacts' as the consequence of any business activity for which the UNGPs (and other international documents) apply. The OHCHR states that '[a]n "adverse human rights impact" occurs when an action removes or reduces the ability of an individual to enjoy his or her human rights'.[54] The Commentary to GP 17 notes that 'potential impacts (i.e. those which have not yet occurred) should be addressed through prevention or mitigation,

---

[49] The Vienna Declaration and Programme of Action, GA Res. 157/23, UN Doc. A/CONF.157/23 (1992), para. 5 provides: '[a]ll human rights are universal, indivisible and interdependent and interrelated.'
[50] Rosemary Hunter, 'Contesting the Dominant Paradigm: Feminist Critiques of Liberal Legalism' in Margaret Davies and Vanessa Munro (eds), *The Ashgate Companion to Feminist Legal Theory* (Routledge, 2016), 13, 15.
[51] Hilary Charlesworth, 'What Are "Women's International Human Rights"?' in Rebecca Cook (ed.), *Human Rights of Women: National and International Perspectives* (University of Pennsylvania Press, 1994), 58, 60. Penelope Simons and Melisa Handl, 'Relations of Ruling: A Feminist Critique of the United Nations Guiding Principles on Business and Human Rights and Violence against Women in the Context of Resource Extraction' (2019) 13 *Canadian Journal of Women and the Law* 113.
[52] Commentaries to GP 3 and GP 18.
[53] WGBHR, Report to the UN Human Rights Committee on 'Gender Dimensions of the UNGPs' UN Doc. A/HRC/41/43 (23 May 2019).
[54] OHCHR, Interpretive Guide, note 24, 5.

while actual impacts—those that have already occurred—should be a subject for remediation (Principle 22).'

The general view is that an 'adverse human rights impact' is the same as a human rights violation or abuse under international human rights law.[55] However, David Birchall has offered an alternative view that 'impacts' are broader than legal or regulatory infractions, and can include, for example, financial actions by businesses which limit access to housing for people even if they appear to be within the law.[56]

6. Types of Conduct

a. Cause, Contribute to, and Directly Linked

The third and last 'foundational' principle of the corporate responsibility to respect human rights is set out in GP 13 (which was referred to in the Introduction to this chapter):

> The responsibility to respect human rights requires that business enterprises:
> (a) Avoid causing or contributing to adverse human rights impacts through their own activities, and address such impacts when they occur;
> (b) Seek to prevent or mitigate adverse human rights impacts that are directly linked to their operations, products or services by their business relationships, even if they have not contributed to those impacts.

The terminology of the key terms here: 'cause', 'contribute to', and 'directly linked', are not defined in the UNGPs or explained by the SRSG. These are called 'participation terms' by Tara van Ho because 'the UNGPs specifically reject the use of legal modes of responsibility and [instead] differentiate a

---

[55] Robert McCorquodale, Lise Smit, Stuart Neely, and Robin Brooks, 'Human Rights Due Diligence in Law and Practice: Good Practices and Challenges for Business Enterprises' (2017) 2 *Business and Human Rights Journal* 195 [McCorquodale, Smit, HRDD], 198. On the supposed difference between a 'violation' (being an act contrary to a treaty obligation on a state) and an 'abuse' (being an act contrary to a human right which is undertaken by a non-state actor) see Andrew Clapham, *Human Rights Obligations of Non-State Actors* (OUP, 2006).

[56] David Birchall, 'Any Act, Any Harm, To Anyone: The Transformative Potential of "Human Rights Impacts" under the UN Guiding Principles on Business and Human Rights' [2019] *University of Oxford Human Rights Hub* 120.

business's responsibility based on how it participates in, or does not participate in, the creation of a harm'.[57] She also notes that these terms are deliberately *sui generis* (or unique) terms removed from legal meanings.[58]

The only significant official attempt to define these terms was by the OHCHR in a response to a request from BankTrack, a civil society organization, in relation to the issues raised by the Thun Bank's Discussion Papers (which were considered in the introduction to this chapter).[59] The OHCHR considered that a business 'causes' an adverse impact when it reduces the realization of a human right by its own activities without the involvement of clients or other stakeholders. In contrast, a business 'contributes to' a human rights impact where that impact occurs as a result of the business's conduct together with that of others, with that contribution having some 'element of causality' and being more than 'trivial or minor'.[60] Rachel Davis has categorized the forms of contribution into three types: where a business may 'facilitate or enable' adverse impact; where it creates 'strong incentives' for a third party to cause adverse impact; or where it undertakes activities 'in parallel with a third party, leading to cumulative [adverse] impacts'.[61] The OHCHR gives an example of contribution as being where a business lends vehicles to security forces that use them for adverse human rights impacts.[62]

The OECD clarified that a business can be 'directly linked' to an adverse impact from its products, services, operations, or business relationships when it neither causes nor contributes to the impact.[63] The meaning of 'business relationships' was initially explained in the Commentary to GP 13 to be 'relationships with business partners, entities in its value chain,

---

[57] Tara van Ho, 'Defining the Relationships: "Cause, Contribute, and Directly Linked to" in the UN Guiding Principles on Business and Human Rights' (2021) 43 *Human Rights Quarterly* 625, 627. I have relied on that article in relation to this section.
[58] Ibid., 630.
[59] See OHCHR, Response to Request from BankTrack for advice Regarding the Application of the UN Guiding Principles on Business and Human Rights in the Context of the Banking Sector (June 2017), www.ohchr.org/Documents/Issues/Business/InterpretationGuidingPri nciples.pdf [OHCHR, Response to BankTrack], 5.
[60] Ibid. Note that the OECD suggests that 'contribution must be substantial': OECD, OECD Due Diligence Guidance for Responsible Business Conduct (2018), https://mneguidelines.oecd.org/OECD-Due-Diligence-Guidance-for-Responsible-Business-Conduct.pdf [OECD, Due Diligence Guidance], 70.
[61] Rachel Davis, 'The UN Guiding Principles on Business and Human Rights and Conflict-Affected Areas: State Obligations and Business Responsibilities' (2012) 94 *International Review of the Red Cross* 961, 973.
[62] OHCHR, Interpretive Guide, note 24, Q39, Answer.
[63] OHCHR, Response to BankTrack, note 59, 16. This requires a relationship between the business and the harm, not merely a relationship between the business and the other party.

and any other non-State or State entity directly linked to its business operations, products or services'. This definition was expanded in the OHCHR Interpretative Guide to 'include indirect business relationships in its value chain, beyond the first tier, and minority as well as majority shareholding positions in joint ventures',[64] and 'the use of the word "include" suggests that [these] examples of business relationships are non-exhaustive and illustrative.'[65]

The OHCHR went further in explaining the situation with regard to financial institutions:

> [T]he determining factor to establish a business relationship in terms of GP 13(b) is whether there is a link between an impact arising from the activities of an entity in which a minority investor holds shares and the operations, products or services of that minority shareholder. The relative size or percentage of the share an institutional investor holds in a company is not a factor in determining whether there is a business relationship for the purposes of GP 13(b). Rather, it can be a factor in determining what measures the institutional investor is expected to take to prevent or mitigate any adverse human rights impacts which are linked to its operations, products or services through the business relationship, as stipulated in GP 19.[66]

Thus, a business that is 'directly linked to' a harm 'has at least direct control or influence over whether the impact occurs'.[67] The OECD provides the following definition:

> 'Linkage' is defined by the relationship between the adverse impact and the enterprise's products, services or operations through another entity (i.e. business relationship). 'Directly linked' is not defined by direct contractual relationships, for example 'direct sourcing'.[68]

---

[64] OHCHR, Interpretive Guide, note 24, 5.
[65] OHCHR, Response to SOMO and OECD Watch (26 April 2013), www.ohchr.org/sites/default/files/Documents/Issues/Business/LetterSOMO.pdf, 3.
[66] Ibid.
[67] OHCHR, Interpretive Guide, note 24, Q46, Answer.
[68] OECD, Due Diligence Guidance, note 60, 71.

This definition of 'directly linked' was expanded upon by Roel Nieuwenkamp, then Chair of the negotiations which led to the 2011 revision of the OECD Guidelines to bring them in line with the UNGPs:

> [Firstly,] it has been stressed multiple times during the 2011 negotiations on the revisions of the Guidelines that *causality is not a factor* in determining whether a company's products, services or operations are 'directly linked' to an adverse impact through a business relationship...
>
> Secondly, it was recognised during the 2011 negotiations that companies' products, services or operations can be directly linked to adverse impacts. It is this direct link to the adverse impact that determines the company's responsibility to carry out due diligence and/or to mitigate adverse impacts. The *amount of leverage of a company does not affect this responsibility* itself, but it does influence the nature and extent of the due diligence...
>
> [Thirdly,] During the 2011 negotiations, we continuously sent out the message that the responsibility to carry out risk-based due diligence *is not limited to first tier business relationships*. There is no quantitative limit regarding this...
>
> [Fourthly,] I would like to stress that the term 'directly' was included in the text in order to ensure that *extremely loosely connected associations would not be covered* by the due diligence provisions. It was never intended to suggest the existence of an 'indirect linkage'. A company's operations, products or services are either 'directly linked' to an adverse impact through a business relationship—or not at all linked as far as the guidelines are concerned.[69]

Based on these statements, it can be concluded that 'directly linked' is considered by reference to a 'business relationship', and that the relevant business relationship (which does not have to be contractual) includes relationships (which extend beyond the first tier) which a business has with business partners, with entities in its value chain (being both the supply chain and the purchasing chain), and with any other entity in connection to its business operations, products, or services. This connection to its

---

[69] Expert Letters and Statements on the Application of the OECD Guidelines for Multinational Enterprises and UN Guiding Principles on Business and Human Rights in the context of the financial sector (June 2014) https://mneguidelines.oecd.org//global-forum/GFRBC-2014-financial-sector-document-3.pdf, 18–20 (emphasis added).

business operations, products, or services is relevant in relation to both actual and potential adverse human rights impact. Causality is not a factor in whether an enterprise is directly linked to an adverse human rights impact, nor is proximity a factor.[70]

The amount of leverage—discussed in the next section—that an enterprise has over its business relationship does not affect whether a business is directly linked to adverse human rights impacts, as leverage is only relevant in terms of the nature and extent of the human rights due diligence to be undertaken by the enterprise. This definition has been applied by the OECD NCPs to a range of circumstances, including in relation to the actions of manufacturers in selling their products to distributors without undertaking human rights due diligence.[71]

Further, there is either a direct link between the products, services, or operations of a business enterprise and an adverse human rights impact through a business relationship or there is no link. As quoted above, extremely loosely connected associations between a business and another entity are not included in the meaning of 'directly linked'. However, as Tara van Ho notes: '[t]he OHCHR's definitions [of these participation terms] seem to suggest that the number of actors involved, and the directness of the relationship between the business and the harm, are the primary considerations for determining a business's responsibility. Both criteria are questionable.'[72]

The need for action by a business which is directly linked to a business relationship where there is an adverse human rights impact is particularly important where the severity of the adverse human rights impact requires a business to terminate its business relationship. According to the Commentary on GP 19: 'the more severe the abuse, the more quickly the enterprise will need to see change before deciding whether to continue the relationship.' Further, for a business to maintain that relevant relationship '[it] should be able to demonstrate ... ongoing efforts to mitigate the impact and be prepared to accept any consequences—reputational, financial or legal—of the continuing connection.'[73]

---

[70] Michael Addo, as Chair of the WGBHR, Letter dated 23 February 2017 to Members of the Thun Group of Banks, www.business-humanrights.org/sites/default/files/documents/20170223%20WG%20BHR%20letter%20to%20Thun%20Group.pdf, 2–3.

[71] UK NCP, Final Statement: Lawyers for Palestinian Human Rights complaint to UK NCP about JCB, https://www.gov.uk/government/publications/lawyers-for-palestinian-human-rights-complaint-to-uk-ncp-about-jcb/final-statement-lawyers-for-palestinian-human-rights-complaint-to-uk-ncp-about-jcb,November 2021.

[72] Tara van Ho, note 57, 635.

[73] Commentary to GP 19.

It is also evident that, while 'cause' is a distinct term, the latter two participation terms ('contribute to' and 'directly linked') are connected. The OHCHR noted this when it stated:

> In practice, there is a *continuum* between 'contributing to' and having a 'direct link' to an adverse human rights impact: a bank's involvement with an impact may shift over time, depending on its own actions and omissions. For example, if a bank identifies or is made aware of an ongoing human rights issue that is directly linked to its operations, products or services through a client relationship, yet over time fails to take reasonable steps to seek to prevent or mitigate the impact—such as bringing up the issue with the client's leadership or board, persuading other banks to join in raising the issue with the client, making further financing contingent upon correcting the situation, etc.— it could eventually be seen to be facilitating the continuance of the situation and thus be in a situation of 'contributing'.[74]

Thus a business can move from being directly linked to an adverse human rights impact to contributing to that impact if it does not take action to prevent or mitigate the business relationship to which it is directly linked, including by undertaking human rights due diligence (discussed below).

Tara van Ho has criticized the existing official guidance on these participatory terms, as she claims that it uses 'the number of actors [e.g. in 'cause' v 'contribute'] involved in a harm as a dominant factor in categorizing businesses' responsibility ... [which] can act as an incentive for businesses to reform their structures to avoid responsibility rather than reforming their practices to avoid human rights impacts'.[75] Rather, she notes the reality of the power of businesses instead of their responsibility, and she proposes a system to enable proactive roles for business in managing their relationships:

> [A] new system of responsibility that moves away from the number of actors to the nature of a business's relationship to the resulting harm. This system is built around five factors: the power (direct, relational, and [power] over social or environmental conditions); independence, and mitigation efforts of the business; and the predictability and severity of

---

[74] OHCHR, Response to BankTrack, note 59, 7 (emphasis added).
[75] Tara van Ho, note 57, 657–8.

the harms ... While there are five factors, they do not carry equal weight in this new system. If a business exercises strong power and independence so that it is 'causing' a harm, the strict nature of the responsibility to respect means the other factors will not reduce its responsibility. The business's mitigation efforts, and the severity and predictability of the harm can otherwise move a business along the continuum in both directions, either towards 'directly linked to' or towards 'causation'.[76]

These understandings of the relationships between these participation terms are helpful in clarifying the responsibilities of businesses and the actions they could take.

b. Leverage

An essential element of a corporate responsibility to respect human rights through being directly linked by its business relationships is the concept of 'leverage'. Leverage is 'considered to exist where the enterprise has the ability to effect change in the wrongful practices of an entity that causes a harm'.[77] This concept of leverage is used to determine whether a business has taken 'appropriate action' in circumstances where it may contribute or be directly linked to an adverse human rights impact.[78]

Leverage is not always straightforward, as businesses may have different leverage over different entities, and may need to coordinate with others to have leverage over some entities, such as states. In other circumstances, a buyer may also be a supplier or may be one of many buyers, such as in the apparel sector, where 'suppliers typically manufacture for a multitude of buyers, with even large brands sometimes only constituting a small proportion of a supplier's total production ... [and] contracts are usually short-term, with buyers switching between producers based on price and quality, rather than social compliance'.[79] The OECD has issued guidance on responsible business conduct in various sectors and these do provide a range of measures which can be taken, from long-term contracts and capacity building to increasing leverage, and the guidance also makes clear that

---

[76] Ibid.
[77] Commentary to GP 19.
[78] GP 19 and Commentary to GP 19.
[79] Justine Nolan and Nana Frishling, 'Human Rights Due Diligence and the (Over) Reliance on Social Auditing in Supply Chains' in Deva and Birchall, BHR, note 19, 108, 126.

this responsibility exists across the entire supply chain.[80] The evidence from practice is that, where leverage is exercised beyond the first tier, it is usually done in one of two ways: either indirectly through the first tier supplier, for example through codes of conduct which require a first tier supplier to impose similar standards on those in the next tier and so on, or through collective engagement with peers or other stakeholders.[81]

The UNGPs' approach is that:

> There are situations in which the enterprise lacks the leverage to prevent or mitigate adverse impacts and is unable to increase its leverage. Here, the enterprise should consider ending the relationship, taking into account credible assessments of potential adverse human rights impacts of doing so.[82]

Ending the business relationship (or termination) is seen as a last resort and may not be available where the business relationship is 'crucial'.[83] However, when terminating a business relationship, the UNGPs expect businesses to assess the 'potential human rights' impacts of doing so, especially the severity of the current impact.[84] This recognizes that termination could have an adverse impact on the lives of the supplier's workers and the local community, and that, once the contract has been terminated, the supplier may no longer be incentivized to raise standards.[85] Also, as Geneviève Paul and Judith Schönsteiner have argued, in situations with widespread or systematic violations, the '"mere presence" of a company might entrench, exacerbate, or condone gross or serious violations' of human rights.[86]

---

[80] OECD, OECD Due Diligence Guidance for Responsible Supply Chains in the Garment and Footwear Sector (OECD Apparel Guidance 2017), 53, 56, 60, 71–3.

[81] Lise Smit, Gabrielle Holly, Robert McCorquodale, and Stuart Neely, 'Human Rights Due Diligence in Global Supply Chains: Evidence of Corporate Practices to Inform a Legal Standard' [2020] *International Journal of Human Rights* 945, 963 [Smit, HRDD Global Supply Chains].

[82] Commentary to GP 19.

[83] Ibid. In that instance the business must still 'demonstrate its own ongoing efforts to mitigate the impact and be prepared to accept any consequences—reputational, financial or legal—of the continuing connection'.

[84] Ibid.

[85] Smit, HRDD in Global Supply Chains, note 81, 955.

[86] Geneviève Paul and Judith Schönsteiner, 'Transitional Justice and the UN Guiding Principles on Business and Human Rights' in Sabine Michalowski (ed.), *Corporate Accountability in the Context of Transitional Justice* (Routledge, 2013), 74, 84.

7. Human Rights Due Diligence

a. Definition

A key aspect of the UNGPs and every related international (and most national) regulation on business and human rights is human rights due diligence (HRDD). In international law, due diligence has played an important role in the responsibility of states for private actors, as discussed in Chapter 4.[87] In that context 'due diligence' refers to an obligation of conduct by a state rather than an obligation of result, which means that the primary focus is on the behaviour of the state duty-bearer rather than on the outcome of their behaviour.[88] The *Max Planck Encyclopaedia of Public International Law* defines due diligence as 'an obligation of conduct on the part of a subject of law ... [the breach of which does not consist in] failing to achieve the desired result ... [but rather in] failing to take the necessary, diligent steps towards that end'.[89] As such, due diligence in international law tends to inquire whether a state has taken reasonable and appropriate steps to prevent or mitigate breaches of international law by private persons.[90]

However, the due diligence duty on states is distinct from the HRDD on business in the UNGPs. Indeed, the use of the term 'due diligence' in the UNGPs appears to be an innovative, clever, and deliberate tactic, as it is a term which is familiar to those working in business, those working in human rights and those working in states.[91] Indeed, while 'due diligence' has been used in some national instruments prior to the UNGPs, and it 'resonates with existing standards of duty of care in tort law and comparable concepts in civil law',[92] it had not been generally used in relation to human

---

[87] Timo Koivurova, 'Due Diligence' in Rüdiger Wolfrum (ed.), *Max Planck Encyclopaedia of Public International Law* (OUP, 2010).
[88] ILA Study Group on Due Diligence in International Law, Second Report (July 2016) [ILA DD Report], 2.
[89] Koivurova, note 87, para. 3.
[90] ILA DD Report, note 88, 3.
[91] The concept of due diligence as part of a state's human rights obligations was first expressed by the Inter-American Court of Human Rights in *Velasquez Rodriguez v. Honduras*, Judgment (Merits), 29 July 1988, para. 172—as discussed in Chapter 4.
[92] Andreas Rühmkorf and Lena Walker, 'Assessment of the Concept of "Duty of Care" in European Legal Systems for Amnesty International' (European Institutions Office, September 2018). Note that the concept of due diligence as a standard of care originated from Roman law: John Jefferson Bray, 'Possible Guidance from Roman Law' [1968] *Adelaide Law Review* 145, 150.

(b) Will vary in complexity with the size of the business enterprise, the risk of severe human rights impacts, and the nature and context of its operations;
(c) Should be ongoing, recognizing that the human rights risks may change over time as the business enterprise's operations and operating context evolve.

Human rights due diligence has been summarized in the OHCHR's Interpretive Guide as 'an ongoing management process that a reasonable and prudent enterprise needs to undertake, in light of its circumstances (including sector, operating context, size and similar factors) to meet its responsibility to respect human rights'.[96] The OECD has been very active in producing guidance on HRDD, including a very clear general guidance on HRDD for responsible business conduct, which clarifies some of the information set out in this section.[97]

To compare HRDD with the business understanding of due diligence, a general difference is that, while human rights lawyers use 'due diligence' as a standard of conduct required to discharge an obligation where the risk is to the individual or group,[98] those in business management normally consider 'due diligence' as a process to manage business risks, where the risk is to the business alone.[99] Indeed, there are five main distinctions between business due diligence and HRDD:[100]

1. Risk to the business in contrast to risk to the rights holder. The focus of the business human rights due diligence is about risk to the business itself, while HRDD is about the risk to those humans who are or might be impacted by the business activities.[101]
2. One responsibility for each business in contrast to having many responsibilities to rightsholders. Business due diligence considers that

---

[96] OHCHR, Interpretive Guide, note 24, 6.
[97] OECD Due Diligence Guidance, OECD-Due-Diligence-Guidance-for-Responsible-Business-Conduct.pdf.
[98] Koivurova, note 87.
[99] Olga Martin-Ortega, 'Human Rights Due Diligence for Corporations: From Voluntary Standards to Hard Law at Last?' (2013) 31 *Netherlands Quarterly of Human Rights* 44, 51.
[100] This distinction is set out in Robert McCorquodale, 'Human Rights Due Diligence Instruments: Evaluating the Current Legislative Landscape' in Axel Marx, Geert Van Calster, and Jan Wouters (eds), *Global Governance, Business and Human Rights* (Edward Elgar, 2022), 121, 123.
[101] Björn Fasterling, 'Human Rights Due Diligence as Risk Management: Social Risk Versus Human Rights Risk' (2016) 2 *Business and Human Rights Journal* 225.

each business has the one responsibility, which is in relation to its own business activity, while there are different responsibilities in HRDD depending on the actions of the business. The latter includes responsibilities for a business enterprise's own adverse human rights impacts which it has caused or which it has contributed to, as well as responsibilities for the human rights impacts of third parties with which the business has business relationships.[102]

3. Due diligence requirements vary only as to product or financial matters in contrast to HRDD requirements which vary as to size, risk, and context of operations. While the level of business due diligence usually depends on the specific financial or product issues involved, the level of HRDD expected will vary in complexity depending on the size of the business enterprise, the risk of severe human rights impacts, and the nature and context of its operations.[103]

4. One-off due diligence in contrast to ongoing HRDD. Business due diligence is usually a one-off activity, such as for a merger or acquisition, while HRDD is ongoing. The latter recognizes that the human rights risks may change over time as the business enterprise's operations and operating context evolve.[104]

5. Corporate social responsibility in contrast to human rights law. Business due diligence can often be seen as part of corporate social responsibility (CSR) and with a tick-box approach, while HRDD has a human rights law foundation, which includes remediation responsibilities, and also includes the responsibility of compliance.[105]

It is, therefore, crucial that the term used in relation to business and human rights is *'human rights* due diligence' and *not* just 'due diligence'. Interestingly, the Draft Treaty on Business and Human Rights 2020 corrected the terminology in a previous draft from 'due diligence' to 'human rights due diligence' for this reason.[106]

---

[102] GP 13—discussed above.
[103] GP 17.
[104] Ibid.
[105] Anita Ramasastry, 'Corporate Social Responsibility versus Business and Human Rights: Bridging the Gap Between Responsibility and Accountability' (2015) 14 *Journal of Human Rights* 237.
[106] Robert McCorquodale and Lise Smit, 'Human Rights, Responsibilities and Due Diligence: Key Issues for a Treaty' in Surya Deva and David Bilchitz (eds), *Building A Treaty on Business and Human Rights: Context and Contours* (CUP, 2017), 216. For a discussion on the draft treaty see Chapter 8.

HRDD is expected of all businesses and not just some, as the OECD has stated:

> Each enterprise in a business relationship has its own responsibility to identify and address adverse impacts. The due diligence recommendations of the OECD Guidelines for MNEs [multinational enterprises] are not intended to shift responsibilities from governments to enterprises, or from enterprises causing or contributing to adverse impacts to the enterprises that are directly linked to adverse impacts through their business relationships. Instead, they recommend that each enterprise addresses its own responsibility with respect to adverse impacts. In cases where impacts are directly linked to an enterprise's operations, products or services, the enterprise should seek, to the extent possible, to use its leverage to effect change, individually or in collaboration with others.[107]

Therefore, '[t]he responsibility for the impact remains with the entity or entities that are causing or contributing to the impacts'.[108] Human rights due diligence cannot be used to shift the corporate responsibilities to respect human rights.

Although HRDD was defined in relation to human rights (see above) in the UNGPs, other international regulation has extended it to include environmental impacts. For example, the OECD Guidelines provide:

> [Business] enterprises should, within the framework of laws, regulations and administrative practices in the countries in which they operate, and in consideration of relevant international agreements, principles, objectives, and standards, take due account of the need to protect *the environment*, public health and safety, and generally to conduct their activities in a manner contributing to the wider goal of sustainable development.[109]

This extension in the OECD Guidelines includes encouraging, in their supply chain, '[the] development and provision of products or services that

---

[107] OECD, Due Diligence Guidance for Responsible Business Conduct (OECD, 2018), [OECD DD Guidance], 17.
[108] Ibid., 77.
[109] OECD Guidelines, Section VI Environment (emphasis added).

have no undue environmental impacts; are safe in their intended use; reduce greenhouse gas emissions; are efficient in their consumption of energy and natural resources; can be reused, recycled, or disposed of safely'.[110] Further extension to climate change is considered in Chapter 8.

b. Application

The terminology of HRDD includes four elements, as set out in GP 17, and which are expanded upon in GPs 18–21. These are:

- identifying and assessing actual and potential human rights impacts;
- integrating and acting upon the findings;
- tracking the effectiveness of actions taken; and
- communicating how impacts are addressed.[111]

Each of these requires businesses to take specific action in their undertaking and implementation of HRDD. These four elements will now be considered.

i. Human Rights Impact Assessment

The UNGPs refer to the 'initial step'[112] in conducting HRDD as being to 'identify and assess any actual or potential adverse human rights impacts with which they may be involved either through their own activities or as a result of their business relationships'.[113] The usual means of doing this is through a human rights impact assessment (HRIA), which provides an overview of actual or potential human rights impacts relevant to a business's activities both at the operational level and in its value chain. In practice, HRIAs are also frequently used to determine whether, once the impacts are discerned, certain human rights risks should be prioritized over others.[114]

The action of a HRIA includes:

> [A]ssessing the human rights context prior to a proposed business activity, where possible; identifying who may be affected; cataloguing the

---

[110] Ibid., Art. 6.
[111] GP 17.
[112] Commentary to GP 18.
[113] GP 18.
[114] McCorquodale, Smit, HRDD, note 55.

relevant human rights standards and issues; and projecting how the proposed activity and associated business relationships could have adverse human rights impacts on those identified.[115]

The UNGPs highlight the importance of undertaking regular HRIA, as human rights impacts may change over time.[116] Human rights impact assessments may be integrated into existing risk management processes, such as labour reviews and health and safety processes, in order to assist in mainstreaming human rights into the existing businesses practices and structures, though the evidence shows that these processes need to include specific human rights risk factors for them to identify most potential human rights impacts.[117]

For example, Nestlé, a Swiss domiciled business, has identified HRIAs as an invaluable tool fundamental to their human rights commitments,[118] while it has acknowledged that they are complex and resource intensive, due to the nature of human rights as they cut across a number of different issues and functions throughout the value chain of the business.[119] Further, Nestlé argues that HRIAs serve a different function from audits, by uncovering areas for improvement for its overall approach to human rights rather than identifying non-compliance with predetermined standards of policies or benchmarks, which is all an audit can do, and so HRIAs can build capacity and raise awareness at the operational level.[120] Indeed, the OECD notes that actions under HRDD 'should include commitments regarding its own activities and should articulate the enterprise's expectations of its business partners—including suppliers, licensees and intermediaries—across the full length of its supply chain'.[121]

In order to conduct effective HRIA, the UNGPs make clear that consultation with all potentially affected stakeholders is crucial:

---

[115] Commentary to GP 18.
[116] Ibid.
[117] McCorquodale, Smit, HRDD, note 55.
[118] Nestlé and the Danish Institute for Human Rights (DIHR), *Talking the Human Rights Walk: Nestle's Experience Assessing Human Rights Impacts in its Business Activities* (DIHR, 2013), 8.
[119] Ibid., 9, 14.
[120] Ibid.
[121] OECD, OECD Due Diligence Guidance for Responsible Supply Chains in the Garment and Footwear Sector (OECD, 2017), 38.

To enable business enterprises to assess their human rights impacts accurately, they should seek to understand the concerns of potentially affected stakeholders by consulting them directly in a manner that takes into account language and other potential barriers to effective engagement. In situations where such consultation is not possible, business enterprises should consider reasonable alternatives such as consulting credible, independent expert resources, including human rights defenders and others from civil society.[122]

This consultation must be 'meaningful [and be] ... appropriate to the size of the business enterprise and the nature and context of the operation'.[123] For example, a part of the review by the Independent Review Mechanism of the African Development Bank of the South African Eskom/Medupi Power Project, partly funded by that Bank, was the adequacy of the consultation process by the business in a culturally, racially, linguistically, and economically diverse community.[124] The review panel noted that, although it was clear the business had made an extensive effort to consult the affected community, nevertheless 'neither the languages of the medium used to inform people about the public consultations (English and Afrikaans language newspapers) nor the languages of the written submissions (English and Afrikaans) are the languages spoken by the majority of people in the area'.[125] Accordingly, the Bank was not compliant with the policy requirement 'that the efforts at public consultation incorporate all affected populations groups, particularly the poor and the marginalized'.[126]

There is empirical evidence showing that there is considerable variation in business practices concerning consultations with stakeholders. For example, consultation with employees is fairly routine in most sectors and, in sectors such as the extractive sector, the consultations with local communities are fairly commonplace, though this may be due to operational risks connected to community dissent.[127] However, other

---

[122] Commentary to GP 18.
[123] GP 18.
[124] Daniel Bradlow and Andria Naudé Fourie, 'The Multilateral Development Banks and the Management of the Human Rights Impacts of their Operations' in Deva and Birchall, BHR, note 19, 315, 327.
[125] AFDB-IRM, 'Medupi Power Project', Compliance Review, , https://www.afdb.org/fileadmin/uploads/afdb/Documents/Compliance-Review/Medupi%20Power%20Project%20Q20102%20%20%281%29.pdf, page vii.
[126] Ibid.
[127] McCorquodale, Smit, HRDD, note 55.

stakeholder groups, such as end-users or transportation providers, may be entirely overlooked in being consulted, or there may be a very selective choice by the business with whom in a community it chooses to consult.[128] There is also evidence of a lack of free, prior, and informed consent by Indigenous people[129]—which is possibly a matter of customary international law[130]—before business takes actions which affect them.[131] Such poor consultation approaches may result in a business missing valuable information regarding the effectiveness of its HRDD, and can cause concerns to investors.[132]

ii. Integration

In order for the findings of the HRIA to be 'properly understood, given due weight, and acted upon',[133] it is necessary that a business integrate and act upon the HRIA. Guiding Principle 19 establishes the main elements of integration as part of HRDD:

> In order to prevent and mitigate adverse human rights impacts, business enterprises should integrate the findings from their impact assessments across relevant internal functions and processes, and take appropriate action.
> (a) Effective integration requires that:
> (i) Responsibility for addressing such impacts is assigned to the appropriate level and function within the business enterprise;
> (ii) Internal decision-making, budget allocations and oversight processes enable effective responses to such impacts.

---

[128] Local Authority Pension Fund (LAPFF), Mining and Human Rights: An Investor Perspective, https://lapfforum.org/wp-content/uploads/2022/04/Mining-and-Human-Rights-An-Investor-Perspective.pdf

[129] UN General Assembly, 'United Nations Declaration on the Rights of Indigenous Peoples' UN Doc. A/RES/61/295 (2 October 2007) and Human Rights Council, 'Free, Prior and Informed Consent: A Human Rights-Based Approach, Study of the Expert Mechanism on the Rights of Indigenous Peoples' UN Doc. A/HRC/39/62 (10 August 2018).

[130] Jernej Letnar Černič, 'Business and Indigenous Peoples' Human Rights' in Deva and Birchall, BHR, note 19, 335.

[131] Nancy Tapias Torrado, 'Overcoming Silencing Practices: Indigenous Women Defending Human Rights from Abuses Committed in Connection to Mega-Projects: A Case in Colombia' (2022) 7 *Business and Human Rights Journal* 29 and Anirudha Nagar, 'The Juukan Gorge Incident: Key Lessons on Free, Prior and Informed Consent' (2021) 6 *Business and Human Rights Journal* 377.

[132] Local Authority Pension Fund, note 128.

[133] Commentary to GP 19.

What is required by integration is for a business to ensure that HRDD is part of all its activities, across all levels of its operations, and consistent with its commitments in its human rights policy. As Florian Wettstein comments:

> The commitments of the human rights policy ought to be integrated in operational policies and procedures and embedded and implemented throughout the enterprise. After all, for a policy to life to be brought to life, it must have an impact not only on what the company believes in but on what it *does*.[134]

This comment notes the necessity for a business to ensure that the policy statement—set out in GP 15—reflects the reality of activity within the business,[135] not least as a human rights policy statement without integration into the actual operation of a company may lead to, for example, litigation risks.[136] This is also relevant for parent companies, as 'the parent(s) also exercise direct or indirect control of subsidiary management through operational integration, overlapping directors and officers, or contractual means'.[137] This statement indicates the need for integration to be about substantive action by a business and not only words.

Further, integration—and the corporate responsibility to respect generally—includes particular consideration for those who are vulnerable:

> In this process, business enterprises should pay special attention to any particular human rights impacts on individuals from groups or populations that may be at heightened risk of vulnerability or marginalization, and bear in mind the different risks that may be faced by women and men.[138]

Penelope Simons and Melisa Handl have shown the particular vulnerability of women to the activity of businesses, and the failure of regulation in this area to acknowledge women's experiences or to protect women's rights, with the risk that the business activities can perpetuate the patriarchal and

---

[134] Florian Wettstein, *Business and Human Rights: Ethical, Legal, and Managerial Perspectives* (CUP, 2022), 146 (his emphasis).

[135] The policy aspect is expanded upon in GP 16, to make clear that the human rights policy has to be approved at a senior level and communicated.

[136] See the cases discussed in Chapter 6.

[137] Virginia Harper Ho, 'Theories of Corporate Groups: Corporate Identity Reconceived' (2012) 42 *Seton Hall Law Review* 122, 122.

[138] Commentary to GP 18.

neoliberal structures that oppress women.[139] The WGBHR has produced a clear and insightful report on the need for gender perspectives in the interpretation and application of the UNGPs.[140] It noted multiple ways in which women are particularly affected by business activities, from gender stereotypes in business marketing and commodification of women, to sexual violence and sexual trafficking, as well as lack of access to remedies.[141]

The WGBHR Report on Gender Dimensions also offers some clear recommendations for action, including in relation to integration:

Illustrative actions:
(a) Depending on the impact assessment findings, gender-transformative measures may include:
  (i) Revising the gender-equality policy and management processes and practices to address systematic concerns related to adverse impacts on women's human rights;
  (ii) Modifying an ongoing project to prevent or minimize adverse impacts on women;
  (iii) Increasing gender sensitivity among enterprise personnel across all departments and supporting business partners in developing gender-responsive management systems;
  (iv) Building the capacity of the enterprise's own personnel and business partners to effectively handle sexual harassment and gender-based violence;
  (v) Adopting affirmative action policies to overcome underrepresentation of women in managerial positions and on boards;
  (vi) Developing collaborative partnerships with women's organizations;
  (vii) Providing effective transformative remedies for, or cooperating in the remediation of, adverse impacts that have already occurred;
(b) In appropriate cases, business enterprises should also conduct advocacy in support of gender equality.[142]

---

[139] Penelope Simons and Melisa Handl, 'Relations of Ruling: A Feminist Critique of the *United Nations Guiding Principles on Business and Human Rights* and Violence against Women in the Context of Resource Extraction' note 51. See also Grace Mutung'u, 'The United Nations Guiding Principles on Business and Human Rights, Women and Digital ID in Kenya: A Decolonial Perspective' (2022) 7 *Business and Human Rights Journal* 117.

[140] WGBHR, 'Gender Dimensions of the UNGPs' Report to the UN General Assembly' UN Doc. A/HC/41/43 (23 May 2019).

[141] Ibid., paras 11–21.

[142] Ibid.

This is an important statement, which also extends across all other actions by businesses and states in this area. There are, of course, other vulnerable groups who are particularly affected by business activities. For example, the WGBHR considered that:

> [I]ndigenous peoples are among the groups most severely affected by the activities of the extractive, agro-industrial and energy sectors. Reported adverse impacts range from impacts on the right of indigenous peoples to maintain their chosen traditional way of life, with their distinct cultural identity to discrimination in employment and access to goods and services (including financial services), access to land and security of land tenure, to displacement through forced or economic resettlement and associated serious abuses of civil and political rights, including impacts on human rights defenders, the right to life and bodily integrity.[143]

Other vulnerable groups include children[144] and persons with disabilities,[145] each of whom must be considered by businesses when taking the necessary action as part of HRDD, as well as being part of all aspects of HRDD and remedies (see Chapter 6).

iii. Tracking

Human rights due diligence requires a business to ensure that it tracks its actions and policies made in response to the HRIA. This must be done both at the operational level and in its value chain. The idea is that, by tracking their own activities, businesses can assess the extent of adverse human rights impacts and respond to them in their further actions. This is because '[t]racking is necessary in order for a business enterprise to know if its human rights policies are being implemented optimally, whether it has responded effectively to the identified human rights impacts, and to drive continuous improvement'.[146] In this way, HRDD should be an ongoing and

---

[143] WGBHR, 'Adverse Impacts of Business-Related Activities on the Rights of Indigenous Peoples' General Assembly, UN Doc. A/68/279 (7 August 2013), para. 1. Also Jernej Letnar Černič, 'Business and Indigenous Peoples' Human Rights' in Deva and Birchall, BHR, note 19, 335.

[144] Jonathan Kolieb, 'Protecting the Most Vulnerable: Embedding Children's Rights in the Business and Human Rights Project' in Deva and Birchall, BHR, note 19, 354.

[145] Michael Stein and Ilias Bantekas, 'Including Disability in Business and Human Rights Discourse and Corporate Practice' (2021) 6 *Business and Human Rights Journal* 490.

[146] Commentary to GP 20.

evidence-based process. Indeed, the key term used in GP 20, which deals with tracking, is 'effectiveness' and that tracking should be based on 'qualitative and quantitative indicators' and with internal and external feedback.[147]

Trying to determine 'effectiveness' in this context is not easy, as it is not defined by the UNGPs. An analysis of the effectiveness of HRDD generally has considered that the term 'effectiveness' is about 'the extent to which prevention through HRDD has pushed the development of new practices by states and businesses so as to improve responsiveness by them of dealing with adverse human rights impacts of business activities'.[148] Thus effectiveness will, inevitably, turn on both evidence of business practices and the use of indicators. For example, since 2017 the Corporate Human Rights Benchmark (CHRB) has produced research which aims to 'provid[e] a comparative snapshot year-on-year of the largest companies on the planet [in certain sectors], looking at the policies, processes, and practices they have in place to systematise their human rights approach and how they respond to serious allegations'.[149] The overall conclusion of the 2020 CHRB, however, was that 'only a minority of companies demonstrate the willingness and commitment to take human rights seriously ... [however, there is a] disconnect between commitments and processes on the one hand and actual performance and results on the other'.[150]

GP 20 suggests some indicators which could be used to check the effectiveness of tracking, being 'performance contracts and reviews as well as surveys and audits, using gender-disaggregated data where relevant, [and feedback from] operational-level grievance mechanisms'.[151] The audits referred to there are generally known as 'social audits' in this area:

> Social auditing is a process by which a company verifies supplier compliance with human rights standards, typically set out in a code of conduct. While the precise nature of a social audit will vary depending on the industry in question and the organisation undertaking the audit, it generally involves a physical inspection of a facility (for example a

---

[147] GP 20.
[148] Robert McCorquodale and Justine Nolan, 'The Effectiveness of Human Rights Due Diligence for Preventing Business Human Rights Abuses' [2021] *Netherlands International Law Review* 455, 465.
[149] Corporate Human Rights Benchmark (CHRB), which is now a part of the World Benchmarking Alliance, ttps://www.worldbenchmarkingalliance.org/corporate-human-rights-benchmark.
[150] Ibid., Key Finding 5.
[151] Commentary to GP 20.

factory, farm, mine or vessel), combined with a review of documents (to the extent that records are kept) and interviews with management and employees.[152]

Justine Nolan and Nana Frishling have argued that, '[a]ccording to some estimates, social auditing accounts for up to 80% of ethical sourcing budgets, and amounts to an estimated US$50 billion industry … [and is] the most common tool utilised by multi-stakeholder and corporate-led initiatives set up to address the human rights impacts of global supply chains'.[153] However, they have shown that there are real problems with businesses tracking their actions under HRDD by principally relying on social auditing:

> [There is] growing consensus that social auditing is in and of itself, a very limited tool, capable of delivering only superficial and short-term outcomes at best, and wholly inadequate for detecting and addressing more serious and systemic human rights violations. In particular, inherent limitations in the manner that social auditing is conducted, as well as broader structural impediments raise serious questions about its suitability for assessing, responding to, and tracking human rights impacts …[T]he fact that auditors may be paid (either by buyer brands or supplier factories), combined with their often-limited experience in human rights and labour issues raises questions about the quality, independence and veracity of social audits.[154]

In addition to these concerns, there is also an argument that the use of such simple metrics may mean that 'human rights are reshaped, minimized, and sometimes lost altogether. For example, tracking instances of child labour within supply chains may be possible through this technique, but comprehensively respecting the right to just work may not.'[155]

The use of technology to track business actions in this area, such as the use of workplace surveillance, has been criticized for being too intrusive.[156] There are, however, potential ways forward through using technology, with,

---

[152] Justine Nolan and Nana Frishling, 'Human Rights Due Diligence and the (Over) Reliance on Social Auditing in Supply Chains' in Deva and Birchall, BHR, note 19, 108.
[153] Ibid., 119.
[154] Ibid., 121–2.
[155] David Birchall, 'The Role of Civil Society and Human Rights Defenders in Corporate Accountability' in Deva and Birchall, BHR, note 19, 422, 426.
[156] Alexander Kriebitz and Christoph Lütge, 'Artificial Intelligence and Human Rights: A Business Ethical Assessment' (2020) 5 *Business and Human Rights Journal* 84.

for example, blockchain technology being advanced as having some possibilities for enhancing traceability within complex corporate value chains, although it is very dependent on reliable data input.[157] Others note that having effective trade unions or workplace representation can be a valuable way of ensuring that tracking is effective, transparent, and accountable.[158]

iv. Communication

Communicating about the outcomes of the HRDD undertaken by a business is the fourth aspect of the HRDD process. GP 21 states:

> In order to account for how they address their human rights impacts, business enterprises should be prepared to communicate this externally, particularly when concerns are raised by or on behalf of affected stakeholders. Business enterprises whose operations or operating contexts pose risks of severe human rights impacts should report formally on how they address them.

The need for having external communication is part of the UNGPs' approach that businesses 'need to know and show that they respect human rights'.[159] The rationale for this is that '[s]howing involves communication, providing a measure of transparency and accountability to individuals or groups who may be impacted and to other relevant stakeholders, including investors'.[160] Thus, for communication to be both useful and legitimate, it should be about the HRDD undertaken and its effectiveness, as it must 'provide information that is sufficient to evaluate the adequacy of an enterprise's response to the particular human rights impact involved'.[161]

There are, though, concerns about certain types of communication, which do not provide the information required by HRDD. This is often known as 'blue-washing', as Florian Wettstein explains:

---

[157] William Crumpler, 'The Human Rights Risks and Opportunities in Blockchain' (Center for Strategic and International Studies, 2021) htttps://www.csis.org/analysis/human-rights-risks-and-opportunities-blockchain.

[158] Anne Trebilcock, 'Due Diligence on Labour Issues—Opportunities and Limits of the UN Guiding Principles on Business and Human Rights' in Adelle Blackett and Anne Trebilcock (eds), *Research Handbook on Transnational Labour Law* (Edward Elgar, 2015).

[159] Commentary to GP 15.

[160] Commentary to GP 21.

[161] GP 21(b).

There remains a concern that companies with less than stellar corporate responsibility track records would use [links to UN regulation in this area] as a tool to enhance their public image, while changing little about their actual business practices ... The term 'bluewashing' alludes to the official color of the UN and was used in analogy to the more familiar term 'green-washing'.[162]

Thus, communication alone should not be mistaken for HRDD if there is no evidence of HRIA, integration, and tracking within a business. For example, a 2020 report examining the modern slavery statements of 79 asset management firms in the UK 'found that less than one-third conduct some form of due diligence on human rights in their portfolio companies'.[163] This low response rate is borne out by the results of the CHRB noted in the previous section, the methodology of which is based on the documents produced by businesses themselves. The broader concerns about reporting in terms of access to remedies is discussed in Chapter 6.

The type of communication under HRDD can take a variety of forms, such as 'in-person meetings, online dialogues, consultation with affected stakeholders, and formal public reports'.[164] This also includes wider public engagement and consultation with stakeholders, and internal engagement. Empirical research has found that one effective way of doing the latter is by training of all employees (and suppliers) in identification, implementation, and responding to human rights impacts.[165] However, '[d]espite the frequent emphasis which survey respondents and interviewees placed on the importance of training, few companies presently provide training specifically around human rights ... [so] it appears that companies are not currently capitalising on the full advantage of human rights training'.[166]

Communicating about an adverse human rights impact can be very difficult for businesses. For example, disclosures relating to a business's supply chain may make directors and senior management concerned that it could expose the business to litigation risk where public statements potentially materially overstate the extent of the business's efforts to address human

---

[162] Wettstein, note 134, 216–17.
[163] Walk Free (2020), ttps://www.walkfree.org/reports/beyond-compliance-in-the-finance-sector/, p.19..
[164] Ibid.
[165] McCorquodale, Smit, HRDD, note 55, 198.
[166] Ibid., 205.

rights issues in its operations and supply chains. There is, however, evidence that such public communication can be beneficial:

> Another interviewee [from a company] confirmed the benefits of publicly reporting on the human rights issues identified in their supply chain. They indicated that this decision was 'counterintuitive [and] took us a long time to sell internally'. [However] no-one reacted negatively. People were happy to see we were honest'. This positive reaction, in turn, helped them to 'educate people internally'. They concluded that 'in fact, there is no taboo, in the end, to communicate'.[167]

In addition, the US courts have recognized a 'safe harbour' doctrine for disclosures made under the California Transparency in Supply Chains Act 2010,[168] which, though contentious, could prove to be an incentive for businesses to communicate more information about their HRDD processes.[169] Further, it has been shown that there can be an economic benefit if businesses undertake HRDD and communicate it properly, as the 'economic benefits can accrue for brand image and reputation, human resources, risk management and operational efficiency, as well as stock/financial performance or capital cost'.[170]

c. Breadth of HRDD

In undertaking HRDD, the UNGPs and OECD Guidelines do recognize that, while HRDD should take place 'as early as possible',[171] its application may vary in certain situations. For example:

> Where business enterprises have large numbers of entities in their value chains it may be unreasonably difficult to conduct due diligence

---

[167] Smit, HRDD in Global Supply Chains, note 81, 960.
[168] *Barber v. Nestlé USA Inc.* No. 8:2015cv01364 (C.D. Cal. December 14, 2015) 778. See further in Chapter 7.
[169] There is a discussion on defences in Chapter 7.
[170] Lise Smit, Claire Bright, Robert McCorquodale, Matthias Bauer, Hanna Deringer, Daniela Baeza-Breinbauer, Francisca Torres-Cortés, Frank Alleweldt, Senda Kara, and Camille Salinier and Héctor Tejero Tobed for the European Commission DG Justice and Consumers, *Study on Due Diligence Requirements through the Supply Chain*, 24 February 2020, https://op.europa.eu/en/publication-detail/-/publication/8ba0a8fd-4c83-11ea-b8b7-01aa7 5ed71a1/language-en [Smit, EC Study], Table 8.63.
[171] Commentary to GP 17.

for adverse human rights impacts across them all. If so, business enterprises should identify general areas where the risk of adverse human rights impacts is most significant, whether due to certain suppliers' or clients' operating context, the particular operations, products or services involved, or other relevant considerations, and prioritize these for human rights due diligence.[172]

Hence, it is possible for a business to prioritize some areas for taking action, provided that priority is given to those risks that are most severe or irremediable.[173] Some have called this a reflection of what are the 'salient' human rights for a business,[174] though 'salience' and 'severity' are not the same concept, as 'salience is not a cut-off line, but a principled basis for sequencing how [business] resources [initially] get applied'.[175] Thus, a business must first determine its human rights impacts *before* it prioritizes its human-rights-related remedial actions. It should not predetermine its potential adverse human rights impacts.

Further, it can be difficult for many businesses to undertake HRDD across all their value chains, if these are large, complex, and dynamic.[176] An extensive study for the European Commission on due diligence through the supply chain[177] showed that just over half of businesses which are undertaking HRDD only do so with respect to their first tier suppliers.[178] Similarly, the evidence showed that there were far less developed HRDD processes undertaken for the downstream value chain,[179] which would include those entities which buy the business's goods and services. Much of this difficulty in undertaking HRDD can be due to competition reasons, where first tier suppliers (or purchasers) do not wish to reveal their own suppliers/clients. Other research has shown that it can still be possible to

---

[172] Ibid.
[173] GP 24.
[174] OHCHR, Interpretive Guide, note 24, 9: 'The most salient human rights for a business enterprise are those that stand out as being most at risk. This will typically vary according to its sector and operating context. The GPs make clear that an enterprise should not focus exclusively on the most salient human rights issues and ignore others that might arise. But the most salient rights will logically be the ones on which it concentrates its primary efforts.'
[175] Caroline Rees and Rachel Davis, 'Salient Human Rights Issues: When Severe Risks to People Intersect with Risks to Business' in Dorothée Baumann-Pauly and Justine Nolan (eds), *Business and Human Rights: From Principles to Practice* (Routledge, 2016), 103, 104.
[176] For example, the Commentary to GP 19.
[177] Smit, EC Study, note 170, 166.
[178] Ibid., 65.
[179] Ibid., 65–7.

undertake whole of value chain HRDD if a business is willing to do so, with various examples of businesses taking proactive and innovative steps to engage with suppliers as part of their HRDD.[180]

Indeed, it is argued that the ability to trace human rights along the value chain through technology, coupled with growing regulatory and internal corporate priority around HRDD in value chains, may reduce management risk.[181] The OECD has produced sector-specific guidelines for conducting HRDD for responsible supply chain management of, for example, conflict minerals, for the garment and footwear sectors, and for agricultural supply chains,[182] each of which provides some valuable information on the implementation of HRDD. The OECD Guidelines also provide examples of how a business's HRDD can be adapted to reflect its leverage and resources.[183]

Yet, there may be situations where there are heightened expectations of HRDD. For example, 'because the risk of gross human rights abuses is heightened in conflict-affected areas',[184] states need to take this into account in their regulation of business activity. Also, '[s]ome operating environments, such as conflict-affected areas, may increase the risks of enterprises being complicit in gross human rights abuses committed by other actors (security forces, for example).'[185] A report by the WGBHR states that 'business should exercise heightened due diligence in conflict-affected contexts because of the increased risk of being involved in serious human rights abuses'.[186] The report notes:

> In conflict-affected situations, the complexity will be increased by the operating context, where State structures are weak or non-existent; business relationships, as some actors may be active participants to the conflict, former combatants or abusers; and the severity of potential

---

[180] Smit, HRDD in Global Supply Chains, note 81, 945.

[181] Ibid.

[182] For example, OECD, OECD Due Diligence Guidance for Responsible Supply Chains of Minerals from Conflict-Affected and High-Risk Areas (OECD, 3rd ed., 2016); OECD, OECD Due Diligence Guidance for Responsible Supply Chains in the Garment and Footwear Sector (OECD, 2017); and OECD/FAO, OECD-FAO Guidance for Responsible Agricultural Supply Chains (OECD, 2016).

[183] For example, OECD, Responsible Business Conduct for Institutional Investors: Key Considerations for Due Diligence under the OECD Guidelines for Multinational Enterprises (OECD, 2017).

[184] GP 7.

[185] Commentary to GP 23.

[186] WGBHR, 'Business, Human Rights and Conflict-Affected Regions: Towards Heightened Action', Report to UN General Assembly (21 July 2020), para. 22.

human rights abuses. Activities linking businesses to conflict are often not perceived as salient human rights issues and therefore might be ignored or under prioritized in standard human rights impact assessments... Businesses are not neutral actors; their presence is not without impact. Even if business does not take a side in the conflict, the impact of their operations will necessarily influence conflict dynamics.

In conflict contexts, therefore, while human rights due diligence requiring business to assess, avoid or mitigate adverse human rights impacts remains valid and necessary, it needs to be complemented by a conflict-sensitive approach. This involves gaining a sound understanding of the two-way interaction between activities and context, and acting to minimize negative impacts.[187]

The WGBHR Report also notes that this heightened HRDD should also take place in post-conflict situations,[188] and in all situations there should be an understanding of the impact of any engagement with armed non-state actors.[189] This warning is particularly relevant as there have been instances of criminal cases against businesses for acting in concert with armed non-state actors; this is discussed in Chapter 6.

An additional element in relation to HRDD is that one of the expectations on business is that, not only should they prevent and mitigate potential adverse human rights impacts through HRDD, they should, where actual impacts have occurred, remediate them.[190] Remediation is provided for where a business causes or contributes to adverse human rights impacts and not when it is directly linked (and see the discussion on developing case law in Chapter 6), though, in the latter instance, it 'may take a role in doing so'.[191] This remediation, as set out in GP 22, should take place through 'legitimate processes'. This is a direct link to Pillar III discussed in Chapter 6. The justification for remediation in these situations is that '[e]ven with the best policies and practices, a business enterprise may cause or contribute to an adverse human rights impact that it has not foreseen or been able to prevent'.[192]

---

[187] Ibid., paras 41–44.
[188] Ibid., paras 72–80.
[189] Ibid., paras 55–61.
[190] Commentaries to GP 15 and GP 17.
[191] Commentary to GP 22.
[192] Ibid.

8. Conclusions

The corporate responsibility to respect human rights is a vital aspect of the developing law and practice on business and human rights. It indicates the significant development which has occurred in the acceptance by states and businesses that businesses do have responsibility in relation to their actions which have adverse human rights impacts. While this responsibility is not (yet) seen as an international legal responsibility equivalent to that of state responsibility, it is part of the changes in the understanding of business within international law, as seen in Chapter 2.

The framing of the corporate responsibility to respect human rights into the typology of cause, contribute to, and being directly linked, sets out the ways in which businesses can participate in adverse human rights impacts. Yet these are not completely distinct, as John Ruggie noted as a part of his response to the Thun Group's Discussion Paper, considered in the Introduction to this chapter. He wrote:

> There is a continuum between contribution and linkage. A variety of factors can determine where on that continuum a particular instance may sit. They include the extent to which a business enabled, encouraged, or motivated human rights harm by another; the extent to which it could or should have known about such harm; and the quality of any mitigating steps it has taken to address it.[193]

Therefore, there is still a great deal for business to do to ensure that they are acting appropriately in their implementation of their business and human rights responsibilities.

A key part of any business response should be to undertake HRDD. This is the core of the corporate responsibility to respect human rights. If a business undertakes HRDD in accordance with the UNGPs it will identify, through an HRIA, the actual and potential human rights risks to rightsholders, integrate this assessment into its actions, track the effectiveness of its actions and revise its assessments, and then communicate its actions publicly. However, HRDD does not automatically provide any remedy for rightsholders. This is the topic of the next chapter.

---

[193] John Ruggie, Letter to the OECD, note 3.

6
Access to Remedies for Victims

1. Context

Royal Dutch Shell, a joint British and Dutch transnational business with subsidiaries around the world, has been involved in oil production in Nigeria for many decades. As seen in Chapter 4, legal action had been taken against the government of Nigeria on the basis of state responsibility under international human rights law before a regional human rights body for the activities of oil companies, including Royal Dutch Shell (Shell).[1] Subsequently, a series of civil claims by Nigerians, based on the human consequences of oil pollution, including impacts on water, land, and livelihoods, have been brought in national courts against Shell (as the parent company) and its Nigerian subsidiary, Shell Petroleum Development Company of Nigeria (Shell Nigeria).[2]

A number of these cases were brought before the courts of the Netherlands, with the jurisdiction being based on the domicile of Shell (then a joint Dutch-UK domiciled business). These cases concerned leaks from Shell Nigeria's oil pipeline and well-heads from 2004 in the Nigerian villages of Goi, Oruma, and Ikot Ada Udo, all being in the Niger Delta. The claims were made on the basis of the tort of negligence, arguing that Shell and Shell Nigeria (the defendants in these cases) were jointly liable for the origin of the leaks, failing to respond adequately to the leaks, failing to clean up properly after the leaks, and causing damage to the claimants' farmlands and fishing grounds. In order to make out such a negligence claim there are a number of key elements that must be shown by the claimants, including that the defendants owed a duty of care to them, that the defendants' actions

---

[1] *Social and Economic Rights Action Center and the Economic and Social Rights Action Center v. Nigeria*, African Commission, Communication No. 155/96 (2001–02) 1985–84.
[2] For example, *Kiobel v. Royal Dutch Petroleum Co.*, 133 S. Ct. 1659 (2013) (US) (discussed below) and *The Bodo Community and Others v. The Shell Petroleum Development Company of Nigeria Ltd* [2014] EWHC 1973 (TCC) (UK).

or omissions breached that duty of care, and that there were consequent damages to the claimants.³

The Hague Court of Appeal held that both Shell and Shell Nigeria did have a duty of care in respect of these leaks.⁴ In relation to the duty of Shell, as the parent company, the court relied on the ground-breaking decision by the UK Supreme Court in *Vedanta v. Lungowe*.⁵ That decision was confirmed by a later case in the UK courts against Shell and Shell Nigeria, *Okpabi v. Shell*.⁶ In the case in the Netherlands, the Dutch court summarized the position of the parent company's duty of care:

> [I]f the parent company knows or should know that its subsidiary unlawfully inflicts damage on third parties in an area where the parent company involves itself in the subsidiary, the starting point is that the parent company has a duty of care in respect of the third parties to intervene.⁷

After considering the evidence and the relevant law, the Court held that Shell Nigeria was strictly liable (i.e. irrespective of negligence) for damages caused by leaks in two of the oil pipelines and that it had acted negligently in its initial response to those leaks. It also held that Shell itself had a duty of care to ensure that particular safety measures were installed in pipelines operated by Shell Nigeria, as Shell needed to do more to prevent these oil spills.⁸ The court also held that Shell and/or Shell Nigeria had to clean up the oil, install leak detection systems on its pipelines, and compensate the claimants,⁹ as well as there being 'a judicially imposed penalty for every day (a part of a day qualified as a day) that it does not comply with this order [to instal a leak detection system] of €100,000.00'.¹⁰

---

³ Cees Van Dam 'Tort Law and Human Rights: Brothers in Arms—On the Role of Tort Law in the Area of Business and Human Rights' [2011] *Journal of European Tort Law* 221.
⁴ *Four Nigerian Farmers v Shell*,The Hague Court of Appeal, 29 January 2021, ECLI:NL:GHDHA:2021 [*Four Nigerian Farmers*].
⁵ *Vedanta Resources plc v. Lungowe* [2019] UKSC 20 [*Vedanta*]. This case is discussed below.
⁶ *Okpabi and Others v. Royal Dutch Shell plc and Another* [2021] UKSC 3 [*Okpabi v. Shell*].
⁷ *Four Nigerian Farmers*, note 4, (Oruma), para. 3.31.
⁸ Lucas Roorda, 'Broken English: A Critique of the Dutch Court of Appeal decision in *Four Nigerian Farmers and Milieudefensie v Shell*' (2021) 12 *Transnational Legal Theory* 144.
⁹ Milieudefensie, 'Milieudefensie and Nigerian Farmers Win Landmark Court Case against Shell' (29 January 2021), https://en.milieudefensie.nl/shell-in-nigeria/milieudefensie-and-nigerian-win-landmark-court-case-against-shell.
¹⁰ *Four Nigerian Farmers*, note 4, Decision. Compensation of $US16m has been agreed to be paid by Shell: https://www.bbc.co.uk/news/world-africa-64075146.

This case is very important as it is the first time that a court anywhere in the world has found that a parent company has breached its duty of care to victims of actions by its subsidiary based in another jurisdiction, and that the parent company (and its subsidiary) has to pay damages to the victims. Unfortunately for all involved, it took 17 years from the first oil spill until the decision in the case, mainly due to the many barriers to access to remedies (discussed below). Nevertheless, this is a significant development for victims in seeking to obtain remedies against businesses directly for their actions which cause adverse human rights and environmental impacts.

This issue of access to remedies for victims in relation to adverse human rights impacts by business activity is the subject of this chapter. The United Nations Guiding Principles on Business and Human Rights 2011 (UNGPs) makes clear that the responsibility of states and businesses in relation to human rights abuses by businesses includes access to a remedy. Pillar III includes access to judicial and non-judicial remedies by the state and access to non-judicial remedies by businesses. These will be considered in turn, as well as relevant case law, with relevant legislation considered in the next chapter.

2. International Legal Obligations on States to Provide Remedies

a. Right to a Remedy

The only 'foundational' principle of the UNGPs in Pillar III is GP 25. It provides:

> As part of their duty to protect against business-related human rights abuse, States must take appropriate steps to ensure, through judicial, administrative, legislative or other appropriate means, that when such abuses occur within their territory and/or jurisdiction those affected have access to effective remedy.

The rationale for the wording of GP 25 is that '[u]nless States take appropriate steps to investigate, punish and redress business-related human rights abuses when they do occur, the State duty to protect can be rendered weak or even meaningless'.[11] This is consistent with the general position that

---

[11] Commentary to GP 25.

there is 'a close relationship between rights and remedies... [and] remedies should be effective, lest rights mean little in practice'.[12] Guiding Principle 25 is also one of only two of the UNGPs that are expressed in mandatory (i.e. compulsory) terms.[13]

As such, this GP is intended to be reflective of the general international human rights law obligations on a state to provide a remedy for a breach of a human right. The right to a remedy is set out in most of the major international human rights treaties.[14] It is also considered that the right to a remedy is implied in every international human rights treaty (and is possibly part of customary international law) because '[f]or rights to have meaning, effective remedies must first be available to redress violations. This requirement is implicit in the Convention [on the Rights of the Child] and consistently referred to in the other six major international human rights treaties.'[15] More generally, the Office of the UN High Commissioner for Human Rights (OHCHR) has stated that the 'right to an effective remedy for harm is a core tenet of international human rights law'.[16] Thus there is an international legal obligation on a state to take steps to ensure that those who have had their human rights abused by businesses have access to an effective remedy.

b. Transnational/Extraterritorial

As discussed in Chapter 4, a key issue of debate concerning the UNGPs has been the extent of the state's international obligations beyond its territory. This applies equally in relation to the right to an effective remedy in situations where the business actions occurred outside the territory of a state

---

[12] WGBHR, 'Access to Effective Remedies', Report to General Assembly, UN Doc. A/GA/72/162 (18 July 2017), para. 2.
[13] GP 1 provides that '[s]tates *must* protect against human rights abuse within their territory and/or jurisdiction by third parties, including business enterprises' (emphasis added), and 'must' is also used in GP 25.
[14] For example, Art. 2(3) of the International Covenant on Civil and Political Rights (ICCPR) and Art. 13 of the European Convention on Human Rights (ECHR).
[15] UN Committee on the Rights of the Child, 'Effective Remedy and Corporate Violations of Children's Rights' (2011), www.unicef.org/csr/css/effectiveremedy_10Oct11.pdf, para. 1.2. See also Amnesty International, *Injustice Incorporated: Corporate Abuses and the Human Rights to a Remedy* (2014), 16–20.
[16] OHCHR, 'Improving Accountability and Access to Remedy for Victims of Business-Related Human Rights Abuse', Report to the UN Human Rights Council, UN Doc. A/HRC/32/19 (10 May 2016) [ARP I], para. 6.

where the claim is made (forum state) and the victims are also outside the territory of the forum state (as they usually live in the host state).

For example, the host state may object to the forum state accepting a claim from victims on the basis that to do so would infringe the host state's sovereignty. Thus, South Africa initially objected to the hearing of claims in the US under the US Alien Torts Claims Act concerning actions on South African territory, and Zambia sought to resist the UK courts having jurisdiction over a claim where the harm occurred in Zambian territory.[17] Similarly, the use of *forum non conveniens*, which means that the forum state is not the best place to hear a case in terms of the location of the parties and the evidence, and the relevant law, is often based on the international legal principle that a forum state should not extend the territorial reach of its laws as to do so would infringe the sovereignty or territorial jurisdiction of another state. There is also a debate as to whether cases brought before home states (being states in which the business is domiciled) for harm done in host states (being the state where the activity occurred) by that business are a form of neo-colonialism.[18] In addition, in a few instances a court in a forum state has been asked to limit its decision-making powers in order to defer to its own government's foreign relations activities.[19]

The position of international human rights supervisory bodies seems to indicate that a part of a state's international human rights obligations includes the obligation to provide redress to victims of human rights due to business activity beyond its territory. This has been summarized by the UN Committee on Economic, Social and Cultural Rights:

> The extraterritorial obligation to protect requires States Parties to take steps to prevent and redress infringements of Covenant rights that occur outside their territories due to the activities of business entities over which they can exercise control, especially in cases where the remedies

---

[17] Christin Gowar, 'The Alien Tort Claims Act and the South African Apartheid Litigation: Is the End Nigh?' [2012] *Speculum Juris* 4 and the Intervention of the Minister for Justice of the Republic of Zambia in *Vedanta Resources plc v. Lungowe*, note 5, para. 92.

[18] Caroline Omari Lichuma, '(Laws) Made in the "First World": A TWAIL Critique of the Use of Domestic Legislation to Extraterritorially Regulate Global Value Chains' [2021] *Zeitschrift für Ausländisches Öffentliches Recht und Völkerrecht* 81 and Dalia Palombo, 'Transnational Business and Human Rights Litigation: An Imperialist Project?' (2022) 22 *Human Rights Law Review* 1 .

[19] *Nevsun Resources Ltd v. Araya*, 2020 SCC 5, Supreme Court of Canada (discussed below).

available to victims before the domestic courts of the State where the harm occurs are unavailable or ineffective.[20]

Indeed, the OECD Guidelines, which have National Contact Points (NCPs) in every OECD state to supervise compliance with them (discussed below), provide the basis for every NCP to accept complaints against businesses located in an OECD state about actions which that business or one of its subsidiaries (or through a business relationship) undertook in another state. For example, *Fivas v. Norconsult*[21] was a complaint filed with the Norwegian NCP against a Norwegian business, Norconsult, arising from human rights impacts on Indigenous peoples in Malaysia. The Indigenous peoples claimed that they had been forced to relocate within Indonesia due to construction of some dams, the construction of which had been aided by the technical assistance provided by Norconsult and its affiliated businesses. In a settlement, the Norwegian business agreed to respect the human rights of Indigenous people in future and to implement a full human rights due diligence process.[22]

Nevertheless, the issue of transnational/extraterritorial jurisdiction of a forum court to consider claims made by those who claim to be victims of adverse human rights impacts of corporate activities remains a matter of contention. As will be seen below, there have been developments in the past few years which have clarified some of these issues.

3. Remedy

a. Definition

The terminology of the UNGPs, and other international regulations on business and human rights, is about 'access to effective remedies'. The WGBHR has noted that, although there are effectiveness criteria for non-judicial grievance mechanisms set out in GP 31, there is no explanation of

---

[20] ESCR Committee, General Comment No. 24, State Obligations under the International Covenant on Economic, Social and Cultural Rights in the Context of Business Activities, UN Doc. E/C.12/GC/24 (23 June 2017), para. 30.

[21] *Fivas v. Norconsult AS/NorPower Sdn Bhd* (2014):https://www.responsiblebusiness.no/dialogue-and-mediation/specific-instances/fivas-vs-norconsult-asnorpower-sdn-bhd/.

[22] Joint statement by Norconsult AS/NorPower Sdn Bhd and FIVAS (2015): https://files.net tsteder.regjeringen.no/wpuploads01/blogs.dir/263/files/2021/02/150622-Joint-Statement-by-Norconsult-AS-and-FIVAS_FINAL.pdf.

what amounts to an effective remedy. Hence, it has clarified the difference between the right to an effective remedy under international human rights law, access to an effective remedy under the UNGPs, and access to justice:

> To realize the right to an effective remedy, access to appropriate remedial mechanisms should be provided by the bearers of a duty or responsibility concerning this right. It can thus be said that the concept of access to effective remedies is derived from, and dependent on, the right to an effective remedy … Access to justice, on the other hand, is a concept that is more elastic than the notions of the right to an effective remedy and access to an effective remedy. In a narrow sense, access to justice can be equated with the right or access to effective judicial remedies, and in this sense effective remedies should often result in justice being provided to rights holders. Nevertheless, access to justice can also be used in a broader sense to deal with larger issues of injustice that may not be addressed through individualized remedies offered for a given set of human rights abuses, but would require more fundamental changes in social, political or economic structures.[23]

Accordingly, much of Pillar III of the UNGPs is focused upon mechanisms to ensure access to an effective remedy for victims.

A remedy for the purposes of the UNGPs is clarified by the Commentary to GP 25 as having both procedural and substantive aspects. The former is where specific public steps need to be taken by the business, while the purpose of a substantive remedy is 'to counteract or make good any human rights harms that have occurred'.[24] The Commentary also notes that 'a grievance is understood to be a perceived injustice evoking an individual's or a group's sense of entitlement, which may be based on law, contract, explicit or implicit promises, customary practice, or general notions of fairness of aggrieved communities'.[25] The Commentary then sets out a range of possible types of appropriate remedy within the context of the UNGPs:

> Remedy may include apologies, restitution, rehabilitation, financial or non-financial compensation and punitive sanctions (whether criminal or administrative, such as fines), as well as the prevention of harm

---

[23] WGBHR, note 12, paras 14 and 16.
[24] Commentary to GP 25.
[25] Ibid.

through, for example, injunctions or guarantees of non-repetition. Procedures for the provision of remedy should be impartial, protected from corruption and free from political or other attempts to influence the outcome.[26]

These constitute a non-exclusive list, as the effective remedy for a victim will depend on a variety of circumstances, including the nature of the abuses and the personal position (such as a being a person with a disability) and preferences of affected rights holders.[27]

An effective remedy, therefore, should be one which 'makes good' any human rights harms in relation to the 'perceived injustice' of an individual or group. Indeed, the Special Representative of the Secretary-General (SRSG) noted that '[v]ictims face particular challenges when seeking personal compensation or reparation as opposed to more general sanction of the corporation through a fine or administrative remedies'.[28] Hence, the focus is on an effective remedy *to the victim* and not on the sanction to the business. This is reinforced by the WGBHR:

> [R]ights holders should be central to the entire remedy process, including to the question of effectiveness. It is they who suffer harm owing to business-related human rights abuses. Any process to remedy such harm should therefore take both the rights holders and their suffering seriously, lest remedies not be regarded as effective by those whose opinion should matter the most.[29]

Further, 'available remedies should combine preventive, redressive and deterrent elements … [to ensure] the overall effectiveness … [so that reparations go beyond guarantees of non-repetition to also comprise] restitution, compensation, rehabilitation, [and] satisfaction.'[30]

---

[26] Ibid.
[27] In the WGBHR, note 12, this variety of remedies is called, rather unusually, a 'bouquet' of remedies—para. 38.
[28] Report of the SRSG to the UN Human Rights Council, 'Protect, Respect and Remedy: A Framework for Business and Human Rights', Human Rights Council Eighth Session, UN Doc. A/HRC/8/5 (7 April 2008),[Framework Report], para. 88.
[29] WGBHR, note 12, para. 19.
[30] Surya Deva, 'Statement by Mr. Surya Deva, Chairperson of the [WGBHR] at the 3rd Session of the open-ended intergovernmental working group on transnational corporations and other business enterprises with respect to human rights' (25 October 2017), www.ohchr.org/EN/NewsEvents/Pages/DisplayNews.aspx?NewsID=22303&LangID=E.

Sometimes the remedy may consist of structural or systemic improvement of the lives of victims and potential victims,[31] though there would need to be substantial evidence of a preventative or non-repetition effect of such a remedy for it to be considered an effective remedy to the victim.[32] Further, the WGBHR argues:

> The right (or access) to an effective remedy has a close relationship with the notion of corporate accountability. If remedies for human rights abuses are construed holistically, as articulated herein, to address 'both individual and societal goals', effective remedies should result in some form of corporate accountability. Conversely, corporate accountability should contribute to some form of remedies, which may or may not be effective. The starting point should therefore be to provide effective remedies to the victims of corporate human rights abuses, which in turn should inevitably result in corporate accountability.[33]

This linking of remedies for victims to business accountability in the above statement extends the corporate responsibility to respect human rights in Pillar II to the availability of remedies in Pillar III.

b. Operational Grievance Mechanisms

As noted above, much of Pillar III the UNGPs is focused upon mechanisms to ensure access to an effective remedy for victims to ensure both substantive and procedural remedies. The Commentary to GP 25 clarifies what is meant by a 'grievance mechanism':

> The term grievance mechanism is used to indicate any routinized, State-based or non-State-based, judicial or non-judicial process through which grievances concerning business-related human rights abuse can be raised and remedy can be sought. State-based grievance mechanisms may be administered by a branch or agency of the State, or by an

---

[31] Francesca Capone, 'Remedies' in Rüdiger Wolfrum (ed.), *Max Planck Encyclopaedia of Public International Law* (OUP, 2012).

[32] This is sometimes termed a 'guarantee of non-repetition': Francesca Capone, Kristin Hausler, Duncan Fairgrieve, and Conor McCarthy, *Education and the Law of Reparations* (BIICL, 2013), 37–8.

[33] WGBHR, note 12, para. 17.

independent body on a statutory or constitutional basis. They may be judicial or non-judicial. In some mechanisms, those affected are directly involved in seeking remedy; in others, an intermediary seeks remedy on their behalf. Examples include the courts (for both criminal and civil actions), labour tribunals, national human rights institutions, National Contact Points under the Guidelines for Multinational Enterprises of the Organisation for Economic Co-operation and Development, many ombudsperson offices, and Government-run complaints offices.[34]

The rationale for this approach was given in the Framework Report, as being that '[s]tate regulation proscribing certain corporate conduct will have little impact without accompanying mechanisms to investigate, punish, and redress abuses'.[35] The main examples of grievance mechanisms provided in the quotation above will be considered in this chapter.

In addition, there is an obligation on states to ensure that victims of human rights harms by businesses are aware of the means of access to a remedy, because 'ensuring access to remedy for business-related human rights abuses requires also that States facilitate public awareness and understanding of these mechanisms, how they can be accessed, and any support (financial or expert) for doing so'.[36] Thus, there is a need for public awareness of the mechanisms available to victims. However, 'merely providing access to remedial mechanisms will not suffice: there should be an effective remedy in practice at the end of the process.'[37]

4. Judicial Mechanisms

a. Types of Judicial Mechanism

Effective state-based judicial mechanisms are 'at the core of ensuring access to remedy'.[38] Hence, GP 26 provides:

> States should take appropriate steps to ensure the effectiveness of domestic judicial mechanisms when addressing business-related human

---

[34] Commentary to GP 25.
[35] Framework Report, note 28, para. 82.
[36] Commentary to GP 25.
[37] WGBHR, note 12, para. 15.
[38] Commentary to GP 26.

rights abuses, including considering ways to reduce legal, practical and other relevant barriers that could lead to a denial of access to remedy.

The particular legal system within a state, such as the structure and core elements of that legal system, and the procedures within it, will affect a claim for remedies by a victim of a business action.[39] A legal system can also 'exacerbate inequalities in the extent to which victims will have access to remedy, create legal uncertainty for both victims and companies, reinforce concerns about impunity and place obstacles in the way of future international cooperation'.[40] However, these differences in legal systems, while relevant for the actual litigation process, are not relevant in terms of the need for a state to have effective judicial mechanisms, within whatever legal system/s operate in that state. Therefore, the particular type of judicial mechanism—as long as its function is that of a body with judicial powers—is not in issue here.

However, while a domestic judicial mechanism is necessary for access to a remedy, it has to be more than the mere existence of a mechanism. As the UN General Assembly made clear in its Declaration on the Rule of Law:

> We are convinced that the independence of the judicial system, together with its impartiality and integrity, is an essential prerequisite for upholding the rule of law and ensuring that there is no discrimination in the administration of justice.[41]

Therefore, a state's obligation in regard to access to an effective remedy includes the provision of judicial mechanisms which are independent, impartial, operate with integrity, and do not discriminate in their administration of justice. Other aspects include 'a fair and open hearing, and a reasonable period within which the case is heard and decided'.[42] It is often the absence

---

[39] Robert McCorquodale, 'The Litigation Landscape of Business and Human Rights' in Richard Meeran (ed.), *Human Rights Litigation against Multinationals in Practice* (OUP, 2021) [Meeran, Litigation], 1.

[40] Jennifer Zerk, 'Corporate Liability for Gross Human Rights Abuses' (OHCHR, 2014), https://www.ohchr.org/sites/default/files/Documents/Issues/Business/DomesticLawRemedies/StudyDomesticeLawRemedies.pdf. , 7.

[41] Declaration of the High-level Meeting of the General Assembly on the Rule of Law at the National and International Levels', UN General Assembly Res. 67/1, adopted by consensus on 30 November 2012, para. 13.

[42] European Commission for Democracy through Law (Venice Commission), Report on the Rule of Law, adopted at its 86th plenary session (Venice, March 2011), www.venice.coe.int/webforms/documents/?pdf=CDL-AD(2011)003rev-e, para. 53.

of these elements, and more generally the absence of the rule of law in many states, which has been one reason why there is very limited access to an effective remedy for victims of activities by businesses.[43]

b. Barriers to Judicial Remedies

Much of the focus of GP 26 is on the barriers or obstacles faced by victims in accessing judicial remedies.[44] Indeed, in the Framework Report on business and human rights, this was emphasized:

> Some complainants have sought remedy outside the State where the harm occurred, particularly through home State courts, but have faced extensive obstacles. Costs may be prohibitive, especially without legal aid; non-citizens may lack legal standing; and claims may be barred by statutes of limitations... Even the most independent judiciaries may be influenced by governments arguing for dismissal based on various 'matters of State.' These obstacles may deter claims or leave the victim with a remedy that is difficult to enforce.[45]

The starting point for many victims is that their home state (which might be in the Global South) does not have an effective rule of law and so there may not be any practically available access to remedies against transnational businesses.[46] Capacity-building should be an important way forward for this, as 'the extent of international cooperation in cross-border cases has a crucial bearing on accountability and access to remedy in practice.'[47]

---

[43] Tom Bingham, *The Rule of Law* (Allen Lane, 2010), 91–2: '[t]he right to a fair trial is a cardinal requirement of the rule of law ... and that fairness means fairness to both sides ... and independence of judicial decision-makers.'

[44] Commentary to GP 26 notes: 'states should ensure that they do not erect barriers to prevent legitimate cases from being brought before the courts in situations where judicial recourse is an essential part of accessing remedy or alternative sources of effective remedy are unavailable.'

[45] Framework Report, note 28, para. 89.

[46] Lise Smit, Claire Bright, Robert McCorquodale, Matthias Bauer, Hanna Deringer, Daniela Baeza-Breinbauer, Francisca Torres-Cortés, Frank Alleweldt, Senda Kara, and Camille Salinier and Héctor Tejero Tobed for the European Commission DG Justice and Consumers, *Study on Due Diligence Requirements through the Supply Chain*, 24 February 2020, https://op.europa.eu/en/publication-detail/-/publication/8ba0a8fd-4c83-11ea-b8b7-01aa7 5ed71a1/language-en [Smit, EC Study], 228.

[47] ARP I, note 16, para. 25.

Consequently, some victims attempt to bring their claims in the relevant transnational business's home state, which is often in the Global North. There they face many barriers—both legal and practical—to accessing legal remedies.[48] Examples of such barriers to access to remedies by victims include:[49]

- Difficulties and costs for claimants to secure legal representation;
- Lack of resources and time required to prove claimants' onus of proof;
- Difficulties in obtaining relevant information from business sources;
- Restrictive time-limits on bringing claims;
- Immunities and non-justiciability doctrines by the courts;
- Issues relating to the applicable law and the limitations of private international law;
- The complexity of corporate structures and the attribution of legal responsibility among the members of a corporate group;
- Proving human rights violations in terms of the nature of the claim; and
- Enforcement of any remedies in other jurisdictions.

It is these types of barriers, and the means by which they can be overcome through state action, of which the Framework Report was very aware:

> States should strengthen judicial capacity to hear complaints and enforce remedies against all corporations operating or based in their territory, while also protecting against frivolous claims. States should address obstacles to access to justice, including for foreign plaintiffs especially where alleged abuses reach the level of widespread and systematic human rights violations.[50]

---

[48] See generally, Gwynne Skinner with Rachel Chambers and Sarah McGrath, *Transnational Corporations and Human Rights: Overcoming Barriers to Judicial Remedy* (CUP, 2020).

[49] This list is based on Axel Marx, Claire Bright, and Jan Wouters, *Access to Legal Remedies for Victims of Corporate Human Rights Abuses in Third Countries* (European Parliament, 2019), www.europarl.europa.eu/RegData/etudes/STUD/2019/603475/EXPO_STU(2019)603475_EN.pdf and Gwynne Skinner, Robert McCorquodale, Olivier De Schutter, and Andie Lambe, *The Third Pillar: Access to Judicial Remedies for Human Rights Violations by Transnational Business* (ICAR, 2013), https://corporatejustice.org/publications/the-third-pillar-access-to-judicial-remedies-for-human-rights-violations-by-transnational-business/ [Skinner].

[50] Framework Report, note 28, paras 89–90.

The OHCHR has provided a series of reports and recommendations to states to enable them to address these obstacles through guidance for improving the effectiveness of state-based judicial mechanisms as a means of delivering accountability and remedy in cases of business-related human rights abuses.[51]

c. Case Law

It is beyond the scope of this book to set out the case law in depth. Some indicative cases in the few states where these issues have been considered at any depth in domestic law will be examined.

i. United States of America

The first major series of cases brought in domestic courts for adverse human rights impacts of companies were in the US.[52] These were primarily under the federal Alien Tort Statute (ATS).[53] The ATS gave US federal courts jurisdiction over tort claims by non-citizens for violations of 'the law of nations' (being customary international law). For almost two centuries there was almost no relevant litigation under the ATS. However, a 1980 case, *Filartiga v. Pena-Irala*,[54] confirmed that the ATS could be used to bring a claim against defendants, regardless of both their citizenship and where the violations occurred, as long as the defendant was present in the US and the violation was a breach of customary international law (such as the right not to be subjected to torture). Since that time, it is estimated that over 200 cases have been brought against businesses and individuals for violations of customary international law.[55] Many have been dismissed, some are still pending in courts, and a few have resulted in settlements (i.e. the parties to the case agreed privately to settle the case, usually with payment of money to the claimants and an acceptance of no liability by the business).[56]

These growing series of cases were significantly affected by the decision of the US Supreme Court in *Kiobel v. Royal Dutch Petroleum Co.* (*Kiobel*) in

---

[51] ARP I, note 15.
[52] For a broader history, see Nadia Bernaz, *Business and Human Rights: History, Law and Policy—Bridging the Accountability Gap* (Routledge, 2017).
[53] There are also claims under the federal Torture Victim Protection Act (TVPA) and under US state laws.
[54] *Filartiga v. Pena-Irala* 630 F.2d 876 (2d Cir. 1980).
[55] Skinner, note 49, 19.
[56] Ibid.

2013.⁵⁷ In *Kiobel*—another case against Shell, as noted in the Introduction to this chapter—the court held that the presumption against the extraterritorial application of US law applies to the ATS, though the court left open the possibility that claims that 'touch and concern the territory of the United States ... with sufficient force' could rebut that presumption.⁵⁸ In that case, the 'mere presence' of a foreign business in the US was not sufficient to meet this test, as was the situation with Shell, and so the claim did not succeed. This slim possibility of bringing a claim against a non-US business largely ended with the US Supreme Court decisions in *Jesner v. Arab Bank*⁵⁹ and *Nestlé and Cargill v. Doe*.⁶⁰ Together these cases effectively concluded that the ATS could not be used against non-US businesses because, for the ATS to apply, the business's conduct must occur in the US. Any future claims against non-US based businesses will now probably be through US state common law claims or arising from any relevant legislation.⁶¹

ii. United Kingdom

The other domestic legal system where there has been a long history of claims for adverse human rights impacts of businesses is that of the UK (or, more specifically, the jurisdiction of England and Wales). One of the first cases was *Connelly v. RTZ Corporation plc*,⁶² decided in 1998, which concerned a claim by a Scottish worker who contracted cancer after working at a mine owned by Rio Tinto in Namibia. The judicial House of Lords refused to strike out the claim that the parent company, Rio Tinto, which was domiciled in the UK, had negligently devised and implemented its subsidiary's policy on health, safety, and environment, although the claim failed on other grounds.

In *Lubbe v. Cape plc*,⁶³ a claim brought against a UK parent company for negligent control of the health and safety of its South African subsidiary's asbestos mining operations, was accepted by the judicial House of Lords at the preliminary stage (i.e. before the merits of the evidence in the

---

⁵⁷ *Kiobel v. Royal Dutch Petroleum Co.*, 133 S. Ct. 1659 (2013).
⁵⁸ Ibid., 1673.
⁵⁹ *Jesner v. Arab Bank plc* 138 S. Ct. 1386 (2018).
⁶⁰ *Nestlé and Cargill v. Doe* 151 S. Ct. 1931 (2021).
⁶¹ Rachel Chambers and Gerlinde Berger-Walliser, 'The Future of International Corporate Human Rights Litigation: A Transatlantic Comparison' (2021) 58 *American Business Law Journal* 579.
⁶² *Connelly v. RTZ Corporation plc* [1998] AC 854.
⁶³ *Lubbe and Others v. Cape plc* [2000] 1 WLR 1545.

case were reviewed). In reaching their decision the senior judge, Lord Bingham, noted:

> Resolution of this issue [of a duty of care] will be likely to involve an inquiry into what part the defendant played in controlling the operations of the group, what its directors and employees knew or ought to have known, what action was taken and not taken, whether the defendant owed a duty of care to employees of group companies overseas and whether, if so, that duty was broken. Much of the evidence material to this inquiry would, in the ordinary way, be documentary and much of it would be found in the offices of the parent corporation, including minutes of meetings, reports by directors and employees on visits overseas and correspondence.[64]

While this statement of principle was important, the first time an English court directly applied a duty of care on a parent company was in *Chandler v. Cape plc*.[65] This case involved allegations of unsafe health and safety systems in a subsidiary, which had since been dissolved, of a UK parent company, and the duty of care on the parent company was applied on the basis that the parent company had some degree of control and knowledge of the subsidiary's actions. In reaching this decision, the Court of Appeal was very clear that it was not 'piercing the corporate veil'—i.e. breaking down the separate corporate personality of each business—even if the businesses were all part of one corporate matrix:

> I would emphatically reject any suggestion that this court is in any way concerned with what is usually referred to as piercing the corporate veil. A subsidiary and its company are separate entities. There is no imposition or assumption of responsibility by reason only that a company is the parent company of another company. The question is simply whether what the parent company did amounted to taking on a direct duty to the subsidiary's employees [who alleged that they were harmed].[66]

This led to an important case before the UK's Supreme Court (which succeeded the judicial House of Lords): *Vedanta Resources plc v. Lungowe*.[67]

---

[64] Ibid., para. 20.
[65] *Chandler v. Cape plc* [2012] 1 WLR 3111.
[66] Ibid., paras 69–70 (Lady Justice Arden for the whole court).
[67] *Vedanta*, note 5. The author was an advocate before the UK Supreme Court in this case.

This case concerned claims by Zambian farmers that their lands had been polluted by a copper mine owned by a subsidiary (incorporated in Zambia) of Vedanta Resources plc (a business incorporated in the UK). The unanimous Supreme Court accepted that a parent company can have a duty of care to those affected by the actions of its subsidiary which had adverse impacts on the claimants, no matter in which state that subsidiary is located. The court was pragmatic about the realities of such businesses in stating that '[t]here is no limit to the models of management and control which may be put in place within a multinational group of companies'.[68]

Whether a duty of care arises was held by the court to depend on 'the extent to which, and the way in which, the parent [company] availed itself of the opportunity to take over, intervene in, control, supervise or advise the management of the relevant operations ... of the subsidiary'.[69] The court went further in deciding:

> Even where group-wide policies do not of themselves give rise to such a duty of care to third parties, they may do so if the parent does not merely proclaim them, but takes active steps, by training, supervision and enforcement, to see that they are implemented by relevant subsidiaries. Similarly, it seems to [the court] that the parent may incur the relevant responsibility to third parties if, in published materials, it holds itself out as exercising that degree of supervision and control of its subsidiaries, even if it does not in fact do so. In such circumstances its very omission may constitute the abdication of a responsibility which it has publicly undertaken.[70]

On this basis, a parent company can have a duty of care to those affected, for both its acts and omissions, and the courts can rely on public statements made by the parent company about its activities, such as in annual reports and other corporate documents. The case was subsequently settled with a large payment to the claimants.[71]

A later case before the UK Supreme Court, *Okpabi v. Royal Dutch Shell plc*,[72] confirmed the decision in *Vedanta v. Lungowe*, and made clear that

---

[68] Ibid., para. 51.
[69] Ibid., para. 49.
[70] Ibid., para. 53.
[71] Daniel Leader, 'Human Rights Litigation Against MNCs: UK Lessons' in Meeran, Litigation, note 39, 61.
[72] *Okpabi v. Shell*, note 6.

control by the parent company over its subsidiary was not the determining factor:

> [C]ontrol is just a starting point. The issue is the extent to which the parent did take over or share with the subsidiary the management of the relevant activity (here the pipeline operation). That may or may not be demonstrated by the parent controlling the subsidiary. In a sense, all parents control their subsidiaries. That control gives the parent the opportunity to get involved in management. But control of a company and de facto management of part of its activities are two different things. A subsidiary may maintain de jure control of its activities, but nonetheless delegate de facto management of part of them to emissaries of its parent.[73]

It is, therefore, clear that, at least in UK law, a parent company can have a duty of care for the actions of its subsidiary which have led to adverse human rights and environmental impacts.[74] This is a significant development in the law to enable remedies for victims of corporate actions around the world.

iii. Other States

The *Vedanta* decision has been taken up in the Netherlands, as discussed in the Introduction to this chapter. The cases in the Netherlands also include ones concerning climate change, as will be considered in Chapter 8.[75] Other cases in the European Union (EU) include *Jabir and Others v. KiK Textilien und Non-Food GmbH*,[76] where the German courts dismissed a claim brought by family members of workers who died in a fire in a textile factory in Pakistan against a German textile business and large customer of the factory, on the basis that the claims were time-barred under Pakistani law.[77]

---

[73] Ibid., para. 147.
[74] Marilyn Croser, Martyn Day, Mariëtte Van Huijstee, and Channa Samkalden, 'Vedanta v Lungowe and Kiobel v Shell: The Implications for Parent Company Accountability' (2020) 5 *Business and Human Rights Journal* 130.
[75] *Milieudefensie v. Royal Dutch Shell plc* [2021] C/09/571932; see Chapter 8.
[76] *Jabir and Others v. KiK Textilien und Non-Food GmbH* Case No. 7 O 95/15, Regional Court of Dortmund.
[77] Philipp Wesche and Miriam Saage-Maaß, 'Holding Companies Liable for Human Rights Abuses Related to Foreign Subsidiaries and Suppliers before German Civil Courts: Lessons from Jabir and Others v KiK' (2016) 16 *Human Rights Law Review* 370.

There have been a growing number of cases in Canada, at least from the time of *Choc v. Hudbay Minerals Inc.*[78] in 2013, where the courts have indicated that they were prepared to accept that a duty of care could arise for parent companies.[79] In 2020, the majority of the Canadian Supreme Court held in *Nevsun Resources Ltd v. Araya*[80] that customary international law's prohibitions against slavery, forced labour, crimes against humanity, and cruel, inhuman, and degrading treatment, could be applicable directly to a business, even though these prohibitions had been created as obligations on states alone.[81] Accordingly, the court allowed the claim to proceed without needing a new tort against a business to be determined. That case, like many others, was later settled between the parties.[82] There have also been some cases in other common law states.[83]

The cases considered above are all before courts in the Global North. This is due to the reality that most major transnational businesses are based in the Global North, with the events giving rise to the claims usually taking place in the Global South.[84] There have, though, been some cases in the Global South which have also developed the law in relation to access to remedies for victims affected by business activities. For example, in the *Owina Ouru Lead Poisoning Case*,[85] the public law claim before the Kenyan High Court concerned the exposure of the residents of the Owina Uhuru neighbourhood to lead contamination from a nearby lead-smelting plant. The claim was against both the operators of the plant (a Kenyan business) and the relevant public authorities, on the basis that both had a duty to prevent environmental pollution and other adverse human rights impacts. The court found in favour of the claimants and apportioned damages between the various defendants. It also held that 'officials from [the government agencies] had furtively assisted [the business] in breaching the law by

---

[78] *Choc v. Hudbay Minerals Inc.* 2013 ONSC 1414 (Superior Court of Ontario).
[79] Also *Das v. George Weston Ltd* 2018 ONCA 1053 (Court of Appeal for Ontario), concerning a retailer of goods.
[80] *Nevsun Resources Ltd v. Araya*, 2020 SCC 5.
[81] Ibid., para. 128.
[82] Penelope Simons, 'Developments in Canada on Business and Human Rights; One Step Forward Two Steps Back' [2023] *Leiden Journal of International Law* 1.
[83] For example, *James Hardie Industries plc v. White* [2018] NZCA 580 (Court of Appeal of New Zealand) and *Sanda v. PTTEP Australasia (Ashmore Cartier) Pty Ltd (No. 7)* [2021] FCA 237 (Federal Court of Australia).
[84] Muhammad Azeem, 'The KiK Case: A Critical Perspective from the South' in Miriam Saage-Maaß, Peer Zumbansen, Michael Bader, and Palvasha Shahab (eds), *Transnational Legal Activism in Global Value Chains* (Springer, 2021), 279.
[85] *KM & 9 Others v. Attorney General and 7 Others* [2020] eKLR (Environment and Land Court), http://kenyalaw.org/caselaw/cases/view/198619/.

disingenuously creating a trail of official communication and a record of warnings, inspections, and closures to create the appearance that they were enforcing environmental standards in good faith, while the opposite was in fact the case'.[86]

iv. Criminal Law

While all these cases above, with the exception of the Kenyan case, have been brought as private law claims (i.e. between individuals and a business directly), there have been cases brought against businesses, and even business executives, under criminal law. These have been for their actions that had adverse human rights impacts, which have often been linked to international humanitarian law.[87] These include cases in France against Lafarge, a major cement business, for complicity in crimes against humanity for their actions in Syria,[88] and against Amesys and Nexa, which are software manufacturers, for complicity in torture and enforced disappearances, for the use of their software in Libya.[89] Similarly, in Sweden charges have been brought against Lundin mining executives for complicity in war crimes in Sudan.[90]

These criminal law cases all occurred in the European civil law legal systems. The approach to taking criminal legal proceedings in the civil law system more than by civil legal proceedings is consistent with the findings of a survey of legal proceedings against businesses:

> [A]round 30 [sets of legal proceedings] were commenced in common law jurisdictions and around 17 in civil law jurisdictions. Of the cases

---

[86] Rosemary Mwanza, 'Toxic Spaces, Community Voices, and the Promise of Environmental Human Rights: Lessons on the Owino Uhuru Pollution Incident in Kenya' (2020) 38 *Nordic Journal of Human Rights* 279, 284–5.

[87] David Turns, 'The Law of Armed Conflict (International Humanitarian Law)' in Malcolm Evans (ed.), *International Law* (OUP, 5th ed., 2018).

[88] Business & Human Rights Resource Centre, 'Lafarge Lawsuit (re Complicity in Crimes against Humanity in Syria)' https://www.business-humanrights.org/en/latest-news/lafarge-lawsuit-re-complicity-in-crimes-against-humanity-in-syria.

[89] Business & Human Rights Resource Centre, 'French Technology Firm Nexa Indicted for 'complicity in torture and enforced disappearances' in Egypt and Libya https://www.business-humanrights.org/en/latest-news/french-technology-firm-nexa-indicted-for-complicity-in-torture-and-enforced-disappearances-in-egypt-and-libya.

[90] Business & Human Rights Resource Centre, 'Sweden: In Historic Indictment, Public Prosecutor Charges Lundin Energy Executives with Complicity in Sudan War Crimes' https://www.business-humanrights.org/en/latest-news/swedens-public-prosecutor-charges-lundin-energy-executives-with-complicity-in-sudan-war-crimes.See also Chiara Albanese, Sergio Di Pasquale, and Kelly Gilblom, 'Eni, Shell to Face Trial in Italy in $1 Billion Bribery Case' *Bloomberg* (20 December 2017).

commenced in common law jurisdictions, all but one are private law (i.e. tort-based) actions for compensation. On the other hand, of the legal proceedings that have been commenced in civil law jurisdictions, well over half were commenced as criminal law complaints.[91]

Therefore, the nature of the legal system can have an influence on the type of claims commenced.[92]

d. Human Rights

There is a general lack of claims in any domestic legal system based explicitly on a violation of a human right (though the human rights abuse will normally be argued in court). Because claims about an abuse of human rights by businesses are normally brought within the tort law or criminal law framework of the domestic legal system, it forces claimants to fit their claims within certain restrictive legal parameters, and it privileges only those human rights abuses that can be expressed in tort or criminal claim terminology.[93] This can make it very puzzling and exclusionary for the many claimants who consider that their human rights have been abused but see the claim not specifically expressed as a human rights claim. It also means that some human rights violations, such as denial of access to education and infringing the cultural rights of Indigenous communities, may not be able to be brought as a claim against a business at all without some legislative basis in domestic law.[94] This lack of legal expression diminishes the potential significance of the UNGPs' clear statement—as examined in Chapter 5—that businesses can violate the full range of human rights and so restricts the possible claims that can be brought to domestic courts.

Further, there is still only limited case law which refers directly to the UNGPs or the OECD Guidelines as a basis for a court's decision, as is considered in Chapter 3. This absence is evident even when these international standard-setting documents are pleaded before a domestic court but not referred to by the domestic court,[95] and despite a number

---

[91] Zerk, note 40, para. 91.
[92] McCorquodale in Meeran, Litigation, note 39, 1.
[93] Skinner, note 49, 37.
[94] McCorquodale in Meeran, Litigation, note 39, 1, 18.
[95] This occurred, for example, in both *Vedanta Resources plc v. Lungowe* and *Okpabi v. Royal Dutch Shell plc*, as well as the *Owina Ouru Lead Poisoning Case*, discussed above.

of major businesses expressly referring to these standards in their public documents.⁹⁶

5. State-Based Non-Judicial Mechanisms

The UNGPs also encourage state-based non-judicial mechanisms to enable effective and appropriate access to remedies for victims. The Commentary to GP 27 insists that:

> Gaps in the provision of remedy for business-related human rights abuses could be filled, where appropriate, by expanding the mandates of existing non-judicial mechanisms and/or by adding new mechanisms. These may be mediation-based, adjudicative or follow other culturally appropriate and rights-compatible processes—or involve some combination of these—depending on the issues concerned, any public interest involved, and the potential needs of the parties ... National human rights institutions have a particularly important role to play in this regard.

Most states have a range of administrative mechanisms, arbitration, and mediation to enable different types of disputes to be resolved. In so doing, there should be acknowledgement of 'imbalances between the parties to business-related human rights claims and any additional barriers to access faced by individuals from groups or populations at heightened risk of vulnerability or marginalization'.⁹⁷ There are also many human rights (including labour rights) treaty bodies and some national human rights institutions which might be considered state non-judicial mechanisms, even though not specifically designed for business and human rights disputes.⁹⁸

The most widespread state-based non-judicial mechanism which is designed to deal specifically with business and human rights claims is that of the NCPs of the OECD Guidelines; these Guidelines were set out

---

⁹⁶ For example, Shell's corporate website lists a series of 'external voluntary codes' that it supports, including the UNGPs, the Global Compact, and the OECD Guidelines: https://www.shell.com/sustainability/our-approach/external-voluntary-codes.html .

⁹⁷ Commentary to GP 27.

⁹⁸ Mariëtte van Huijstee and Joseph Wilde-Ramsing, 'The Relationship between Non-Judicial Grievance Mechanisms and Access to Remedy for Business-Related Human Rights Abuses' in Surya Deva and David Birchall (eds), *Research Handbook on Business and Human Rights* (Edward Elgar, 2020) [Deva and Birchall, BHR], 471.

in Chapter 3. Each OECD member state is meant to establish an NCP to which complaints may be made that a business is in breach of the OECD Guidelines.[99] Over 50 member states and non-member adhering states have established NCPs.[100] These states are generally considered to be those with a free market economy, and so it is argued that '[t]he institutional foundations of the Guidelines are symptomatic of an international economic order rooted in multinational power, Global North–South power imbalances, democratic interference and social and political unrest, that also contributes to understanding the operational effectiveness of NCPs today'.[101]

While the NCPs were created before the 2011 revision of the OECD Guidelines, it was only after that revision that the NCPs could handle claims relating to human rights matters.[102] Complaints can be brought to an NCP by an interested party, which may be an individual or community, and can be brought by a trade union or other civil society entity on behalf of a complainant. The complaint must relate to one of the matters listed in the OECD Guidelines, such as environment, taxation, consumer issues, and human rights, including labour rights, with the largest number currently being in regard to human rights.[103]

Once a complaint is made, the procedures are that the NCP will make an initial assessment as to whether to accept the complaint, provide an offer of good offices (i.e. mediation) to settle the complaint, and then reach a final statement, with an optional last step of follow-up. The first stage of admissibility is key, as a large number of complaints do not succeed at this stage. An NCP decision will typically take into account 'whether it is the correct NCP to handle the Specific Instance [as the complaint is known], whether the

---

[99] Paragraph 11 of the OECD Guidelines provides that adhering states 'will establish' National Contact Points, and Part I of its Amendment provides that adhering states 'shall set up' National Contact Points'.

[100] OECD member states are: Australia, Austria, Belgium, Canada, Chile, Colombia, Czech Republic, Denmark, Estonia, Finland, France, Germany, Greece, Hungary, Iceland, Ireland, Israel, Italy, Japan, Korea, Latvia, Lithuania, Luxembourg, Mexico, Netherlands, New Zealand, Norway, Poland, Portugal, Slovak Republic, Slovenia, Spain, Sweden, Switzerland, Turkey, United Kingdom, and United States; Non-member adhering states: Argentina, Brazil, Costa Rica, Croatia, Egypt, Jordan, Kazakhstan, Morocco, Peru, Romania, Tunisia, Ukraine, and Uruguay.

[101] Kinnari Bhatt and Gamze Erdem Türkelli, 'OECD National Contact Points as Sites of Effective Remedy: New Expressions of the Role and Rule of Law within Market Globalization?' (2021) 6 *Business and Human Rights Journal* 423, 429. See also the discussion in Chapter 3.

[102] Karin Buhmann, 'Public Regulators and CSR: The Social Licence to Operate in Recent United Nations Instruments on Business and Human Rights and the Juridication of CSR' [2016] *Journal of Business Ethics* 136.

[103] NCP database, https://mneguidelines.oecd.org//database/.

alleged breach is indeed a breach of the Guidelines, if it is material and substantiated, and whether taking on the case will contribute to further the effectiveness of the Guidelines'.[104] There is no substantive appeal available to any other forum (as is consistent with some other non-judicial processes) if the complaint is rejected at the initial assessment stage.[105]

The Commentary to the OECD Guidelines notes that 'since governments are accorded flexibility in the way they organise NCPs, NCPs should function in a visible, accessible, transparent, and accountable manner … [and in a way that is] impartial, predictable, equitable and compatible with the principles and standards of the Guidelines'.[106] In reality, there is a great deal of diversity in how NCPs operate, with some housed within government ministries and others being distinct and separate; some are comprised entirely of government officials and others include all or some independent experts, and they vary significantly in terms of staff numbers and budget.[107]

In addition, the 'NCPs differ in how they determine admissibility of a complaint, including how they determine jurisdiction, who is eligible to bring complaints, and whether there is a time limit by which a complaint must be brought after an alleged incident occurred'.[108] This has led to considerable criticism of how they operate, especially for the lack of clarity and uncertainty for victims seeking a remedy through this process.[109] Indeed, annual reports by the civil society organization, OECD Watch, show how rare it is for a victim to receive a remedy directly, as even final statements by NCPs which find a breach by a business often only request that a business

---

[104] Kari Otteburn and Axel Marx, 'Seeking Remedies for Corporate Human Rights Abuses: What is the Contribution of OECD National Contact Points?' in Axel Marx, Geert Van Calster, and Jan Wouters with Kari Otteburn (eds), *Research Handbook on Global Governance, Business and Human Rights* (Edward Elgar, 2022), 228, 234.

[105] A review might be available to those NCPs which have an advisory board, though this tends to be only for procedural errors in the investigation, e.g. under the UK NCP: https://www.gov.uk/government/publications/complaints-brought-under-the-oecd-guidelines-for-multinational-enterprises-to-the-uk-national-contact-point-review-procedure/steering-board-review-of-uk-ncp-procedures..

[106] Part I.9 of the Commentary on the Implementation Procedures of the OECD Guidelines for Multinational Enterprises, 71–2.

[107] Juan Carlos Ochoa Sanchez, 'An Empirical Examination of the Function of the OECD National Contact Points to Handle Complaints on an Alleged Breach of the OECD Guidelines for Multinational Enterprises' in Roger Blanpain (ed.), *Protecting Labour Rights in a Multi-Polar Supply Chain and Mobile Global Economy* (Wolters Kluwer, 2014), 159.

[108] Ibid., 240.

[109] OECD Watch, Remedy Remains Rare (2015), https://www.oecdwatch.org/remedy-remains-rare/ and Amnesty International, Obstacle Course: How the UK's National Contact Point handles Human Rights Complaints under the OECD Guidelines for Multinational Enterprises (2020), https://www.amnesty.org.uk/files/uk_ncp_complaints_handling_full_report_lores_0.pdf.

undertake human rights due diligence (or similar outcomes) without any direct remedy on the ground for the victims.[110] National Contact Points also have no enforcement mechanism,[111] and rely on publicity and pressure. However, it is argued that 'when a conflict arises [for a business] between pursuing profits, and observing human rights, soft law might be just a bit too soft to lean the balance in favor of human rights'.[112]

There are some examples where NCPs have clarified the requirements on businesses under the OECD Guidelines. There are also some NCP cases where victims have received remedies. A few of these cases will be considered here (and some have been considered elsewhere in this book).

In *Equitable Cambodia and Inclusive Development International v. Australia and New Zealand Bank* (ECIDI v. ANZ),[113] the complaint concerned almost 700 Cambodian families who were forcibly displaced and dispossessed of their land and houses (among other alleged human rights abuses) to make way for a sugar plantation and refinery operated by Phnom Penh Sugar Company (PPS). The refinery was partly financed by Australia and New Zealand Bank (ANZ), a bank incorporated in Australia. The Australian NCP reviewed the facts, including ANZ's published documents on internal policies and procedures, and also relied on the OECD's Responsible Business Conduct for Institutional Investors guidance,[114] which applied human rights due diligence responsibilities to financial institutions. The NCP determined that:

> [T]here is some doubt in this case around the extent to which ANZ's actual business practices aligned with its stated approach to human rights ... When its human rights standards were applied to ANZ's commercial relationship with its former client PPS, it is arguable that most (if not all) of them would not be satisfactorily met.[115]

---

[110] For example, OECD Watch, 'State of Remedy 2022' (19 July 2023), https://www.oecdwatch.org/state-of-remedy-2022/

[111] Stéfanie Khoury and David Whyte, 'Sidelining Corporate Human Rights Violations: The Failure of the OECD's Regulatory Consensus' (2019) 18 *Journal of Human Rights* 363.

[112] Ramona Cîrlig, 'Business and Human Rights: From Soft Law to Hard Law?' (2016) 6 *Juridical Tribune* 228, 233.

[113] OECD Watch, *EC and IDI vs. Australia and New Zealand Banking Group* (2018), https://www.oecdwatch.org/complaint/ec-and-idi-vs-australia-and-new-zealand-banking-group/

[114] OECD Guidance for Institutional Investors, https://mneguidelines.oecd.org/RBC-for-Institutional-Investors.pdf.

[115] OECD Watch, note 113, paras 37–8.

The NCP concluded that ANZ should ensure that its practices meet OECD standards and strengthen its human rights due diligence arrangements and institutional grievance mechanisms. Subsequently, ANZ has paid an amount of damages equal to its profit from the loan to the victims and has created grievance mechanisms.[116]

Similarly, in *Society for Threatened Peoples Switzerland Complaint to Swiss NCP regarding UBS Group AG*,[117] the complaint concerned possible human rights abuses in the context of the provision of financial services through investment by a Swiss financial institution—UBS—in shares in Hikvision, a Chinese business. It was claimed that Hikvision manufactured technology used for surveillance of the Uyghurs and other Turkic minorities living in the Xinjiang Uyghur Autonomous Region in China. In its initial assessment, the Swiss NCP stated:

> By investing in shares of Hikvision, the UBS fund contributes to the funding of Hikvision. As the state of China is an important shareholder of Hikvision, the NCP assumes that a direct link between the UBS Fund and the alleged human rights violations could not be excluded, when Hikvision shares were part of the fund ... The Swiss NCP concludes that a business relationship according to the OECD Guidelines between UBS and Hikvision and a direct link between UBS' products and services and the alleged human rights violations could not be excluded with regard to the UBS Fund.[118]

However, the Swiss NCP considered that where a financial institution holds nominee shares (i.e. on behalf of a client of the financial institution) then it could not be directly linked to the abuse of human rights. This decision was subsequently clarified as being incorrect by the OHCHR, on the basis that a 'direct link is created by the fact that the service [provided by the financial institution] entails holding and trading shares in the investee', with the

---

[116] Inclusive Development International, 'ANZ Payment to Displaced Cambodian Families Brings Landmark Human Rights Case to a Close' (November 2021), https://media.business-humanrights.org/media/documents/ANZ_Settlement_Final_Distribution_Press_Release__11-2-21_.pdf.

[117] OECD Watch, *Society for Threatened Peoples Switzerland vs. UBS Group* (22 June 2020), https://www.oecdwatch.org/complaint/society-for-threatened-peoples-switzerland-vs-ubs-group.

[118] Ibid., 7–8.

only issue being about the degree of leverage.[119] These two cases do, though, confirm that the responsibility to respect human rights applies to financial institutions (as discussed in Chapter 5).

A different example is a case before the Dutch NCP, where a complaint was brought by former employees of a subsidiary, based in the Democratic Republic of Congo (DRC), of a Dutch beer company, Heineken, concerning unlawful dismissals, abusive treatment, and failure to pay wages.[120] In *Bralima and Heineken* the mediation by the NCP occurred in Uganda, which was near to the location of most of the victims (and, in this instance, the travel costs of the victims were partly paid by the Dutch government). At the end of the NCP mediation, Heineken paid substantial damages to the complainants.[121] This unusual outcome has been attributed to 'accessibility, political and commercial will, and the wide publicity of the case',[122] as well as the fact that, unlike most other NCPs, the Dutch NCP is not located within a government department and has sound financial support.[123]

The above are examples of cases where an NCP has accepted the complaint, clarified the situation, and, in two cases, provided a remedy to the victims. Nevertheless, as Kinnari Bhatt and Gamze Erdem Türkellí have noted:

> Currently, the potential of NCPs to provide effective remedy, both in procedural and implementation terms... remains curtailed by various limitations. These include their inability to compel businesses to take part in problem-solving processes, mandates restricted to non-adversarial measures and the provision of light 'good offices', the structural and ethical issues stemming from being located in a single government department, inadequate resources in dealing with claims from affected persons, and lack of independent oversight mechanisms... [U]nder current circumstances, the ability of NCPs to offer effective remedy is severely limited, inconsistent and unpredictable.[124]

---

[119] OHCHR response to BankTrack, 30 August 2021, https://www.ohchr.org/sites/default/files/Documents/Issues/Business/finance-2021-response-nominee-shareholders.pdf, 4-5; 4– see Introduction to Chapter 5.
[120] OECD Watch, *Former Employees v. Heineken* (2017), https://www.oecdwatch.org/complaint/former-employees-vs-heineken/
[121] Ibid.
[122] Bhatt and Türkellí, note 101, 438.
[123] Jernej Letnar Černic, 'Corporate Responsibility Human Rights: A Critical Analysis of the OECD Guidelines for Multinational enterprises' (2008) 4 *Hanse Law Review* 71.
[124] Bhatt and Türkellí, note 101, 441–2, 447.

Indeed, the OHCHR's Accountability and Remedy Project has found, through a review of over 430 business and human rights related events, allegations, and disputes, that it is usually state-based non-judicial mechanisms, such as NCPs, that do *not* offer an accessible or realistic route to an effective remedy.[125] Indeed, some NCPs seem very reluctant to see the provision of a remedy to victims as being part of their responsibilities on the basis that '[t]he NCP cannot impose liability or sanctions on companies'.[126]

6. Business Operational Grievance Mechanisms

The last four GPs in the UNGPs all deal with non-state non-judicial grievance mechanisms. GP 28 encourages states to support them, GP 29 expects that 'business enterprises should establish or participate in effective operational-level grievance mechanisms', and GP 30 suggests that '[i]ndustry, multi-stakeholder and other collaborative initiatives that are based on respect for human rights-related standards' should ensure that effective grievance mechanisms are available.

A key aspect for each of them is the term 'effective'. Hence, GP 31 defines what are the effectiveness criteria for such non-judicial grievance mechanisms. The criteria are: legitimate; accessible; predictable; equitable; transparent; rights-compatible; a source of continuous learning; and based on engagement and dialogue.[127] The OHCHR has produced a report, which provides a series of suggestions as to how different types of grievance mechanisms can meet each of the effectiveness criteria in practice in a wide range of operating contexts, reflecting on how these criteria have been largely accepted by businesses, benchmark systems, and regulators.[128]

---

[125] OHCHR, 'State-Based Non-Judicial Mechanisms for Accountability and Remedy for Business-Related Human Rights Abuses: Supporting Actors or Lead Players?' Discussion paper prepared for the 6th UN Annual Forum on Business and Human Rights, Geneva' (27–9 November 2017), 15–16, www.ohchr.org/Documents/Issues/Business/DomesticLawRemedies/ARPII_%20DiscussionpaperonPhase2forUNForum_FINAL.

[126] Danish NCP, Final Statement—*CCC vs PWT Group* (17 October 2016); https://www.oecdwatch.org/complaint/pwt-groups-role-in-the-rana-plaza-collapse/. Also discussion in van Huijstee and Wilde-Ramsing, note 98, 478–9.

[127] GP 31. These are expanded upon in OHCHR, 'Improving Accountability and Access to Remedy for Victims of Business-Related Human Rights Abuse through Non-State-Based Grievance Mechanisms' UN Doc. A/HRC/44/32 (July 2020) (ARP III).

[128] OHCHR, note 127. Also SGSR Report, 'Piloting Principles for Effective Company/Stakeholder Grievance Mechanisms: A Report of Lessons Learned' (21 May 2011), https://www.ohchr.org/sites/default/files/Documents/Issues/Business/A-HRC-17-31-Add1.pdf.

The scale and complexity of operational-level grievance mechanisms (OGMs) will vary depending on the circumstances, and they can be shared with other entities, such as industry associations and multi-stakeholder initiatives referred to in GP 30. Some OGMs might be limited to some stakeholders, such as employees or local communities, and some may be broader. While focused on human rights issues, an effective OGM should not be limited to addressing grievances that appear to amount to alleged breaches of human rights. This is because there may be those grievances which, if ignored, could lead to adverse human rights impacts, and those which could be systemic and, if left unaddressed, could lead to broad unrest and/or conflict.[129]

These OGMs are not to be located geographically distant from where the business is operating; hence the idea that they are 'operational-level' grievance mechanisms. They are meant to operate as communication and dialogue channels established on-site wherever a business operates (which may not be where it is incorporated), which aim to enable all relevant affected stakeholders, such as workers and community members—with special regard to vulnerable and marginalized groups—to voice their grievances, and to have swift, effective, and appropriate responses by the business to address them.[130]

There is a strong argument that OGMs should never be used, directly or indirectly, to preclude access to other judicial or non-judicial remedial mechanisms, as it is the victims who are meant to be able to choose the forum for the resolution of their grievances.[131] In addition, OGMs do not have the sanctioning power to force a party to provide a remedy in the same way as judicial mechanisms, and so are often not focused on providing a long-term or systemic remedy.[132]

It is also evident that these OGMs should be in place as soon as the business explores the possibility of operating in a location, not least as it can help to ease the possibility of tensions with the local communities. This would combine with the consultations which are a necessary part of human rights due diligence (discussed in Chapter 5), and its ongoing tracking, as '[o]perational-level grievance mechanisms can also provide important

---

[129] Florian Wettstein, *Business and Human Rights: Ethical, Legal, and Managerial Perspectives* (CUP, 2022), 149.
[130] Jonathan Kaufman and Katherine McDonnell, 'Community-Driven Operational Grievance Mechanisms' (2015) 1 *Business and Human Rights Journal* 125, 128.
[131] Commentary to GP 29 and WGBHR, note 12, para. 71.
[132] van Huijstee and Wilde-Ramsing, note 98.

feedback on the effectiveness of the business enterprise's human rights due diligence from those directly affected.[133] Effective grievance mechanisms can also assist businesses to build positive relationships with all rights holders by showing that the business does take seriously their concerns and the impacts on their human rights. This is also relevant for investors.[134] It could also lead to the prevention of future human rights impacts and reduce business risks.

Despite these reasons for having OGMs, there appears to be to-date limited use of them by businesses, especially beyond the first tier of suppliers.[135] Some high-profile OGMs have been strongly criticized.[136] One empirical analysis of 18 voluntary sustainability standards concluded that most OGMs fail to meet the criteria for effective access to remedy because, for example, they are not communicated in languages or formats accessible to rightsholders (if communicated at all), and they lacked clear timelines, processes, and transparency protocols.[137] Some industry associations have developed good practice guidance, such as that of the International Council on Mining and Metals in relation to Indigenous peoples, as it urges their members that 'as part of good engagement practice, companies should seek agreement with indigenous groups on effective, culturally appropriate processes and structures for pre-empting, responding to and resolving community concerns and grievances'.[138]

---

[133] Commentary to GP 20.

[134] Investor Alliance for Human Rights, https://investorsforhumanrights.org and Local Authority Pension Fund Forum (LAPFF), https://lapfforum.org/wp-content/uploads/2022/04/Mining-and-Human-Rights-An-Investor-Perspective.pdf.

[135] Lise Smit, Gabrielle Holly, Robert McCorquodale, and Stuart Neely, 'Human Rights Due Diligence in Global Supply Chains: Evidence of Corporate Practices to Inform a Legal Standard' [2020] *International Journal of Human Rights* 945.

[136] For example, Enodo Rights, 'Assessment of Barrick Gold's Grievance Mechanism' (2015), https://atelieraftab.com/insight/assessment-of-barrick-gold-grievance-mechanism, p. 1: 'Claimants were thus exposed to a process which failed adequately to protect them and which they did not understand. In the end, successful claimants received remedies that were equitable, even generous, under international law. Nevertheless, many were left disaffected, stigmatized and abused.'

[137] MSI (Multi-Stakeholder Integrity), 'Not Fit-for-Purpose: The Grand Experiment of Multi-Stakeholder Initiatives in Corporate Accountability, Human Rights and Global Governance' (2020). Also Daniel Bradlow and Andria Naudé Fourie, 'The Multilateral Development Banks and the Management of the Human Rights Impacts of their Operations' in Deva and Birchall, BHR, note 98, 315.

[138] The International Council on Mining and Metals, 'Good Practice Guide: Indigenous Peoples and Mining' (2015) tool 12, 87–90, https://www.icmm.com/en-gb/guidance/social-performance/2015/indigenous-peoples-mining. Also Jernej Letnar Černič, 'Business and Indigenous Peoples' Human Rights' in Deva and Birchall, BHR, note 98, 335.

There are a few examples of good practice regarding OGMs:

> Some companies are using innovative methods for their human rights grievance mechanisms ... [such as] the use of smartphone apps which link with worker voice programmes [across their supply chain] ... The programme educates members of the community on human rights, and provides each participant with a smartphone containing an app which records data. For example, around forced labour issues, the app may ask questions such as whether the smartphone holder can leave their job when they want or whether they have to pay their employer. The results are collated and provided to the company as independent and anonymous data from the community.[139]

In addition, the ILO's Multinational Enterprises Declaration expects that businesses should participate in all such legitimate processes and also comply with their remedial decisions.[140]

At the same time, there can be an issue of lack of trust by rightsholders in any grievance mechanisms which are administered by the business itself, meaning that some OGMs which exist may not be used. Therefore, it has been argued that it is better if businesses involve independent third parties and include possibilities for recourse to external institutions in their OGMs.[141] For example, there are some independent bodies which offer mediation as part of such a grievance process, which enables flexibility and responsiveness to the different stakeholders to be respected speedily and effectively.[142] Other innovative proposals include ones for an arbitration system for helping to resolve these types of disputes.[143]

---

[139] Smit, HRDD in the Supply Chain, note 135, 958.

[140] WGBHR, note 12, para. 68.

[141] Shift, 'Remediation, Grievance Mechanisms, and the Corporate Responsibility to Respect Human Rights' (2014) https://shiftproject.org/resource/remediation-grievance-mechanisms-and-the-corporate-responsibility-to-respect-human-rights.

[142] Centre for Effective Dispute Resolution, 'Mediation for Business and Human Rights', https://www.cedr.com/foundation/currentprojects/mediation-for-business-and-human-rights/.

[143] Center for International Legal Cooperation, The-Hague-Rules-on-Business-and-Human-Rights-Arbitration_CILC-digital-version.pdf (December 2019).

7. Conclusions

Access to effective remedies is a key part of business and human rights and is consistent with the right to a remedy under international human rights law. This remedy, to be effective, must be a remedy to the victim/s, rather than being only a sanction, such as a fine, to the business, and it should be relevant to the particular circumstances of the victim/s. The WGBHR, in its Report on Access to Remedies, concluded:

> The concept of effective remedies is closely connected to the idea of corporate accountability. Effective remedies for business-related human rights abuses, taken in a holistic sense to fulfil individual and societal goals, should result in some form of corporate accountability and vice versa.
>
> Rights holders should be central to the entire remedy process. Such centrality would, among other elements, mean that remedial mechanisms are responsive to the diverse experiences and expectations of rights holders; that remedies are accessible, affordable, adequate and timely from the perspective of those seeking them; that the affected rights holders are not victimized when seeking remedies; and that ... preventive, redressive and deterrent remedies are available for each business-related human rights abuse.[144]

Therefore, there is an obligation on states to provide access to effective remedies in their judicial mechanisms for adverse human rights impacts of business activities. However, the evidence is that there are significant barriers to accessing these mechanisms by those claiming that their human rights have been adversely impacted. Despite this, a number of cases, primarily in the Global North, have gradually broadened the ability for civil claims to be made, such as against parent companies and for claims that were originally devised in terms of state obligations, and there have also been some cases based on criminal law.

In terms of non-judicial mechanisms, the NCPs under the OECD Guidelines have been used as a state-based mechanism, though with limited remedies to victims. In relation to businesses, there is a responsibility to have operational grievance mechanisms, as a means of dealing

---

[144] WGBHR, note 12, paras 80–1.

with the victims' concerns early and in the location where they occurred. Unfortunately, there are still too few businesses which have created effective operational grievance mechanisms.

The evidence from this chapter indicates that there is still a gap between the expectations of the UNGPs and the reality on the ground for most rightsholders. Accordingly, there has been pressure brought on states to create legislation in this area. This is considered in Chapter 7.

7
National Regulation of International Human Rights Responsibilities of Business

1. Context

For a long time it was assumed that all businesses would lobby against any proposal for national legislation which imposed legal obligations on them, based on international law, in relation to their activities which might have adverse human rights and environmental impacts.[1] This was reinforced by strong statements by some businesses, industry associations, and politicians against the (then) proposed legislation on this issue in France and Germany:

> [W]e fear that this [French] bill will betray the spirit of CSR [Corporate Social Responsibility], based on taking responsibility, initiative and voluntary approach, which have already proven their worth ... Let's not force companies to set up a vigilance plan; instead, let us encourage voluntary approaches ... We must choose: should we be a leader in this field by initiating this reform [in the legislation], at the risk of making our companies bear an additional constraint and thus placing them in a position of high inequality compared to their competitors on the European market, and this in a context of crisis?[2]

---

[1] Surya Deva, 'From "Business or Human Rights" to "Business and Human Rights": What Next?' in Surya Deva and David Birchall (eds), *Research Handbook on Business and Human Rights* (Edward Elgar, 2020) [Deva and Birchall, BHR], 1.

[2] Maina Sage, Deputy for the Tapura Hiraatira party, French Assembly debates, 23 March 2016, For more detail, see Maria-Therese Gustafsson, Almut Schilling-Vacaflor, and Andrea Lenschow, 'Foreign Corporate Accountability: The Contested Institutionalization of Mandatory Due Diligence in France and Germany' (2022) 16 *Regulation & Governance* 891.

158   National Regulation

The German non-ferrous metals industry is generally in favour of a voluntary approach and industry solutions. We therefore take a critical view of the [proposed German] national law on corporate due diligence.[3]

In contrast, there have been other businesses and industry associations who have made clear statements in favour of such legislation, particularly in regard to the European Union's (EU) proposed legislation, now known as the Corporate Sustainability Due Diligence Directive (CSDDD):

We, the undersigned companies, business associations, and investors, are strongly in support of mandatory human rights and environmental due diligence (mHREDD) legislation. We believe mHREDD is key to ensure that efforts by companies that respect people and the planet, both during and post COVID-19, are not undercut by the lack of a uniform standard of conduct applying to all business actors based in the EU or active on the EU market. We see the upcoming EU framework on mHREDD as a vital and long overdue step in the right direction that sends a strong signal that corporate responsibility for human rights and the environment is a duty and not a voluntary matter.[4]

We remain convinced that the mHREDD legislation can bring about a paradigm shift if it succeeds in driving better outcomes for people and planet across globalised value chains. For the initiative to achieve this, it is critical that requirements fully align with the international standards of the UN Guiding Principles on Business and Human Rights (UNGPs) and the OECD Guidelines for Multinational Enterprises.[5]

---

[3] WVMetal (2021) Lieferkettengesetz—Stellungnahme WVMetalle in BMAS—Due Diligence Act; Statements made to consultation by German Federal Ministry of Labour and Social Affairs, https://www.bmas.de/SharedDocs/Downloads/DE/Gesetze/Stellungnahmen/sorgfaltspflichtengesetz-wvmetalle.pdf?__blob=publicationFile&v=1..

[4] Business Statement of Engagement, https://media.business-humanrights.org/media/documents/Business_Statement_Engagement_MHREDD_finalv3_1011.pdf.More generally, Business and Human Rights Resource Centre (BHRRC), List of large businesses, associations & investors with public statements & endorsements in support of mandatory due diligence regulation, https://www.business-humanrights.org/en/latest-news/list-of-large-businesses-associations-investors-with-public-statements-endorsements-in-support-of-mandatory-due-diligence-regulation.

[5] EU Business Statement, February 2022 tps://www.business-humanrights.org/en/latest-news/making-eu-legislation-on-mandatory-human-rights-and-environmental-due-diligence-effective.

Further, a comprehensive survey of businesses and other stakeholders, which was undertaken for a report to the European Commission about whether to introduce legislation on supply chain HRDD, found:

> Overall, the majority of stakeholders interviewed and surveyed considered existing laws on due diligence requirements for human rights and environmental impacts not to be effective, efficient and coherent. Moreover, the majority of general survey respondents indicated that the current legal landscape does not provide companies with legal certainty about their human rights and environmental due diligence obligations.[6]

Therefore, it is evident that an assumption that all businesses will oppose regulation in this area is no longer sustainable. Indeed, John Ruggie had predicted this when he wrote:

> Governments should not assume they are helping business by failing to provide adequate guidance for, or regulation of, the human rights impact of corporate activities. On the contrary, the less governments do, the more they increase reputational and other risks to business.[7]

This warning has proved pertinent, as will be shown.

This chapter will consider the change over time of states' responses to regulation in this field, especially since the adoption of the UNGPs. It will do so by reviewing some of the main pieces of national legislation in the area of business and human rights. It will also cover the proposed EU legislation (as of the time of writing) since, should it be enacted, it will directly influence the national legislation of the 27 EU Member States. These pieces of legislation will be briefly summarized, as more detailed explanations are found elsewhere.[8] The focus of the summaries will be on the extent to which

---

[6] Lise Smit, Claire Bright, Robert McCorquodale, Matthias Bauer, Hanna Deringer, Daniela Baeza-Breinbauer, Francisca Torres-Cortés, Frank Alleweldt, Senda Kara and Camille Salinier, and Héctor Tejero Tobed for the European Commission DG Justice and Consumers, *Study on Due Diligence Requirements through the Supply Chain*, 24 February 2020, https://op.europa.eu/en/publication-detail/-/publication/8ba0a8fd-4c83-11ea-b8b7-01aa75ed71a1/language-en [Smit, EC Study].

[7] Report of the SRSG, 'Framework of Protect, Respect and Remedy', UN Human Rights Council, UN Doc. A/HRC/8/5 (7 April 2008) www.reports-and-materials.org/Ruggie-report-7-Apr-2008.pdf [Framework Report], para. 22.

[8] For example, European Coalition on Corporate Justice (ECCJ), Comparative Table: Corporate due diligence laws and legislative proposals in Europe https://corporatejustice.org/publications/comparative-table-corporate-due-diligence-laws-and-legislative-proposals-in-europe-2/. Parts of this chapter are based on Robert McCorquodale, 'Human Rights

human rights due diligence (HRDD) and corporate liability are provided for in national legislation,[9] because these particular aspects of business and human rights law highlight all three pillars of the UNGPs: state action; corporate responsibility to respect human rights; and access to remedies by victims.

2. Examples of Legislation Prior to the UNGPs

a. South Africa Broad-Based Black Empowerment Act 2003

The South Africa Broad-Based Black Empowerment Act 2003 was a response to apartheid in South Africa.[10] Its aim was to increase the participation of black people in the management, ownership, and control of South Africa's economy by measuring the economic involvement of black people over a range of specified elements and to have sector codes of conduct.[11] This piece of legislation was passed in accordance with the South African Constitution 1996, which also required that government purchasing—public procurement—combat 'unfair discrimination'.[12] HRDD is not mentioned in the legislation and there is no direct enforcement under the Act.

However, a business with a turnover of more than ZAR10m will need to comply with these rules if applying for government services, and certain industries, such as the extractive sector, require evidence of compliance in order to obtain a licence.[13] Thus, there is a form of indirect sanction. However, there have been instances where bilateral investment treaties

---

Due Diligence Instruments: Evaluating the Current Legislative Landscape' in Axel Marx, Geert Van Calster, and Jan Wouters (eds), *Global Governance, Business and Human Rights* (Edward Elgar, 2022), 121.

[9] As of June 2023.
[10] There were other attempts to restrict corporate activity which impacted on human rights under the South African apartheid regime, such as the Sullivan Principles 1977, which provided that businesses should uphold human rights as a priority over domestic laws: Florian Wettstein, *Business and Human Rights: Ethical, Legal, and Managerial Perspectives* (CUP, 2022), 12–13.
[11] Broad-Based Black Empowerment Act 53 of 2003 (South Africa).
[12] Geo Quinot, 'Constitutionalising Public Procurement through Human Rights: Lessons from South Africa' in Olga Martin-Ortega and Claire Methven O'Brien (eds), *Public Procurement and Human Rights* (Edward Elgar, 2019), 78.
[13] Hogan Lovells LLP, 'BBBEE for Doing Business in South Africa' (December 2017) https://www.hoganlovells.com/en/publications/bbbee-for-doing-business-in-south-africa.

(BITs) entered into by South Africa have been found to be contrary to the Act, enabling other states to bring claims against South Africa under those BITs, and to avoid compliance with the Act by their businesses.[14]

b. Brazil Decree No. 540/2004 ('Dirty List')

In 2004 Brazil passed Decree No. 540, which became known as the 'Dirty List', because it is a register of employers (both people and businesses) found to be exploiting workers under abusive and coercive conditions. An employer subjecting workers to these conditions would usually be fined, and they would be placed on this Dirty List for a period of at least two years and also monitored.[15]

While the Dirty List does not have any HRDD provisions, it does include sanctions for businesses, as any business that is on the list becomes ineligible for loans from the Brazilian state, has restrictions on the sale of their products, and may even lose their property.[16] At one stage, during the course of preparations for the Rio Olympics in 2016, the Brazilian Superior Court issued an injunction to stop the Dirty List, but this was avoided by an amendment to the legislation.[17]

c. California Transparency in Supply Chains Act 2010

The California Transparency in Supply Chains Act 2010 requires certain businesses—retailers or manufacturers doing business in California with annual worldwide gross receipts exceeding $US100,000,000—to report on their specific actions to eradicate slavery and human trafficking in their supply chains. Transparency is a key stated purpose of the Act, as its aim is 'to educate consumers on how to purchase goods produced by companies that responsibly manage their supply chains, and, thereby, to improve the lives of victims of slavery and human trafficking.'[18] The only sanction

---

[14] John Ruggie, *Just Business* (Norton, 2013), 59. BITs are discussed in Chapter 2.
[15] Sarah Pierce, 'Blacklisted: An Overview of Brazil's "Dirty List"' (May 2015) https://humantraffickingsearch.org/blacklisted-an-overview-of-brazils-dirty-list.
[16] Jena Martin, 'The Use of Disclosure-Based Regulation to Advance the State's Duty to Protect' in Deva and Birchall, BHR, note 1, 176.
[17] Pierce, note 15.
[18] California Transparency in Supply Chains Act 2010, Senate Bill 657, s. 2(j).

which can be obtained against a business under this Act is by an injunction brought by the Californian Attorney-General demanding that a business comply with the Act on the basis that the business's failure to disclose potential abuses in the supply chain was a material fact likely to deceive a reasonable consumer.

The California Transparency in Supply Chains Act does not refer to HRDD directly, though some case law under it is relevant. For example, in *Barber v. Nestlé*[19] the claimant alleged that Nestlé had breached the Act for failing to disclose that some ingredients in its cat food products might have been sourced using forced labour. A Californian court dismissed the claim on the basis that the Act had set out what disclosures businesses were required to make to customers about potential forced labour in their supply chains, and, as such, businesses were only required to make disclosures to the extent provided for in that Act and no more. Accordingly, the court held that, because Nestlé had done this, the California Transparency in Supply Chains Act had created a 'safe harbour' whereby a business would be shielded from civil liability in those situations where they truthfully and accurately complied with the requirements of the Act.[20] This decision appears to create a type of defence of reasonable HRDD, which is discussed below.

3. Examples of HRDD Legislation Subsequent to the UNGPs

a. French Duty of Vigilance Act 2017

The French Duty of Vigilance Act 2017 (French Vigilance Act)[21] imposes a general mandatory due diligence requirement for human rights and environmental impacts. Businesses within the scope of the French Vigilance Law have to establish a vigilance plan setting out:

> [R]easonable vigilance measures adequate to identify risks and to prevent severe impacts on human rights and fundamental freedoms, on the health and safety of persons and on the environment, resulting

---

[19] *Barber v. Nestlé USA Inc.* No. 8:2015cv01364 (C.D. Cal. December 14, 2015).
[20] Ibid., 787.
[21] French Law No. 2017-399 of 27 March 2017 on the Duty of Care of Parent Companies and Ordering Companies (French Vigilance Act).

from the activities of the company and of those companies it controls within the meaning of II of article L. 233-16, directly or indirectly, as well as the activities of subcontractors or suppliers with whom there is an established commercial relationship, when these activities are related to this relationship.[22]

Hence, in order to discharge their legal duty, businesses need to implement a 'vigilance plan' which should include reasonable measures to identify risks and prevent serious violations of human rights and the environment. The terminology in the French Vigilance Act refers to 'reasonable vigilance measures' (*mesures de vigilance raisonnable*), rather than the UNGPs' HRDD terminology. While the vigilance obligations under the French Vigilance Act share commonalities with the UNGPs' HRDD process, it has been asserted that the two terminologies, while very similar, are not identical.[23]

The businesses covered under the French Vigilance Act are those French businesses which have 5,000 employees in France or 10,000 employees globally. The Act also includes within its coverage the activities of subsidiaries controlled by the French business 'directly or indirectly, as well as the activities of subcontractors or suppliers with whom there is an established commercial relationship, when these activities are related to this relationship',[24] as well as French-registered subsidiaries of foreign businesses. This legislation uses a threefold definition of the concept of 'control'—legal, de facto, or contractual—as linked to consolidated and group management reports.[25] This Act also expressly adds environmental harms as part of the action plan on human rights impacts needed to be undertaken by business.

The French Vigilance Act does not have a specific monitoring body, but it does provide for civil liability under domestic tort law if the business breaches its vigilance obligations.[26] A few legal actions have already commenced in French courts.[27] In relation to these civil actions, two well-informed commentators have noted:

---

[22] Commercial Code, art. L. 225-102-4.-I, as introduced by the French Vigilance Act.
[23] Stéphane Brabant, Elsa Savourey, and Charlotte Michon, 'The Vigilance Plan: Cornerstone of the Corporate Duty of Vigilance Law' *Revue internationale de la compliance et de l'éthique des affaires* (December 2017), 4.
[24] Commercial Code, note 22.
[25] Ibid., art. L. 233-16.-II.
[26] Commercial Code, note 22.
[27] For example, 'Total Sued under France's New Duty of Vigilance Law' (23 October 2019), https://www.business-humanrights.org/en/latest-news/total-sued-under-frances-new-duty-of-vigilance-law/; Sherpa, 'Sherpa and UNI Global Union Send Formal Notice to

All of the companies targeted had published a vigilance plan in 2019, but these plans were dissimilar in their length and comprehensiveness. In every case, these plans were deemed unsatisfactory by the requesting parties. Their allegations are focused on the impacts generated by the activities of the companies (Total, climate change; XPO), and/or that of their subsidiaries abroad (Teleperfomance; EDF; and Total, Uganda) and that of subcontractors with an alleged established commercial relationship (for part of the activities under scrutiny for Total, Uganda).[28]

This analysis indicates that the French Vigilance Act could have the effect of forcing businesses to ensure that their vigilance plan is accurate, that the plan reflects what is done on the ground and not just in stated policy, and that established business relationships act on the vigilance plan. In addition, the Act applies to businesses (such as subsidiaries of French businesses) which are not incorporated in France, and so it has a global effect in its focus. The existence of the Act, despite its limitations, has probably been crucial in showing that such legislation is possible.[29]

b. The Netherlands Child Labour Due Diligence Act 2019

The Netherlands Child Labour Due Diligence Act (Dutch Due Diligence Act) was passed in May 2019, though it is not yet in force,[30] and may not come into force in light of the EU CSDDD (discussed below).[31] The aim of

---

Teleperformance Calling on the World Leader in Call Centres to Strengthen Workers' Rights' (24 July 2019), www.asso-sherpa.org/sherpa-and-uni-global-union-send-formal-notice-to-teleperformance-calling-on-the-world-leader-in-call-centers-to-strengthen-workers-rights-2; ITF, 'Transport Giant Served Notice under Duty of Vigilance Law in Landmark Legal Move' (1 October 2019), www.itfglobal.org/en/news/transport-giant-served-notice-under-duty-vigilance-law-in-landmark-legal-move.

[28] Stéphane Brabant and Elsa Savourey, 'All Eyes on France', www.cambridge.org/core/blog/2020/01/24/all-eyes-on-france-french-vigilance-law-first-enforcement-cases-1-2-current-cases-and-trends/#_edn13.

[29] Antonella Angelini, 'The Carrots and Sticks of Due Diligence' *Fair Observer* (17 December 2019).

[30] Netherlands Kamerstukken I, 2016/17, 34 506, A (Dutch Due Diligence Act).

[31] There is also a proposed Bill for International Responsible Business Conduct, which may form the basis of Dutch legislation to implement the EU Directive: Gijs Smit and Bas van Niekerk, 'The Netherlands: A Dutch Initiative for a Value Chain Due Diligence', https://sustainablefutures.linklaters.com/post/102i833/the-netherlands-a-dutch-initiative-for-a-value-chain-due-diligence.

this Dutch legislation is to prevent the use of child labour in the production of goods and services being supplied to Dutch end-users, as part of a consumer protection approach by the government. According to the Act: '[t]he company that … investigates whether there is a reasonable presumption that the goods and services to be supplied have been produced using child labour, and that draws up and carries out an action plan in case there is such a reasonable presumption, conducts due diligence.'[32]

The Dutch Due Diligence Act applies to every business, whether domiciled in the Netherlands or not and whether publicly listed or not, which supplies goods or services to Dutch end-users, being 'the natural or legal persons that use or use up the goods or make use of the services'.[33] Also included are foreign businesses that have a branch, or that conduct business, in the Netherlands,[34] though the Act excludes businesses that only transport the goods into the Netherlands. There is a requirement for businesses which are domiciled within Dutch territory to report on activities which they, or those with which they are in a business relationship, have undertaken outside Dutch territory in their supply chains.

The terminology in the Dutch Due Diligence Act is expressly that of 'due diligence' (*gepaste zorgvuldigheid*), though the HRDD requirement is not defined further in the Act. It is stated that more detailed requirements with respect to both the investigation and the action plan will be set by a General Administrative Order, taking account of the existing International Labour Organization Child Labour Guidance Tool for Business.[35]

The Dutch Due Diligence Act enables any natural or legal person (such as a consumer or competitor) whose interests have been affected by the (in) actions of a business to file a complaint with the public supervisor (who has yet to be appointed).[36] There are fines which can be imposed on the business and there is provision for personal criminal liability of the 'compliance officer'.[37] However, as the focus of the Act is on the protection of Dutch consumers, it does not contain provisions relating to access to remedy for the actual victims of child labour, so any remedy in that regard would be

---

[32] Dutch Due Diligence Act, note 30, art. 5(1).
[33] Ibid., Preamble.
[34] Dutch Commercial Register Act, art. 5d.
[35] Dutch Due Diligence Act, note 30, art. 5(2). Interestingly, the term 'due diligence' (in Dutch and English) is also used for the Dutch international responsible business conduct covenants; for an overview and more information, see https://www.imvoconvenanten.nl/agreements?sc_lang=en. .
[36] Ibid., art. 1(d).
[37] Ibid., art. 9.

dependent on general Dutch tort law. It appears that Dutch tort law could be relied upon if the violation of the Act by the business could be construed as an indication of an act contrary to a duty of care to society (see the introduction to Chapter 6).[38]

c. German Corporate Due Diligence Obligations in Supply Chains Act 2021

The German Parliament passed the Corporate Due Diligence Obligations in Supply Chains Act in July 2021 (German Supply Chains Act).[39] This legislation came about because, in 2016, the German government issued its National Action Plan (NAP) to implement the UNGPs.[40] In that NAP the German government indicated that it did not wish to introduce legislation on HRDD if at least half of all businesses in Germany with more than 500 employees had adequately integrated the core elements of HRDD into their corporate processes in a verifiable manner by 2020.[41] Yet a survey commissioned by the German government in 2020 found that only 13–17 per cent of German businesses were able to document that they were adequately meeting the NAP requirements on HRDD.[42] As a consequence, the German government introduced the German Supply Chains Act to remedy this lack of voluntary action by businesses.

The German Supply Chains Act entered into force in January 2023. It applies to businesses domiciled in Germany (i.e. they have their central administration, their principal place of business, their administrative headquarters, or their statutory seat in Germany). It will initially apply to businesses with 3,000 or more employees and, from 2024, to businesses with 1,000 or more employees, in relation to their supply chains. The Act obliges these businesses to fulfil their HRDD obligations in their supply

---

[38] Liesbeth Enneking, *Foreign Direct Liability and Beyond: Exploring the Role of Tort Law in Promoting International Corporate Social Responsibility and Accountability* (Eleven International Publishing, 2012).

[39] Act on Corporate Due Diligence Obligations in Supply Chains of 16 July 2021 [German Supply Chain Act].

[40] German Federal Foreign Office, National Action Plan to Implement the UNGPs (2016), https://www.ohchr.org/sites/default/files/Documents/Issues/Business/ForumSession6/Germany.pdf [German NAP].

[41] Ibid., 28.

[42] Summary given in virtual conference of the Federal Ministry of Labour and Social Affairs: 'Global Supply Chains—Global Responsibility'—EU2020—EN, Workshop #1 (7 October 2020).

chains with regard to respecting internationally recognized human rights and certain environmental standards, which are set out in some detail,[43] and to provide an annual report on this.

There are detailed provisions on HRDD and on risk management, including oversight by senior management of the HRDD process, which must be 'appropriate and effective',[44] as well as on remedial actions where a violation has occurred.[45] Direct civil liability is expressly excluded, though there is regulatory oversight by a supervisory authority, the Federal Office for Economic Affairs and Export Control, which can assess business reports, seek to prevent violations (on its own motion or if there are complaints), and impose administrative fines of up to €500,000 or, in some cases, up to 2 per cent of the annual turnover of very large businesses. A complaint has already been made to the supervisory body since the Act came into force.[46] Businesses that have been subject to such fines may be excluded from public procurement procedures for a maximum of three years.[47]

d. Norwegian Transparency Act 2021

Also in July 2021, the Norwegian Parliament passed an Act relating to Enterprises' Transparency and Work on Fundamental Human Rights and Decent Working Conditions (Norwegian Transparency Act).[48] It came about after an independent Ethics Information Committee recommended legislation and there was public consultation on the issue.[49] It came into force on 1 July 2022, with first reports from businesses due on 30 June 2023.

The Norwegian Transparency Act applies to businesses incorporated in Norway and those offering goods and services in Norway (as long as the

---

[43] German Supply Chain Act, note 39, s. 2(1) and Annex.
[44] Ibid., s. 4(1).
[45] Ibid., s. 7.
[46] First complaint filed under German Supply Chain Due Diligence Act, https://duedilige nce.design/first-case-filed-under-the-german-supply-chain-due-diligence-act-against-tom-tailor-amazon-and-ikea-by-bangladeshi-workers.
[47] Markus Krajewski, Kristel Tonstad, and Franziska Wohltmann, 'Mandatory Human Rights Due Diligence in Germany and Norway: Stepping, or Striding, in the Same Direction?' (2021) 6 *Business and Human Rights Journal* 550.
[48] Act relating to Enterprises' Transparency and Work on Fundamental Human Rights and Decent Working Conditions, LOV-2021-06-18-99 (Norwegian Transparency Act).
[49] Mark Taylor, 'Mandatory Human Rights Due Diligence in Norway—A Right to Know' (12 April 2021) https://www.jus.uio.no/english/research/areas/sustainabilitylaw/blog/companies-markets-and-sustainability/2021/mandatory-human-rights--taylor.html.

latter are subject to Norwegian tax), which exceed the threshold of two of the following three conditions: sales revenue of NOK70 million, a balance sheet total of NOK35 million, and/or 50 full-time employees in the financial year.[50] It applies to subsidiaries of Norwegian parent companies, no matter where they are incorporated, and business partners in their supply chains.[51] It includes provisions on HRDD—with a direct reference being made to the UNGPs and the OECD Guidelines[52]—as well as remediation and compensation when required.

A major focus of the Norwegian Transparency Act (and hence its name) is on provision of information by businesses. A public statement must be provided by businesses on an easily accessible website and updated annually, setting out information regarding actual adverse impacts and significant risks of such impacts, as well as information regarding measures the business has implemented or plans to cease actual adverse impacts, and the results or expected results of these measures.[53] There is also a right to information on request from any person. There is, though, no civil liability provision, with the monitoring and guidance to be undertaken by a supervisory authority, being the Consumer Authority, which can impose administrative fines for breaches of the duties.[54]

e. EU Draft Corporate Sustainability Due Diligence Directive 2022

In February 2022, the European Commission (EC), being the executive body of the EU, issued a draft Directive on Corporate Sustainability Due Diligence (draft EC CSDDD).[55] The process for this legislation arose after civil society pressures across the EU, and as a direct result of an extensive

---

[50] Norwegian Transparency Act, s. 3(a).
[51] Krajewski, Tonstad, and Wohltmann, note 47, at 556, argue that the Norwegian Act may be interpreted as covering both upstream and downstream suppliers.
[52] Norwegian Transparency Act, s. 4(1).
[53] Krajewski, Tonstad, and Wohltmann, note 47.
[54] Taylor, note 49.
[55] European Commission, Proposal for a Directive of the European Parliament and of the Council on Corporate Sustainability Due Diligence and amending Directive (EU), 23 February 2022, https://eur-lex.europa.eu/legal-content/EN/TXT/?uri=CELEX:52022PC0071. Claire Bright and Lise Smit, 'The New European Directive on Corporate Sustainability Due Diligence' (British Institute of International and Comparative Law, 23 February 2022), https://www.biicl.org/blog/32/the-new-european-directive-on-corporate-sustainability-due-diligence.

study for the EC, which study included businesses responses to any such legislation, possible economic impacts, and a comparative analysis of the use of HRDD laws in 12 of the Member States. The study's results showed that:[56]

> [T]he breadth of the areas of national law which have aspects of due diligence for human rights and environmental matters is extensive. It primarily includes many areas of corporate law ... health and safety law, product liability law, employment law and environmental law ... constitutional and public law, consumer law, equality law, and bribery law, as well as in the consideration of public procurement law ... Hence, a use of the term 'due diligence' in relation to human rights and the environment in any EU legislation would not appear to be a problem for harmonisation within the Member States surveyed.[57]

As a consequence, the EC Justice Commissioner announced in April 2020 that the EC would introduce draft legislation requiring mandatory human rights (including environmental) due diligence on businesses across all EU Member States.[58] The draft CSDDD was finally published in February 2022, after there had been a Resolution of the European Parliament addressed to the EC, providing specific recommendations and the introduction of the Parliament's own draft directive on corporate due diligence and corporate accountability.[59] There were, as of October 2023, three possible drafts of the CSDDD: that of the European Commission, that of the European Council (being the body of the EU Member States),[60] and that of the European Parliament[61] The EU draft is the most restrictive in scope of the three drafts with there being considerable differences between all three drafts in relation to, for example, which businesses are in scope, which human rights and

---

[56] Smit, EC Study, note 6.
[57] Ibid., 198–9, 209–10.
[58] EU Parliament Working Group on Responsible Business Conduct, 'Speech by Commissioner Reynders in RBC Webinar on Due Diligence' (30 April 2020), https://responsiblebusinessconduct.eu/wp/2020/04/30/speech-by-commissioner-reynders-in-rbc-webinar-on-due-diligence.
[59] European Parliament, Corporate due diligence and corporate accountability, 10 March 2021, https://www.europarl.europa.eu/doceo/document/TA-9-2021-0073_EN.html.
[60] Council of the European Union, Proposal for a Directive on Corporate Sustainability Due Diligence and amending Directive, 30 November, 2022, https//data.consilium.europa.eu/doc/document/ST-15024-2022-REV-1/en/pdf.
[61] For a timeline and summary, see Business and Human Rights Resource Centre, 'Towards an EU Mandatory Due Diligence and Corporate Accountability Law', https://www.business-humanrights.org/en/latest-news/eu-commissioner-for-justice-commits-to-legislation-on-mandatory-due-diligence-for-companies.

environmental issues are to be addressed, and the extent of liability.[62] The process is that there is now a 'trialogue' between these bodies to finalize the provisions of the EU CSDDD, with the hope that there may be an agreed draft by the end of 2023 or early 2024.

This section focuses on the original draft produced by the European Commission (draft EC CSDDD), as it is the basis for the other drafts and provides a sense of the broad matters being considered by all three parts of the EU for the final draft. The draft EC CSDD sets out five objectives: improving corporate governance practices; avoiding fragmentation of due diligence requirements in the EU and creating legal certainty for businesses and stakeholders; increasing corporate accountability for adverse impacts and ensuring coherence for businesses regarding obligations in the EU; improving access to remedy for those affected by adverse human rights and environmental impacts by businesses; and complementing other measures in force or proposed within the EU through an overarching horizontal framework.[63] The draft EC CDDDD covers all EU domiciled businesses which have more than 500 employees on average and a worldwide net turnover exceeding €150 million in the previous financial year. Within two years it will be extended to include EU domiciled businesses that have more than 250 employees on average and a net turnover of over €40 million in three sectors of 'high impact' on human rights: manufacture and trade of textiles and garments; agriculture, forestry, and fisheries; and extraction, manufacture, and trade in minerals. In addition, it covers all non-EU domiciled businesses which operate in the EU with a net turnover of more than €150 million and, after two years, will also include non-EU domiciled businesses operating in the three high impact sectors with a net turnover of more than €40 million, of which 50 per cent were in those sectors. This includes subsidiaries of EU domiciled parent companies and businesses with which the businesses covered have established business relationships.[64]

The EC CSDD draft includes a wide range of human rights and environmental matters within the HRDD actions and reporting requirements, as well as a climate change plan.[65] It includes civil liability for human rights

---

[62] Nicola Bonucci, Jonathan Drimmer, Tara Giunta, Renata Parras and Daye Cho, 'Corporate Sustainability Due Diligence in the EU: Latest Updates and What to Expect Next', https://www.paulhastings.com/en-GB/insights/client-alerts/corporate-sustainability-due-diligence-in-the-eu-latest-updates; Sophie Flores, 'What is the EU CSDDD?', https://www2.deloitte.com/uk/en/blog/emea-centre-for-regulatory-strategy/2023/what-is-the-european-corporate-sustainability-due-diligence-directive.html
[63] Draft EC CSDDD, note 55, 3.
[64] Bright and Smit, note 61.
[65] EC CSDD draft, note 63, art. 15.

and environmental harms by businesses and by a business relationship, including harms outside the EU. There are defences available to businesses where they had sought contractual assurance in their business relationship, where there was verified compliance and where it would reasonably be expected that the HRDD measures taken were adequate,[66] and it does not include a clear statement on consultation with stakeholders.[67] The main form of enforcement is through national supervisory bodies, which can investigate on their own initiative and order cessation, fines, and interim measures.[68] It is also proposed that there be specific duties on directors of businesses to take account of all stakeholders' views and oversee strategies on human rights, environment, and climate change, which may have ramifications for directors' duties more generally.[69]

4. Examples of Specific Legislation Relating to Business and Human Rights

The pieces of legislation discussed above are all from the Global North because, to date, states in other regions have not taken legislative action directly in implementation of the UNGPs. However, a number of Global South states have either produced policies in this area, through their National Action Plans on Business and Human Rights[70]—which could be considered as public policy statements towards potential action[71]—or drafted legislation without direct reference to the UNGPs, such as Sierra Leone's legislation referred to below.

---

[66] Ibid., s. 7. The contractual defence is strong criticized: Jeffrey Vogt, Ruwan Subasinghe, and Paapa Danqua, 'A Missed Opportunity to Improve Workers' Rights in Global Supply Chains' *Opinio Juris* (18 March 2022).

[67] Christopher Patz, 'The EU's Draft Corporate Sustainability Due Diligence Directive: A First Assessment' (2022) 7 *Business and Human Rights Journal* 291.

[68] Martijn Scheltema and Robert McCorquodale, 'Supervisory Mechanisms and Directors Duties: Innovations in the Proposed EU Directive on Corporate Sustainability Due Diligence' *Business and Human Rights Resource Centre Blog* (24 May 2022), https://www.business-humanrights.org/en/latest-news/supervisory-mechanisms-and-directors-duties-innovations-in-the-proposed-eu-directive-on-corporate-sustainability-due-diligence.

[69] Robert McCorquodale and Stuart Neely, 'Director's Duties and Human Rights: A Comparative Approach' [2022] *Journal of Corporate Legal Studies* 605.

[70] OHCHR, National Action Plans on Business and Human Rights, https://www.ohchr.org/en/special-procedures/wg-business/national-action-plans-business-and-human-rights.

[71] Humberto Cantú Rivera, 'National Action Plans on Business and Human Rights: Progress or Mirage?' (2019) 4 *Business and Human Rights Journal* 213.

There have been pieces of national legislation which are within the business and human rights area, though they do not refer specifically to HRDD. These include the UK Modern Slavery Act 2015, the Australian Modern Slavery Act 2018 and the Canadian Modern Slavery Act 2023.[72] Other legislation includes some HRDD requirements in specific provisions within larger pieces of legislation, such as the US Dodd-Frank Act.[73] There are some pieces of legislation which provide for free, prior, and informed consent of Indigenous people, which is consistent with the consultation aspect of HRDD, such as Sierra Leone's Customary Land Rights Act 2022 and Land Commission Act 2022,[74] or which impose restrictions on the importing of some goods which raise human rights concerns, such as the US Uyghur Forced Labour Prevention Act 2022.[75]

Each of these pieces of legislation has elements which are consistent with the approach of the UNGPs and OECD Guidelines for dealing with adverse human rights impacts of business activities. However, they are limited in their effects, either due to the narrow range of human rights covered (such as modern slavery or forced labour) or the strict geographical location focus (such as in the Democratic Republic of Congo for the Dodd-Frank Act). There are also examples of only using reporting as the primary means of prevention, such as in the UK Modern Slavery Act the Australian Modern Slavery Act and the Canadian Modern Slavery Act.

---

[72] There is also the Australian Illegal Logging Prohibition Act 2012, which prohibits the importation of items made from illegally logged timber and imposes due diligence requirements for certain classes of regulated timber products: Justine Nolan, 'Human Rights and Global Corporate Supply Chains' in Surya Deva and David Bilchitz (eds), *Building a Treaty on Business and Human Rights* (CUP, 2017), 238.

[73] Dodd-Frank Wall Street Reform and Consumer Protection Act 2010, section 1502 requires disclosure by businesses that there has been supply chain due diligence on conflict minerals from some states, such as the DRC. There was also proposed legislation in Switzerland—the Responsible Business Initiative—which went to a popular vote on 29 November 2020 but just failed to pass, and so will not be considered here. Swiss Coalition for Corporate Justice (SCCJ), 'The Initiative Text with Explanations', https://corporatejustice.ch/wp-content/uploads//2018/06/KVI_Factsheet_5_E.pdf. As to the close vote, see www.swissinfo.ch/eng/business/swiss-to-vote-on-holding-companies-accountable-for-supply-chain-abuses/46184500. Nicolas Bueno and Claire Bright, 'Implementing Human Rights Due Diligence through Corporate Civil Liability' (2020) 69 *International and Comparative Law Quarterly* 789.

[74] Umaru Fofana, 'Sierra Leone Passes New Laws to Boost Landowners' Rights' *Reuters* (8 August 2022).

[75] Pillar II, 'The US Uyghur Forced Labour Prevention Act: 5 Things Businesses Need to Know', https://www.pillar-two.com/featured-insights/2022/6/24/the-us-uyghur-forced-labour-prevention-act-5-things-businesses-need-to-know.More generally, see US Department of State, Bureau of Democracy, Human Rights and Labor, *US Government Approach on Business and Human Rights* (2013).

Reporting by itself has been shown to be deeply flawed, not least as disclosure alone is not sufficient evidence of actual practices of the business and, without effective enforcement, there are limited incentives on businesses to comply fully.[76] This is because '[t]ransparency about human rights in global supply chains relies on creating a culture of continuous improvement within the organisation and across [the] value chain', and this is not created by reporting alone.[77]

This means that, without liability and enforcement provisions in these pieces of legislation, there is a heavy burden on civil society—with its limited resources—to act on the small amount of information provided by businesses reporting on their human rights impacts. The ability of civil society and rightsholders to act as a form of regulator may also be restrained by courts, as discussed in Chapter 6.

5. Conclusions

The legislation examined in this chapter indicates the rapid developments which are taking place in some states as they seek to comply with their legal obligations in this area, as expressed in the UNGPs. It has been shown here how there is an increasing amount of state and regional legislation (in addition to the international regulation considered in Chapter 3) which requires or encourages businesses to act in relation to their activities which can cause, contribute to, or be directly linked to adverse human rights impacts.

The summaries of the key pieces of legislation in this area indicate that they vary widely in their scope and enforcement. For example, some are intended to apply to all human rights (e.g. the French Duty of Vigilance Act), while others are limited to certain human rights (e.g. modern slavery), and most do now expressly include environmental impacts (see also Chapter 8). Some extend to all businesses operating in a state (e.g. the Dutch Due Diligence Act), while some extend only to those businesses domiciled in the state, and with a threshold in terms of number of employees (e.g. the German Supply Chains Act) or turnover (e.g. the UK and Australian

---

[76] Genevieve LeBaron, *Combatting Modern Slavery: Why Labour Governance is Failing and What We Can Do About It* (Polity Press, 2020).
[77] Jolyon Ford and Justine Nolan, 'Regulating Transparency on Human Rights and Modern Slavery in Corporate Supply Chains: The Discrepancy Between Human Rights Due Diligence and the Social Audit' (2020) 26 *Australian Journal of Human Rights* 27, 33.

Modern Slavery Acts). Some have a focus on consumer protection (e.g. the Dutch Due Diligence Act) or freedom of information (e.g. the Norwegian Transparency Act), some include civil liability provisions (e.g. the French Duty of Vigilance Act), and others extend to administrative and criminal liability (e.g. the Dutch Due Diligence Act); some, however, seem to have no effective liability linked to specific HRDD requirements (e.g. the UK and Australian Modern Slavery Acts). It is also evident that most of these legislative developments are occurring primarily in the Global North.

These pieces of legislation are all subject to criticisms for what they lack, and how far short they fall of the standards set in the UNGPs and OECD Guidelines.[78] There are differing views as to whether legislation which provides defences for business, whereby a business can show that they have conducted reasonable and appropriate HRDD, should act as incentives for businesses to comply or not, as noted in the discussion of the California Transparency in Supply Chains Act and the draft EU CSDDD.[79] In addition, there is a risk that legislation which simply requires a 'tick box' approach by businesses, such as the EU Non-Financial Reporting Directive 2014[80]—which only requires publicly listed businesses to report on, amongst other things, human rights and environmental issues, with no enforcement requirements—will have limited impact on business decision-making.[81]

Therefore, it is important to balance voluntary activity by business in relation to human rights matters with complementary state enforcement mechanisms, in order to enable effective HRDD implementation.[82] Further, where the legislation has introduced civil, administrative, and/or criminal liability, these still remain to be tested as to their effectiveness, as they are all relatively recent.

---

[78] Jernej Letnar Černič, 'The Human Rights Due Diligence Standard-Setting in the European Union: Bridging the Gap Between Ambition and Reality' (2022) 10 *Global Business Law Review* 1.

[79] Gabriela Quijano and Carlos Lopez, 'Rise of Mandatory Human Rights Due Diligence: A Beacon of Hope or a Double-Edged Sword?' (2021) 6 *Business and Human Rights Journal* 241.

[80] Directive 2014/95/EU of the European Parliament and of the Council of 22 October 2014, amending Directive 2013/34/EU as regards disclosure of non-financial and diversity information by certain large undertakings and groups [2014] OJ L330/1.

[81] Frank Bold, *Comparing the Implementation of the Non-Financial Reporting Directive* (2017), http://www.purposeofcorporation.org/comparing-the-eu-non-financial-reporting-directive.pdf.

[82] Robert McCorquodale and Justine Nolan, 'The Effectiveness of Human Rights Due Diligence for Preventing Business Human Rights Abuses' [2021] *Netherlands International Law Review* 455.

Finally, there is a risk that the liability and enforcement imposed by these pieces of legislation are so limited that they do not operate to prevent business activities which adversely impact on human rights or even change the behaviour of business. Indeed, as Gabriella Quijano and Carlos Lopez conclude after an insightful review of legislative proposals on HRDD in the 10 years since the UNGPs:

> [A]ll those more or less directly involved in processes to bring about new laws must watch out for and ensure the following two critical risks are avoided. Firstly, the risk of creating the appearance of progress with hollow HRDD laws that, while doing little to change the status quo in practice, will effectively bring legislative efforts to an end, at least for the foreseeable future. Secondly, the risk of inadvertently providing companies with a tool that they hitherto did not have to show respect for human rights and rebut charges of liability with little bearing on effective respect for human rights on the ground.[83]

These warnings highlight the need to have effective and appropriate legislation in this field and of being wary of simply having any form of legislation, especially if it is of limited scope. This becomes necessary as developments outside national legislation continue to occur, as is discussed in the next chapter.

---

[83] Quijano and Lopez, note 79, 254.

8
Future Developments in Business and Human Rights Law

1. Context

In May 2021, the Dutch District Court in The Hague gave its judgment on a complaint brought by several civil society organizations, a local authority, and a number of Dutch citizens.[1] The claimants alleged that Royal Dutch Shell (Shell), a major oil producer which is incorporated in the Netherlands, was in breach of its duty of care under the Dutch Civil Code by failing adequately to reduce its greenhouse gas emissions.

In order to decide if there was such a duty of care, the court held:

> In its interpretation of the unwritten standard of care, the court follows the UN Guiding Principles (UNGP). The UNGP constitute an authoritative and internationally endorsed 'soft law' instrument, which set out the responsibilities of states and businesses in relation to human rights. The UNGP reflect current insights. They do not create any new right nor establish legally binding obligations. The UNGP are in line with the content of other, widely accepted soft law instruments, such as the UN Global Compact (UNGC) 'principles' and the OECD Guidelines for Multinational Enterprises (the OECD guidelines). Since 2011, the European Commission has expected European businesses to meet their responsibilities to respect human rights, as formulated in the UNGP. For this reason, the UNGP are suitable as a guideline in the interpretation of the unwritten standard of care. Due to the universally endorsed content

---

[1] *Milieudefensie v. Royal Dutch Shell plc* [2021] C/09/571932, ECLI:NL:RBDHA:2021:5339, Rechtbank Den Haag, C/09/571932/HA ZA 19-379 [*Milieudefensie v. Shell*].

of the UNGP, it is irrelevant whether or not RDS [Royal Dutch Shell] has committed itself to the UNGP.[2]

This was a significant conclusion in relation to the direct influence on national law of the UN Guiding Principles on Business and Human Right (UNGPs). In effect, the court, through its interpretation of the UNGPs as an 'internationally endorsed' instrument, enabled the UNGPs to be enforceable under Dutch law.

The court then considered climate change obligations and did so by reference to the Paris Agreement on Climate Change 2015.[3] It held:

> [T]he goals of the Paris Agreement represent the best available scientific findings in climate science, which is supported by widespread international consensus. The non-binding goals of the Paris Agreement represent a universally endorsed and accepted standard that protects the common interest of preventing dangerous climate change...
> It is also important here that each reduction of greenhouse gas emissions has a positive effect on countering dangerous climate change. After all, each reduction means that there is more room in the carbon budget. The court acknowledges that [Shell] cannot solve this global problem on its own. However, this does not absolve [Shell] of its individual partial responsibility to do its part regarding the emissions of the Shell group, which it can control and influence.[4]

On this basis, the court held that Shell is obliged to reduce the carbon monoxide emissions of its entire corporate group's activities by net 45 per cent by the end of 2030 relative to 2019. This is a significant move towards implying direct international legal obligations on a business in relation to climate change.[5] As will be shown below, this development was outside the original parameters of the UNGPs.

This chapter will consider two areas which will affect developments in the field of business and human rights, being the extension to climate

---

[2] Ibid., para. 4.4.11.
[3] Paris Agreement on Climate Change 2015, UN Framework Convention on Climate Change.
[4] *Milieudefensie v. Shell*, note 1, paras 4.4.27, 4.4.49. Shell has appealed this decision.
[5] Chiara Macchi and Josephine van Zeben, 'Business and Human Rights Implications of Climate Change Litigation: Milieudefensie et al. v Royal Dutch Shell' [2021] *Review of European, Comparative & International Environmental Law* 409.

change and the increase in use of technology, as well as exploring the possibility of a treaty in this area. It will begin by reviewing the key developments since the adoption of the UNGPs in 2011.

2. Reviewing Progress

During 2021, the Working Group on Business and Human Rights (WGBHR) undertook a stocktake of the developments in business and human rights over the ten years since the UNGPs were adopted in 2011.[6] This was followed up by a report to the UN Human Rights Council setting out these developments and proposing the ways forward, known as the Roadmap.[7] The Roadmap was expressly 'inspired by the vision of UNGPs' former SRSG, John Ruggie, that efforts to promote implementation should never lose sight of the need for making a difference where it matters most: in the daily lives of people affected by business on the ground'.[8]

The stocktake revealed many positive actions taken in terms of the UNGPs, such that the UNGPs are now 'providing a globally agreed-upon authoritative standard for what States and businesses need to do respectively to protect and respect the full range of human rights across all business contexts—something which did not exist before 2011'.[9] Further:

> The fast-growing collection of interpretive and practical guidance to support implementation—including by the Working Group—has demonstrated that the regime established by the Guiding Principles is applicable to companies of all sizes and sectors, to all business relationships, in all countries, and for all human rights.[10]

However, the stocktake also showed ongoing issues of concern as 'many— if not most—of the barriers in accessing both judicial and non-judicial

---

[6] WGBHR, 'Guiding Principles on Business and Human Rights at 10: Taking Stock of the First Decade', Report to the UN Human Rights Council (HRC) (22 April 2021), https://documents-dds-ny.un.org/doc/UNDOC/GEN/G21/093/82/PDF/G2109382.pdf?OpenElement [Stocktake].

[7] WGBHR, 'Tenth Anniversary of the Guiding Principles on Business and Human Rights: A Roadmap for the Next Decade of Business and Human Rights—Raising the Ambition, Increasing The Pace', Report to the HRC (8 June 2022), https://documents-dds-ny.un.org/doc/UNDOC/GEN/G22/373/36/PDF/G2237336.pdf?OpenElement [Roadmap].

[8] Ibid., para. 11.

[9] WGBHR, Stocktake, note 6, para. 11.

[10] Ibid., paras 12–14.

mechanisms identified in the Guiding Principles still largely remain... [and] the persistence of business-related abuses is a major concern and a source of deep frustration'.[11] In relation to the latter, the stocktake noted:

> [B]esides a need to expand geographically, a key priority remains driving respect for human rights more broadly across value chains, including among small and medium-sized enterprises that are challenged by limited resources and few practical tailored tools. Similarly, there is an urgent need to also tackle the informal economy, which accounts for more than 6 out of 10 workers and four out of five enterprises in the world.
>
> [B]enchmarking initiatives and stakeholder assessments also highlight, in particular, the apparent disconnect between improvements at the policy level and human rights due diligence in practice—both generally and in relation to specific human rights concerns.
>
> This disconnect also underlines the fact that, just as for States, lack of policy coherence in business practice remains a key challenge to realizing effective implementation of the Guiding Principles.[12]

On this basis, the Roadmap suggested ways forward in the context of, for example, ongoing global economic issues, the Covid-19 pandemic, and the desire for sustainable development. These ways forward were divided into eight key action areas:

- Ensure that the UNGPs are a compass for meeting global challenges;
- Improve state action on policy coherence and mandatory legislation;
- Increase business implementation in practice, including embedding human rights due diligence in corporate governance and business models;
- Improve access to remedies, including reducing barriers to access for victims;
- Increase meaningful stakeholder engagement;
- Improve the use of effective leverage, including in the financial sector and with regulators;
- Ensure better tracking of progress of actions and implementations; and

---

[11] Ibid., paras 93 and 114.
[12] Ibid., paras 63–65.

- Secure more effective international cooperation and implementation support, including within the UN, and enhance capacity-building and coordination globally.[13]

The Roadmap sets out a range of illustrative actions for supporting progress as to how each of these key action areas could be achieved. These are intended to be 'strategic guidance for supporting more ambitious efforts to increase the pace of UNGPs implementation'.[14]

A recurring issue in both the stocktake and the Roadmap is the recognition of increasing global issues affecting this area. In particular, the Roadmap states that an important outcome for the next decade is that 'the UNGPs are embedded across key global agendas for our common future, particularly those for realizing a just transition and tackling climate change'.[15] Therefore, the issue of climate change will be considered next.

3. Climate Change

As seen in the case set out at the introduction to this chapter, one of the new developments in business and human rights is that of linking it to climate change. There is considerable evidence showing that climate change has a broad adverse impact on human rights. For example, the former High Commissioner for Human Rights, Michelle Bachelet, stated that 'the global climate emergency presents perhaps the most profound planet-wide threat to human rights that we have seen since World War II. From the right to life, to health, to food, water and shelter, to our rights to be free of discrimination, to development and to self-determination, its impacts are already making themselves felt.'[16]

This connection between the impacts of climate change and adverse human rights consequences was confirmed by a joint statement from nine UN human rights Special Procedures mandate-holders in September 2019:[17]

---

[13] Roadmap, note 7, para. 13 (the text here is a summary).
[14] Ibid., para. 15.
[15] Ibid., para. 19. WGBHR, 'Extractive Sector, Just Transition and Human Rights (2023).
[16] UN High Commissioner for Human Rights, Michelle Bachelet, Statement on Human Rights Day, 10 December 2019, https://www.ohchr.org/EN/NewsEvents/Pages/DisplayNews.aspx?NewsID=25403.
[17] The nine mandate holders were: Special Rapporteur on human rights and the environment; Special Rapporteur on the right to food; Special Rapporteur on the human rights to safe drinking water and sanitation; Special Rapporteur on the rights of indigenous peoples;

Climate change is already causing increased frequency, intensity and duration of extreme weather events, melting of glaciers and ice sheets, rising sea levels, storm surges, saltwater intrusion, ocean acidification, changes in precipitation, flooding, heatwaves, droughts, wildfires, increased air pollution, desertification, water shortages, the destruction of ecosystems, biodiversity loss and the spread of water-borne and vector-borne disease.

Among the human rights being threatened and violated by climate change are the rights to life, health, food, water and sanitation, a healthy environment, an adequate standard of living, housing, property, self-determination, development and culture.

While fossil fuels have made an enormous contribution to economic prosperity, the environmental and social costs of their use are staggering. Millions of people die prematurely each year because of air pollution, while billions of people are adversely affected by the Earth's changing climate...

A safe climate is a vital element of the right to a healthy environment and is absolutely essential to human life and well-being. In today's global climate emergency, meeting the obligations to respect, protect and fulfil human rights could help to spur the transformative changes that are so urgently required.[18]

Further, climate change has been specifically identified by the Office of the High Commissioner for Human Rights (OHCHR) as a 'cross-cutting thematic issue' since the 'human rights impact of climate change is a critical emerging issue that cuts across several Special Procedures mandates because of climate change's negative impact on, among others, the rights to life, water and sanitation, health, food, an adequate standard of living, housing, property, a healthy environment, culture, self-determination, and development'.[19]

---

the UN Working Group on human rights and transnational corporations and other business enterprises; Special Rapporteur on the right to development; Special Rapporteur on the right to physical and mental health; Special Rapporteur on extreme poverty and human rights; and Special Rapporteur on extrajudicial, summary or arbitrary executions.

[18] United Nations Climate Action Summit, New York, 23 September 2019, https://www.ohchr.org/EN/NewsEvents/Pages/DisplayNews.aspx?NewsID=25003. The right to a clean, healthy, and sustainable environment has been recognized as a human right by the UN Human Rights Council, Res. 48/13 (8 October 2021).

[19] OHCHR, Cross-cutting Thematic Issues, https://ohchr.org/EN/HRBodies/SP/Pages/CrosscuttingThematicIssues.aspx.

While it is evident that the key global human rights bodies now accept climate change as a human rights issue, the UNGPs did not specifically refer to climate change (or the environment). The OECD Guidelines, which do refer to environmental impacts, was updated in 2023 to include, amongst other changes, climate change responsibilities on business:

> [Business] enterprises have an important role in contributing towards net-zero greenhouse gas emissions and a climate-resilient economy, necessary for achieving internationally agreed goals on climate change mitigation and adaptation.... This includes the introduction and implementation of science-based policies, strategies and transition plans on climate change mitigation and adaptation as well as adopting, implementing, monitoring and reporting on short, medium and long-term mitigation targets..[20]

This extension in the OECD Guidelines includes noting that '[business] enterprises play a key role in advancing sustainable economies and can contribute to delivering an effective and progressive response to global, regional and local environmental challenges, including the urgent threat of climate change.'[21] The inclusion of accountability of businesses for environmental damage connected to climate change is also found in some national legislation.[22]

The lack of direct reference to climate change in the main international regulation on business and human rights has been argued to be surmountable if the approach to the interpretation of international instruments is one of dynamic interpretation, and one which takes account of subsequent developments.[23] Indeed, some of the key drafters of the UNGPs have stated

---

[20] OECD Guidelines, Section VI Environment, Commentary paras 76–77.. This includes direct reference to the Paris Agreement.
[21] Ibid., Preamble to Chapter VI.
[22] Robert McCorquodale, 'Overview and Comparative Analysis of Country Reports' in Lise Smit, Claire Bright, Robert McCorquodale, Matthias Bauer, Hanna Deringer, Daniela Baeza-Breinbauer, Francisca Torres-Cortés, Frank Alleweldt, Senda Kara, and Camille Salinier and Héctor Tejero Tobed for the European Commission DG Justice and Consumers, *Study on Due Diligence Requirements through the Supply Chain* (24 February 2020), https://op.europa.eu/en/publication-detail/-/publication/8ba0a8fd-4c83-11ea-b8b7-01aa75ed71a1/language-en [Smit, EC Study], 199.
[23] For example, International Law Commission (ILC), *Fragmentation of International Law: Difficulties Arising from the Diversification and Expansion of International Law* (ILC, 2006), http://legal.un.org/ilc/documentation/english/a_cn4_l682.pdf and Scott Sheeran, 'The Relationship of International Human Rights Law and General International Law: Hermeneutic Constraint or Pushing The Boundaries?' in Scott Sheeran and Nigel Rodley (eds), *Routledge Handbook of International Human Rights Law* (Routledge, 2013), 95.

that the UNGPs should be understood in a 'dynamic dimension, such as [the UNGPs'] capacity to push the development of new norms and practices that go beyond the initial content of the [UN]GPs and improve companies' compliance with human rights standards'.[24] This is also consistent with the Commentary to GP 12 that 'business enterprises may need to consider additional standards [of human rights]' beyond those specifically set out in the UNGPs. This dynamic approach to interpreting the UNGPs can also take into account systemic matters, as the International Court of Justice (ICJ) has stated that 'an international instrument has to be interpreted and applied within the framework of the entire legal system prevailing at the time of the interpretation'.[25]

In relation to climate change, a justification for a dynamic interpretation can be seen in developments in two of the three main international human rights treaties to which the UNGPs specifically refer in GP12, being the International Covenant on Economic, Social and Cultural Rights (ICESCR) and the International Covenant on Civil and Political Rights (ICCPR). The Committee on Economic, Social and Cultural Rights (CESCR) has considered that:

> [A] failure to prevent foreseeable human rights harm caused by climate change, or a failure to mobilize the maximum available resources in an effort to do so, could constitute a breach of [their] obligation [under the ICESCR to respect, protect and fulfil all human rights for all].[26]

Similarly, the UN Human Rights Committee (HRC), the treaty supervisory body of the ICCPR, has stated that:

> [The] obligations of States parties under international environmental law should thus inform the contents of article 6 of the [ICCPR], and the obligation of States parties to respect and ensure the right to life should

---

[24] John Ruggie, Caroline Rees, and Rachel Davis, 'Ten Years After: From UN Guiding Principles to Multi-Fiduciary Obligations' (2021) 6 *Business and Human Rights Journal* 179, 181.

[25] *Advisory Opinion on the Legal Consequences for States of the Continued Presence of South Africa in Namibia* [1971] ICJ Rep. 53.

[26] Committee on Economic, Social and Cultural Rights, 'Statement on Climate Change and the International Covenant on Economic, Social and Cultural Rights' (8 October 2018), www.ohchr.org/en/NewsEvents/Pages/DisplayNews.aspx?NewsID=23691&LangID=E

also inform their relevant obligations under international environmental law.[27]

Other human rights treaty supervisory bodies have also addressed and elaborated human rights obligations regarding climate change since 2011, including by setting out substantive measures which are required to discharge these obligations.[28] In addition, the ILO Declaration on Fundamental Principles and Rights at Work, which is also referred to in GP 12, now includes a 'safe and healthy working environment',[29] and, in 2022, the United Nations General Assembly recognized 'the right to a clean, healthy and sustainable environment' as a human right.[30] Combined, these show systemic changes in international human rights law.[31]

At the same time, there have been relevant developments in international law concerning climate change. As noted above, the Paris Agreement was adopted in 2015.[32] It was adopted by 196 states, which shows near-universal agreement by states as to how to approach climate change. The Paris Agreement, amongst other matters, sets out a global temperature goal intended to limit the worst risks and impacts of climate change, while also prioritizing resilience and adaptation to climate change, and making finance flows consistent with these objectives. It also provides:

> Holding the increase in the global average temperature to well below 2°C above pre-industrial levels and pursuing efforts *to limit the temperature increase to 1.5°C* above pre-industrial levels, recognizing that this would significantly reduce the risks and impacts of climate change.[33]

Accordingly, the OHCHR has stated that '[b]usinesses should set science-based targets throughout their operations to align with limiting global

---

[27] HRC General Comment No. 36, UN Doc. CCPR/C/GC/36, para. 62, https://documents-dds-ny.un.org/doc/UNDOC/GEN/G19/261/15/PDF/G1926115.pdf?OpenElement.

[28] For example, Committee on the Elimination of Discrimination Against Women, General Recommendation No. 37, UN Doc. CEDAW/C/GC/37 (13 March 2018), https://www.ohchr.org/en/documents/general-comments-and-recommendations/general-recommendation-no37-2018-gender-related.

[29] ILO Declaration on Fundamental Principles and Rights at Work.

[30] UN General Assembly Res. A/76/L.75.

[31] WGBHR, 'Information Note on Climate Change and the UNGPs': https://www.ohchr.org/sites/default/files/documents/issues/business/workinggroupbusiness/Information-Note-Climate-Change-and-UNGPs.pdf.

[32] The Paris Agreement on Climate Change 2015, note 3.

[33] Ibid., Art. 4.1 (emphasis added).

warming to well below 2°C above pre-industrial levels and pursuing efforts towards 1.5°C, with efforts towards net-zero greenhouse gas emissions by 2050, as indicated in the Paris Agreement'.[34]

Concerns about business impacts on climate change have led to demands for more renewable energy and a just transition to it, being where labour rights and other human rights are included in the decision-making on the transition. However, there are still concerns about the human rights impacts of some renewable energy business.[35] Karin Buhmann has noted the important role of human rights due diligence (HRDD) for all parts of the extractive sector, including renewable energy technology:

> Human rights due diligence will not solve the dilemma on how to obtain a speedy but fair transition, but it can help provide an informed basis for decisions to be taken. Through the involvement of affected stakeholders, meaningful engagement can help companies identify problems and develop alternative solutions.[36]

It could, therefore, be seen as consistent with these systemic developments and dynamic interpretation that the court in *Milieudefensie v. Shell* linked the UNGPs and Paris Agreement together to indicate that a business could have a duty of care in relation to climate change. As noted above, this duty is likely to extend to the transition to renewable energy. Undoubtedly, future developments will clarify this situation.

4. Technology

In 2019, the editors of the *Business and Human Rights Journal*, a leading journal in this field, published an Editorial which included this statement:

---

[34] OHCHR, 'Human Rights, Climate Change and Business Key Messages', https://www.ohchr.org/sites/default/files/Documents/Issues/ClimateChange/materials/KMBusiness.pdf.

[35] Rights and Accountability in Development (RAID), 'The Road to Ruin? Electric Vehicles and Workers' Rights Abuses at DR Congo's Industrial Cobalt Mines' (November 2021), https://raid-uk.org/wp-content/uploads/2023/03/report_road_to_ruin_evs_cobalt_workers_nov_2021.pdf and Dorothée Baumann-Pauly, 'Making Mining Safe and Fair: Artisanal Cobalt Extraction in the Democratic Republic of the Congo' (16 September 2020), https://bhr.stern.nyu.edu/cobalt-2023.

[36] Karin Buhmann, *Human Rights: A Key Idea for Business and Society* (Routledge, 2022), 194–5.

> We see the continuing development and deployment of AI [Artificial Intelligence] as a critical area of focus for future BHR scholarship—from autonomous weapons, to facial recognition and how AI will impact various human rights such as the right to life, the right to privacy and the right to not be subject to discrimination ... In addition to concerns about the impact of social media on democratic elections and civil discourse, social media companies such as Facebook and Google depend crucially on amassing the personal data, predilections, hobbies and patterns of friendship and associations to sell advertisement space to marketers of commercial products and political campaigns. The human rights implications of such data collection are manifest, but not yet fully understood.[37]

This Editorial indicated that there was a vast field of technology of which business and human rights scholars and practitioners needed to be aware, due to its potential to make profound impacts on human rights. Since then, there has been some further scholarship in this area,[38] and the issue will continue to grow. Of course, there are also potentially positive human rights impacts in the use of technology, such as ensuring that labour rights are continually protected in factories rather than simply relying on occasional audits, and by using technology appropriately in supply chains, such as the use of blockchains.[39]

The UNGPs do not directly raise issues of technology, yet they do cover all businesses, and so would include those businesses which are using technology, from artificial intelligence (AI) to data collection, including the use of algorithms to determine business and legal actions,[40] to social media and network platforms.[41] Yet, considering that there may be 'hundreds of

---

[37] Surya Deva, Anita Ramasastry, Florian Wettstein, and Michael Santoro, 'Editorial: Business and Human Rights Scholarship: Past Trends and Future Directions' (2019) 4 *Business and Human Rights Journal* 201, 211.

[38] For example, Simon Chesterman, *We, The Robots: Regulating Artificial Intelligence and the Limits of Law* (CUP, 2022) and Grace Mutung'u, 'The United Nations Guiding Principles on Business and Human Rights, Women and Digital ID in Kenya: A Decolonial Perspective' (2022) 7 *Business and Human Rights Journal* 117.

[39] William Crumpler, 'The Human Rights Risks and Opportunities in Blockchain' (CSIS, 14 December 2021) https://www.csis.org/analysis/human-rights-risks-and-opportunities-blockchain.

[40] Lorna McGregor, Daragh Murray, and Vivian Ng, 'International Human Rights Law as a Framework for Algorithmic Accountability' (2019) 68 *International and Comparative Law Quarterly* 309.

[41] Stephen Toope, *A Rule of Law for Our New Age of Anxiety* (CUP, 2023), 71–93.

millions (or even billions) of users spread across the world using diverse products, services, technologies, and applications in vastly different human rights environments',[42] identifying relevant human rights impacts through meaningful engagement and consultation with all relevant stakeholders—as expected by GP 18—is difficult. Further, the use of technology without undertaking HRDD can lead to legal consequences as seen, for example, in the criminal charges against Nexus Technologies/Amesys for conspiracy to commit torture due to its selling of surveillance technology to the then government of Libya, which was then used against alleged opponents of that government.[43] Thus, approaches to technology may need to be embedded in the governance structures of businesses.[44]

There are also challenges for businesses to provide remedies for adverse human rights impacts due to technology. For example, some technology is intertwined with the internet, which transcends geographical and national borders, and so a problematic algorithm may impact hundreds of millions of users, which would overburden most operational grievance mechanisms, without there being a clear rule of liability.[45] There are also differing domestic laws on technology, especially AI and data, for example where a government orders businesses to suspend or restrict public access to the internet and telecommunications.[46]

Some sectors, such as the information and communications technology (ICT) sector, have been active in creating specific guidance, with the Principles on Freedom of Expression and Privacy of the Global Network Initiative (GNI), which is a multi-stakeholder initiative in that industry.[47] For example, GNI has outlined the steps that business in the technology sector could take to respond to government requests in a human rights-sensitive way:

---

[42] BSR and Centre for Democracy and Technology, 'Legitimate and Meaningful. Stakeholder Engagement in Human Rights Due Diligence: Challenges and Solutions for ICT Companies' (September 2014), 5, https://www.bsr.org/en/reports/engaging-with-rights-holders.

[43] International Federation for Human Rights, 'Surveillance and Torture in Libya: The Paris Court of Appeal confirms the indictment of AMESYS and its executives, and cancels that of two employees' (21 November 2022), https://www.fidh.org/en/impacts/Surveillance-torture-Libya-Paris-Court-Appeal-indictment-AMESYS..

[44] Alexander Kriebitz and Christoph Lütge, 'Artificial Intelligence and Human Rights: A Business Ethical Assessment' (2020) 5 *Business and Human Rights Journal* 84.

[45] Jacob Turner, *Robot Rules: Regulating Artificial Intelligence* (Springer, 2018).

[46] David Kaye, 'Report of the Special Rapporteur on the Promotion and Protection of the Right to Freedom of Opinion and Expression' (30 March 2017).

[47] Global Network Initiative (GNI), *GNI Principles on Freedom of Expression and Privacy* (May 2017), https://globalnetworkinitiative.org/gni-principles.

If national laws, regulations and policies do not conform to international standards, ICT companies should avoid, minimize, or otherwise address the adverse impact of government demands, laws, or regulations, and seek ways to honor the principles of internationally recognized human rights to the greatest extent possible. ICT companies should also be able to demonstrate their efforts in this regard.[48]

The technology sector also recommends that businesses should ensure that procedural requirements and HRDD are strictly followed,[49] including while handling government demands.[50] In addition, some states have begun to enact legislation on data collection in order to protect individuals, such as the European Union Digital Services Act, which came into force on 16 November 2022.[51]

Therefore, the increasing use of technology has possible benefits and significant challenges for business and human rights.

5. Business and Human Rights Treaty

As seen in Chapter 1, there have been many attempts to provide some form of binding legal obligation in relation to business activities which have adverse human rights impacts. On 26 June 2014, the UN Human Rights Council adopted a resolution, proposed by Ecuador and South Africa, establishing an open-ended intergovernmental working group on transnational corporations and other business enterprises with respect to human rights (Working Group on a BHR Treaty), whose mandate is to 'elaborate an international legally binding instrument to regulate, in international human rights law, the activities of transnational corporations and other business enterprises'.[52]

---

[48] Ibid., 2.
[49] Yael Ronen, 'Big Brother's Little Helpers: The Right to Privacy and the Responsibility of Internet Service Providers' (2015) 31 *Utrecht Journal of International and European Law* 72.
[50] Christopher Soghoian, 'An End to Privacy Theater: Exposing and Discouraging Corporate Disclosure of User Data to the Government' (2011) 12 *Minnesota Journal of Science and Technology* 191.
[51] European Commission, 'The Digital Services Act: Ensuring a Safe and Accountable Online Environment (16 November 2022), https://commission.europa.eu/strategy-and-pol icy/priorities-2019-2024/europe-fit-digital-age/digital-services-act_en..
[52] UN Human Rights Council, 'Elaboration of an International Legally Binding Instrument on Transnational Corporations and Other Business Enterprises with Respect to Human Rights' UN Doc. A/HRC Res. 26/9 (26 June 2014).

a. Reasons for a Treaty

There are many arguments for and against having a treaty in relation to business and human rights issues. A few of the main ones are summarized here.[53]

The key arguments in favour of a treaty include:

- The nature of human rights in international law is such that, no matter what the subject matter, it requires a legally binding treaty to ensure that there is some global standard to which states can be held.[54]
- The voluntary nature of the corporate responsibility to respect human rights has not worked to change business practices substantially or increased state actions in this area.[55]
- Access to remedies by victims of business activities, and the removal of obstacles to their obtaining justice, will not be progressed effectively without a treaty.[56]
- Many of the activities of business which have had adverse human rights impacts have been undertaken by transnational corporations across boundaries. Individual states will struggle to deal effectively with these matters in a coherent manner without an agreed and binding international legal framework.[57]
- A treaty will help resolve some conflicts between the protection of human rights and areas of international law which deal with business

---

[53] See generally, Surya Deva and David Bilchitz (eds), *Building a Treaty on Business and Human Rights: Context and Contours* (CUP, 2017) [Deva and Bilchitz, Treaty] and Jernej Letnar Černič and Nicolás Carrillo-Santarelli (eds), *The Future of Business and Human Rights: Theoretical and Practical Considerations for a U.N Treaty* (Insentia, 2018).

[54] Justine Nolan, 'A Business and Human Rights Treaty' in Dorothée Baumann-Pauly and Justine Nolan (eds), *Business and Human Rights: From Principles to Practice* (Routledge, 2016), 71.

[55] Penelope Simons, 'The Value-Added of a Treaty to Regulate Transnational Organisations and Other Business Enterprises: Moving Forward Strategically' in Deva and Bilchitz, Treaty, note 53, 48, who notes that the soft law framework of the UNGPs cannot effectively protect human rights against powerful businesses. See also the example in Chapter 7 of the survey by the German government in 2020 showing the lack of voluntary action by German businesses.

[56] Radu Mares, 'Draft Treaty on Business and Human Rights' in Axel Marx, Geert Van Calster, and Jan Wouters with Kari Otteburn (eds), *Research Handbook on Global Governance, Business and Human Rights* (Edward Elgar, 2022), 22, who discusses both governance gaps and implementation gaps. .

[57] Claret Vargas, 'A Treaty on Business and Human Rights' in César Rodríguez-Garavito (ed.), *Business and Human Rights: Beyond the End of the Beginning* (CUP, 2017), 111.

activities, such as international investment law and international trade law.⁵⁸

The key arguments against a treaty include:

- The UNGPs should be allowed time to change the behaviour of businesses and states. Indeed, there was a counter-resolution at the Human Rights Council (passed after the treaty resolution) urged by a number of industrialized states, which sought to focus on the implementation of the UNGPs instead, especially through exploring all legal options to increase access to remedy.⁵⁹
- Some business associations have argued that a treaty would undermine the consensus created by the UNGPs and would be 'a genuine setback to the efforts underway to improve the human rights situation and access to remedy on the ground'.⁶⁰
- The length of time it takes to draft a treaty will slow progress, is unlikely to be supported by a diversity of states, and would distract from other measures to improve corporate accountability for adverse human rights impacts.⁶¹
- A treaty by itself, which does not lead to effective enforcement, will raise expectations which cannot be realized, with no substantive changes occurring on the ground.⁶²

It is also argued that there is a middle ground:

> The development of a business and human rights treaty should not be viewed as an either/or narrative but rather as an additional mechanism

---

⁵⁸ Markus Krajewski, 'Framing the Broader Context of Business and Human Rights: The Impact of Trade Agreements on Human Rights' in Surya Deva and David Birchall (eds), *Research Handbook on Business and Human Rights* (Edward Elgar, 2020) [Deva and Birchall, BHR], 269.

⁵⁹ Human Rights Council, Res. 26/22 (2014).

⁶⁰ International Organisation of Employers, 26 June 2014, https://www.ioe-emp.org/fileadmin/ioe_documents/publications/Policy%20Areas/csr/EN/_2014-06-26__G-566_Consensus_on_Business_and_Human_Rights_is_broken_with_the_Adoption_of_the_Ecuador_Initiative.pdf.

⁶¹ John Ruggie, *Just Business* (Norton, 2013), 59. John Ruggie's view on the treaty has changed over time, see, for example, Ruggie, Rees, and Davis, 'Ten Years After: From UN Guiding Principles to Multi-Fiduciary Obligations', note 24.

⁶² Florian Wettstein, *Business and Human Rights: Ethical, Legal, and Managerial Perspectives* (CUP, 2022), 312.

that could help to clarify the legal responsibilities of businesses, be used to encourage the development of consistent national laws and operate in conjunction with more practically focused industry-specific standards and metrics that are being developed from the ground up.[63]

As at the middle of 2023, the process of negotiating and drafting a treaty on business and human rights has continued.[64] There have been a number of drafts of a treaty proposed by the Chair-Rapporteur of the government of Ecuador which have been debated fully in the annual negotiation sessions. As further drafts of a treaty will appear over time, the following is a brief summary of a few aspects of the process and issues which indicate some of the developments to date.

b. Process

The process of negotiation of the draft treaty (called a 'Legally Binding Instrument' by the Working Group on the BHR Treaty) has generally been through an annual session of the Working Group on the BHR Treaty held at the OHCHR in Geneva (though online during the Covid-19 pandemic), though regional consultations between states were held in 2023. An important element of this process has been the active involvement of civil society, and often rights holders directly, in the consultations.[65] This is a continuation of a process for the drafting of a human rights treaty, which accelerated with the drafting of the Convention on the Rights of Persons with Disabilities 2006.[66] There has been less involvement in the negotiations by business, other than a few business associations, and the attendance

---

[63] Justine Nolan, 'A Business and Human Rights Treaty' in Deva and Bilchitz, Treaty, note 53, 72.
[64] HuffPost UK Politics, Statement by Ecuador's Minister for Foreign Affairs, 'Transnational Misconduct Must End' (20 October 2014) (huffingtonpost.co.uk).
[65] Geneviève Paul, 'The Treaty Process Can Serve as a Catalyst for Effective Reforms at Domestic Levels', 20 September 2015)https://www.business-humanrights.org/en/blog/the-treaty-process-can-serve-as-a-catalyst-for-effective-reforms-at-domestic-levels/. Summaries of the treaty drafting sessions can be found on the Business and Human Rights Resource Centre website: Binding Treaty on Business & Human Rights, https://www.business-humanrights.org/en/big-issues/binding-treaty.
[66] Convention on the Rights of Persons with Disabilities 2006 (CRPD). Frédéric Mégret, 'The Disabilities Convention: Human Rights of Persons with Disabilities or Disability Rights?' (2008) 30 *Human Rights Quarterly* 494 and Michael Stein and Ilias Bantekas, 'Including Disability in Business and Human Rights Discourse and Corporate Practice' (2021) 6 *Business and Human Rights Journal* 490.

of states has fluctuated, with limited active engagement by industrialized states in the early sessions.[67]

The process has also led to movements in the location of some of the key provisions in the various drafts of the treaty offered. For example, in the first full draft provided in 2018, called the Zero Draft, the provisions on the rights of victims and prevention were Articles 8 and 9.[68] By 2021, in the Third Revised Draft, the first few substantive Articles were dealing with 'Rights of Victims', 'Protection of Victims', and 'Access to Remedies' (Articles 4, 5, and 7), with Article 6 being 'Prevention'. This indicated a change in priorities in the drafting arising from the process.[69]

c. Issues

In relation to the direct obligations on businesses in international law (discussed in Chapters 2 and 3), a strong argument was made that this treaty should include such direct obligations in relation to international human rights law:

> The proposed business and human rights (BHR) treaty will be unique amongst human rights treaties ... Where [other human rights] treaties lay out obligations, it is generally the state which is expressly identified as being responsible for protecting and realizing those rights. A BHR treaty, in contrast, will, in all likelihood, need to be different ... [as] it will need to focus on the regulation of ... businesses.[70]

While a very early draft indicated that direct international legal obligations would be placed on businesses,[71] later drafts have completely moved away

---

[67] Peter Muchlinksi, *Advanced Introduction to Business and Human Rights* (Edward Elgar, 2022), 168–9.

[68] Zero Draft 2018, https://www.ohchr.org/sites/default/files/Documents/HRBodies/HRCouncil/WGTransCorp/Session3/DraftLBI.pdf.

[69] Gabriela Quijano, 'A New Draft Business and Human Rights Treaty and a Promising Direction of Travel' 10 September 2019), https://www.business-humanrights.org/en/blog/a-new-draft-business-and-human-rights-treaty-and-a-promising-direction-of-travel/..

[70] David Bilchitz, 'Corporate Obligations and a Treaty on Business and Human Rights' in Deva and Bilchitz, Treaty, note 53, 185.

[71] Elements for the Draft Legally Binding Instrument (September 2017), https://www.ohchr.org/sites/default/files/Documents/HRBodies/HRCouncil/WGTransCorp/Session3/LegallyBindingInstrumentTNCs_OBEs.pdf.

from this.⁷² Thus, all the later drafts, while focusing on the regulation of business activity in relation to human rights impacts, do so through the prism of state obligations to put these regulations in place. For example, Article 6.1 of the Updated Revised Draft 2023 of the treaty provides:

> States Parties shall regulate effectively the activities of all business enterprises within their territory, jurisdiction, or otherwise under their control, including transnational corporations and other business enterprises that undertake activities of a transnational character.⁷³

Nevertheless, the Preamble to the Third Revised Draft 2021 noted:

> Underlining that business enterprises, regardless of their size, sector, location, operational context, ownership and structure *have the obligation to respect internationally recognized human rights*, including by avoiding causing or contributing to human rights abuses through their own activities and addressing such abuses when they occur, as well as by preventing or mitigating human rights abuses that are directly linked to their operations, products or services by their business relationships.⁷⁴

This movement from an expectation on businesses to respect human rights as set out in the UNGPs, to being stated as an obligation in the draft treaty, is an interesting one. This statement in a Preamble is, though, not a legally binding one in terms of treaty interpretation.⁷⁵

One issue which was raised on the first day of the first session (in October 2015) of the Working Group on a BHR Treaty was about which businesses were to be included in the treaty. The issue was whether the treaty's scope was to be about 'transnational corporations' only or was to include all businesses. This issue arose due to the original resolution of the Human Rights

---

⁷² For example, First Revised Draft of a Legally Binding Instrument (July 2019), https://www.ohchr.org/sites/default/files/Documents/HRBodies/HRCouncil/WGTransCorp/OEIGWG_RevisedDraft_LBI.pdf.
⁷³ Updated Revised Draft of a Legally Binding Instrument (August 2023), https://www.ohchr.org/sites/default/files/documents/hrbodies/hrcouncil/igwg-transcorp/session9/igwg-9th-updated-draft-lbi-clean.pdf.
⁷⁴ Third Revised Draft 2021, Preamble, para. 11, https://www.ohchr.org/sites/default/files/Documents/HRBodies/HRCouncil/WGTransCorp/Session6/LBI3rdDRAFT.pdf (emphasis added).
⁷⁵ Makane Moïse Mbengue, 'Preamble' in *Max Planck Encyclopedia of International Law* (OUP, 2006).

Council, being Resolution 26/9 of 26 June 2014. That resolution included a footnote to the Preamble: ' "Other business enterprises" denotes all business enterprises that have a transnational character in their operational activities, and does not apply to local businesses registered in terms of relevant domestic law.' At the first session, the EU delegation argued that all businesses should be included, not least because the UNGPs include all businesses.[76] This led to considerable disagreement by other states, many of which considered that the treaty should not include their own local businesses, and also that leverage by Global South states over transnational businesses was needed, and that covering all businesses would make the treaty too unwieldy.[77] A compromise was initially made so that the Zero Draft provided that the scope of the treaty would include 'any business activities of a transnational character'.[78] By the Third Revised Draft the scope of the treaty had become: 'shall apply to all business activities, including business activities of a transnational character'.[79] This was clearly a movement towards much greater inclusion of all businesses within the treaty.

Another issue which was raised by some states and by the business participants in the negotiations was to bring the treaty as close to the UNGPs as possible, on the basis that the UNGPs had been widely agreed and constituted the authoritative standard. With successive drafts, this increased alignment with the UNGPs has occurred, so that, by the Third Revised Draft, there has been 'a noticeable effort to align some of the language with the [UNGPs] when relevant, in response to comments from certain states and stakeholders'.[80] For example, the Second Revised Draft corrected the terminology in a previous draft from 'due diligence' to 'human rights due diligence' for this reason.[81]

However, while the UNGPs are an important framework for a treaty,[82] they do not contain a range of measures which a legally binding treaty

---

[76] Carlos López and Ben Shea, 'Negotiating a Treaty on Business and Human Rights: A Review of the First Intergovernmental Session' (2015) 1 *Business and Human Rights Journal* 111.

[77] Surya Deva, 'Scope of the Proposed Business and Human Rights Treaty' in Deva and Bilchitz, Treaty, note 53, 154, 167–73.

[78] Zero Draft, note 68, Art. 3.

[79] Third Revised Draft, note 74, Art. 3, LBI3rdDRAFT.pdf (ohchr.org).

[80] Carlos López, 'The Third Revised Draft of a Treaty on Business and Human Rights: Modest Steps Forward, But Much of the Same' *Opinio Juris* (3 September 2021).

[81] Robert McCorquodale and Lise Smit, 'Human Rights, Responsibilities and Due Diligence: Key Issues for a Treaty' in Deva and Bilchitz, Treaty, note 53, 216.

[82] There has been an argument that the draft treaty is too detailed and should be changed to a solely framework treaty with limited provisions: Claire Methven O'Brien, 'Bounded Rationality, Metonymy, Humility: Further Arguments for a Framework-Style Business and

would include, such as civil liability and enforcement provisions. These provisions have been some of the most contentious of the treaty negotiations,[83] and deal with many of the matters discussed in Chapter 6 about access to remedies. These are probably the provisions most likely to evolve over time. In that regard, civil society organizations and scholars continue to remind the negotiators of the importance of paying particular attention to women and other vulnerable groups in relation to the protections and remedies provided for in the treaty.[84]

At this stage, after nearly a decade of debate and negotiations, the final content of a treaty on business and human rights is still not clear. Some issues have been resolved, though not to every stakeholder's satisfaction, while others remain unresolved. Actions by states, businesses, and civil society organizations will also affect the negotiations of a treaty, such as progress with the EU's Corporate Sustainability Due Diligence Directive (discussed in Chapter 7). Yet the pressure for some legally binding treaty will remain and, as the WGBHR stated in its Roadmap, 'it is vital to also ensure policy coherence when developing further standards in the area of business and human rights at multi-lateral level, including in relation to the ongoing discussions on a legally binding instrument on business and human rights'.[85]

6. Conclusions

This chapter considered some of the future developments in the international protection of human rights adversely impacted by business activities. It examined two key areas: climate change and technology. It can be

---

Human Rights Treaty' (Völkerrechtsblog, 22 June 2022), 4. This matter was raised previously, see Simons, note 55.

[83] Humberto Cantú Rivera, 'Binding Treaty Negotiations: Considerations on Legal Liability and Access to Justice'(20 October 2022) https://www.business-humanrights.org/fr/blog/the-business-and-human-rights-binding-treaty-negotiations-some-considerations-on-legal-liability-and-access-to-justice/ .

[84] Penelope Simons and Melisa Handl, 'Relations of Ruling: A Feminist Critique of the United Nations Guiding Principles on Business and Human Rights and Violence against Women in the Context of Resource Extraction' (2019) 31 *Canadian Journal of Women and the Law* 113 and Feminists for a Binding Treaty, 'Key Recommendations by Feminists for a Binding Treaty on the Third Revised Draft' (5 October 2021) https://www.business-humanrights.org/en/latest-news/key-recommendations-by-feminists-for-a-binding-treaty-on-the-third-revised-draft.

[85] Roadmap, note 7, para. 43.

seen that climate change is becoming an issue of heightened awareness globally, and that the impacts of climate change on human rights are evident, including those arising from business activities. The case before the Dutch courts discussed in the introduction to this chapter showed the legal developments occurring in this area.[86] It was established that the increasing use of technology has both possible benefits and significant challenges for business and human rights, depending on the use of it.

The progress of the negotiations on a treaty on business and human rights has been slow. Yet there have been significant changes in the drafts over this period, with a clear move towards it containing international legal obligations on states alone, while also aiming to ensure that the regulation of those business activities which impact on human rights is done in a coherent and global manner. These developments also reinforce the changes in the international legal order which the business and human rights field have helped to highlight.

---

[86] The WGBHR has also issued a communication (complaint) in 2023 against Saudi Aramco and a number of investors in that business, and their states of domicile, for the impacts of Saudi Aramco on climate change: https://spcommreports.ohchr.org/TMResultsBase/DownLoadPublicCommunicationFile?gId=28094

9
Conclusions: International Law, Business, and Human Rights

1. Context

This book began by setting out the many—and ongoing—adverse impacts on human rights of the Bhopal incident in 1984 and the lack of legal accountability of the businesses involved. It concluded in Chapter 8 with a decision of a court in 2021 stating that a business had a legal duty of care to the claimants in relation to its global climate change impacts on human rights. That is an extraordinary change in the legal position in less than 40 years.

These international legal developments are also seen in the changing understanding that it is not the state alone which has legal responsibilities for human rights impacts. This is shown in the difference between the decision that the state of Nigeria was the only entity with legal responsibilities for the actions of oil companies, such as Shell, in Chapter 4,[1] to the number of domestic law cases against Shell in the past few years which have successfully relied on international and domestic law to find that Shell itself was potentially or actually legally responsible for similar activities.[2]

These developments are based on increasing international regulation in this field, especially the ground-breaking United Nations Guiding Principles on Business and Human Rights 2011 (UNGPs), as shown in Chapter 3. This international regulation has affected both domestic legislation—with the increasingly mandatory nature of regulation shown in Chapter 7—and business awareness across many sectors, including the finance sector, as was indicated in Chapter 5, and in other areas of international law, such as

---

[1] *Social and Economic Rights Action Center and the Economic and Social Rights Action Center v. Nigeria*, African Commission, Communication No. 155/96 (2001–02) 1985–84; see Chapter 4.
[2] For example, The Hague Court of Appeal, 29 January 2021, ECLI:NL:GHDHA:2021,; and *Okpabi v. Royal Dutch Shell Plc* [2021] UKSC 3; see Chapter 6.

international investment law, as with the *Urbaser v. Argentina* case.³ These situations, with which each chapter began, show the breadth of coverage of business and human rights legal issues.

2. Business and Human Rights as Part of International Law

While international human rights law is a core aspect of business and human rights matters, it is not the only area of public international law for which business and human rights issues are relevant. Other international law areas of which instances have been analysed in this book include international investment law, international humanitarian law, international criminal law, international environmental law, and international legal theory, as well as many of the general principles of public international law, such as state responsibility, jurisdiction and state sovereignty.

In addition, as with some other areas of international law, there are many areas of domestic law which affect business and human rights law, especially in regulation and litigation, which is increasing. For lawyers, judges, prosecutors, and legislators—as well as decision-makers in business and others—to apply this international law effectively, this can require them to have some understanding of domestic corporate law, domestic criminal law, tort/obligations and contract law, domestic human rights law, domestic environmental law, and domestic constitutional law, as well as private international law and comparative law. Of course, business and human rights is not solely a legal issue, with, for example, international relations, corporate management, business ethics, financial management, and organizational studies having vital engagement in, and insights on, issues of business and human rights.

Therefore, it is not surprising that some developments in this field across many states have been slow. This may explain why many of the developments so far in legislation and case law have tended to occur in the Global North. It is hoped that greater experience and exposure to these issues, as well as capacity building, will ensure that these developments take place worldwide.⁴

---

³ *Urbaser S.A. v. Argentina*, ICSID Case No. ARB/07/26, decided 8 December 2016; see Chapter 2.
⁴ WGBHR, 'Report on Building Capacity for the Implementation of the Guiding Principles on Business and Human Rights' UN Doc. A/HRC/53/24 (15 May 2023).

3. Business, Human Rights, and International Law

While businesses have interacted with international law over many centuries, including influencing how international law has been shaped, as seen in Chapter 2, the development of an international legal framework of business and human rights has been much more recent. The creation of the UNGPs was pivotal in developing law at both the national and international levels. Much of this has been soft law, though, with such widespread acceptance of the UNGPs that it has tended 'to legitimise conduct [consistent with it] and make it harder to sustain the legality of opposing positions'.[5] Indeed, as seen in Chapter 7, the UNGPs and related international instruments have provided an authoritative and strong basis for national and international regulation, as well as being relied on or argued before national and international dispute mechanisms. As such, the development of business and human rights—as law—does have an impact on international law.

In terms of specific impacts on international law, business and human rights issues are being considered in many areas of international law, such as international investment law and international humanitarian law (as seen in Chapter 3) and in the broadening of transnational jurisdiction of states (see Chapter 4), as well as in the approach of international organizations.[6] In addition, business and human rights developments have continued the challenge to absolute state sovereignty, with the acceptance that states alone do not have legal obligations in relation to human rights. Indeed, the complete acceptance now that the remit of the Office of the United Nations High Commissioner for Human Rights (OHCHR) should include business actions is a sharp change from the traditional position that states are meant to be the sole focus of a UN human rights body.[7]

---

[5] Alan Boyle and Christine Chinkin, *The Making of International Law* (OUP, 2007), 212.
[6] For example, OHCHR, *Remedy in Development Finance*, (2022) https://www.ohchr.org/en/publications/policy-and-methodological-publications/remedy-development-finance, and Siobhán McInerney-Lankford and Robert McCorquodale (eds), *The Roles of International Law in Development* (OUP, 2023)
[7] WGBHR, 'Tenth Anniversary of the Guiding Principles on Business and Human Rights: A Roadmap for the Next Decade of Business and Human Rights—Raising the Ambition, Increasing The Pace', Report to the HRC (8 June 2022), https://documents-dds-ny.un.org/doc/UNDOC/GEN/G22/373/36/PDF/G2237336.pdf?OpenElement, paras 141–9. For example, in 2022 there were resolutions by the UN Human Rights Council on technology and human rights, and on cyber-security and human rights, all with direct reference to business activities: OHCHR, 51st regular session of the Human Rights Council: Resolutions, decisions, and President's statements.

These actions do indicate both new international law being crafted and new directions for international law. For example, business and human rights issues are now on the global agenda, from climate change to technology, within the broader acknowledgement that businesses can be regulated at an international level. Such developments will continue in the future.

At the domestic law level, international legal issues of sovereignty and jurisdiction are being considered and adapted. Almost all the legislation passed since the UNGPs includes aspects of transnational jurisdiction, as they apply to subsidiaries, and sometimes to suppliers, located outside the territory of the state passing the legislation. They do so through the prism of applying to the businesses which are within the state's territory. In addition, there are some pieces of domestic and regional legislation that apply to businesses operating in a territory even where there is no direct jurisdictional link—such as a parent company registered in that territory or a supply link to a business in the territory—other than providing goods and services in that territory.[8] The responses of other states, especially those in the Global South, have yet to be seen clearly. In addition, domestic case law is using international law increasingly to make businesses accountable for some of their actions which adversely affect human rights, and even adapting state international human rights legal obligations so that they apply directly to businesses..[9]

All these many developments are both a risk (reputational, legal, social, and financial) and an opportunity for businesses, with some businesses keenly aware of the changes and the need to take effective action, while others have so far been reluctant to engage. However, a key challenge remains, which is to enable those whose human rights are abused by the actions of businesses to be able to access justice and obtain an appropriate remedy. As the Working Group on Business and Human Rights (WGBHR) noted:

> By positioning the need for greater access to effective remedy for victims of business-related harms as a core pillar, the Guiding Principles have

---

[8] The issue of the transnational/extraterritorial effects of state action, which would include legislation and court decisions, is discussed in Chapter 4. Nico Krisch, 'Jurisdiction Unbound: (Extra)territorial Regulation as Global Governance' [2022] *European Journal of International Law* 481 and Joanne Scott, 'Extraterritoriality and Territorial Extension in EU Law' (2014) 62 *American Journal of Comparative Law* 87.

[9] *Nevsun Resources Ltd v. Araya*, 2020 SCC 5, discussed in Chapter 6.

also helped shift the focus from corporate philanthropy to accountability as an essential feature of responsible business.

This normative development is easy to overlook but has been an essential step for progress. Norms shape laws, policies and practices. After years of confusion, the transformative concept of an internationally recognized business responsibility to respect human rights has become the authoritative standard that defines responsible business.[10]

This normative change is important and is based on many of the materials considered throughout this book, including in case law, national legislative action, international regulation, and corporate responses, from across the world. Within this change, the language of human rights due diligence has become an accepted 'normative innovation'.[11] Above all, it is the transformative idea of businesses having human rights responsibilities which has had clear effects on international law.

---

[10] WGBHR, 'Guiding Principles on Business and Human Rights at 10: Taking Stock of the First Decade', Report to the UN Human Rights Council (HRC) (22 April 2021), https://documents-dds-ny.un.org/doc/UNDOC/GEN/G21/093/82/PDF/G2109382.pdf?OpenElement, paras 12–14.

[11] Ibid., para. 18.

Bibliography

International Documents

United Nations Guiding Principles on Business and Human Rights 2011 =
United Nations Human Rights Council, 'Mandate of the Special Representative of the Secretary-General on the issue of human rights and transnational corporations and other business enterprises' (2008), UN Doc. Res. 8/7
—— Resolution adopting UNGPs (2011), UN Doc. A/HRC/RES/17/4
—— (2014) 'Elaboration of an International Legally Binding Instrument on Transnational Corporations and Other Business Enterprises with Respect to Human Rights' A/HRC Res. 26/9
Report of the Special Representative of the Secretary-General on the Issue of Human Rights and Transnational Corporations and Other Business Enterprises (2006) E/CN.4/2006/97
—— (2007) A/HRC/4/35
—— Framework Report (2008) A/HRC/8/5
—— (2009) A/HRC/11/13
—— (2010) A/HRC/14/27
—— Guidelines Report (2011) A/HRC/17/31
—— Presentation of Report (2011), Opening Statement to United Nations Human Rights Council
Working Group on Business and Human Rights
—— Report (2013) on 'Adverse Impacts of Business-Related Activities on the Rights of Indigenous Peoples' A/68/279
—— Report (2016) on 'State-Owned Entities', A/HRC/32/45
—— Report (2017) on 'Access to Effective Remedies', A/GA/72/162
—— Report (2018) on 'The State as an Economic Actor' A/HEC/38/48
—— Report (2018) on 'Corporate Human Rights Due Diligence—Emerging Practices, Challenges and Ways Forward', A/73/163
—— Report (2019) on 'Gender Dimensions of the UNGPs', A/HRC/41/43
—— Report (2020) on 'Business, Human Rights and Conflict-Affected Regions: Towards Heightened Action'
—— Report (2021) on 'Guiding Principles on Business and Human Rights at 10: Taking Stock of the First Decade'
—— Report (2021) on 'Tenth Anniversary of the Guiding Principles on Business and Human Rights: A Roadmap for the Next Decade of Business and Human Rights—Raising the Ambition, Increasing The Pace'
—— Report (2023) on 'Development Finance Institutions and Human Rights'

—— Report (2023) on 'Building Capacity for the Implementation of the Guiding Principles on Business and Climate Change and the UNGPs':
—— Report (2023) on 'Extractive Sector, Just Transition and Human Rights
—— Thun Group of Banks (2017) Letter
Office of the High Commissioner on Human Rights (OHCHR)
—— Information Note (2023) on 'Human Rights'
—— (2011) 'Piloting Principles for Effective Company/Stakeholder Grievance Mechanisms: A Report of Lessons Learned'
—— (2012) 'The Corporate Responsibility to Respect Human Rights: An Interpretive Guide', UN Doc. HR/PUB/12/02
—— (2013) Response to SOMO and OECD Watch,
—— (2016) Improving Accountability and Access to Remedy for Victims of Business-Related Human Rights Abuse'
—— (2016) 'Human Rights, Climate Change and Business Key Messages'
—— (2017) *Human Rights Translated 2.0: A Business Reference Guide*,
—— (2017) Response to Request from BankTrack for Advice Regarding the Application of the UN Guiding Principles on Business and Human Rights in the Context of the Banking Sector
—— (2017) Tackling Discrimination Against Lesbian, Gay, Bi, Trans, & Intersex People: Standards of Conduct for Business
—— (2020) 'Improving Accountability and Access to Remedy for Victims of Business-Related Human Rights Abuse through Non-State-Based Grievance Mechanisms'
—— (2022) *Remedy in Development Finance*
United Nations General Assembly
—— Report (1992) of the President of the General Assembly on a Code of Conduct on Transnational Corporations, UN Doc. A/47/446
—— Report (2022) of the UN Secretary-General to the UN General Assembly, 'Responsibility of States for Internationally Wrongful Acts: Compilation of Decisions of International Courts, Tribunals and Other Bodies', UN Doc. A/77/74
United Nations Economic and Social Council (2003) 'Draft Norms on the Responsibilities of Transnational Corporations and Other Business Enterprises with Regard to Human Rights'
Organisation of Economic Cooperation and Development (OECD)
—— (2011) The OECD Guidelines for Multinational Enterprises, *OECD Declaration and Decisions on International Investment and Multinational Enterprises: Basic Texts* (Updated 2023)
—— (2014) *Expert Letters and Statements on the Application of the OECD Guidelines for Multinational Enterprises and UN Guiding Principles on Business and Human Rights in the context of the financial sector*, June 2014
—— (2015) OECD Guidelines on Corporate Governance of State-Owned Enterprises
—— (2016) OECD Responsible Business Conduct for Institutional Investors: Key Considerations for Due Diligence under the OECD Guidelines for MNEs

—— (2016) Due Diligence Guidance for Responsible Supply Chains of Minerals from Conflict-Affected and High-Risk Areas
—— (2016) OECD-FAO Guidance for Responsible Agricultural Supply Chains
—— (2017) OECD Due Diligence Guidance for Responsible Supply Chains in the Garment and Footwear Sector
—— (2018) Due Diligence Guidance for Responsible Business Conduct,
International Labour Organization (ILO)
—— (1977) Tripartite Declaration of Principles concerning Multinational Enterprises and Social Policy, adopted by the Governing Body of the International Labour Office at its 204th Session and subsequently revised
—— Declaration on Fundamental Principles and Rights at Work 1998 (amended 2022)

Treaty Supervisory Bodies

Committee on Economic Social and Cultural Rights
—— (1997) General Comment No. 8, 'The Relationship between Economic Sanctions and Respect for Economic, Social and Cultural Rights'
Committee on Economic Social and Cultural Rights
—— (2017) General Comment No. 24 on 'State Obligations under the International Covenant on Economic, Social and Cultural Rights in the Context of Business Activities'
—— (2018) 'Statement on Climate Change and the International Covenant on Economic, Social and Cultural Rights',
Committee on the Rights of the Child (2011) 'Effective Remedy and Corporate Violations of Children's Rights'
European Union
—— (2011) 'A Renewed EU Strategy 2011–14 for Corporate Social Responsibility', COM (2011) 681 final
—— (2012) Council Regulation (EU) No. 1215/2012 of 12 December 2012 of the European Parliament and of the Council on Jurisdiction and the Recognition and Enforcement of Judgments in Civil and Commercial Matters [2012] OJ L351, 20.12.2012 (Recast Brussels Regulation)
—— (2014) Directive 2014/95/EU as regards disclosure of non-financial and diversity information by certain large undertakings and groups
—— (2022) European Commission Proposal for a Directive of the European Parliament and of the Council on Corporate Sustainability Due Diligence and amending Directive (EU) 2019/1937, COM/2022/71 final,
—— European Parliament, Texts adopted—Corporate due diligence and corporate accountability—Wednesday, 10 March 2021
Paris Agreement on Climate Change 2015 (The Paris Agreement) United Nations Framework Convention on Climate Change

Bibliography

Books and Articles

Note: Books and Articles are included but not chapters in books (as the edited book is included)

Addo, M. (ed.) (1999) *Human Rights Standards and the Responsibility of Transnational Corporations* (Kluwer)

Adeyemi, A. (2014) 'Changing the Face of Sustainable Development in Developing Countries: The Role of the International Finance Corporation' 16 *Environmental Law Review* 91

Alam, S., Atapattu, S., Gonzalez, C., and Razzaque, J. (eds) (2015) *International Environmental Law and the Global South* (Cambridge University Press)

Allott, P. (1988) 'State Responsibility and the Unmaking of International Law' 29 *Harvard International Law Journal* 1

—— (2014) *Clouds of Injustice, India: Summary of Clouds of Injustice—Bhopal Disaster 20 Years on* (Amnesty International)

—— (2014) *Injustice Incorporated: Corporate Abuses and the Human Rights to a Remedy, Injustice Incorporated: Corporate Abuses and the Human Right to Remedy* (Amnesty International)

—— (2020) *Obstacle Course: How the UK's National Contact Point handles Human Rights Complaints under the OECD Guidelines for Multinational Enterprises*

Anghie, A. (2005) *Imperialism, Sovereignty and the Making of International Law* (Cambridge University Press)

Azaria, D. (2019) 'The International Law Commission's Return to the Law of Sources of International Law, 13 Florida International University Law Review' 13 *Transnational Legal Activism in Global Value Chains* 989

Baars, G., and Spicer, A. (eds) (2017) *The Corporation: A Critical, Multidisciplinary Handbook* (Cambridge University Press)

Barnes, M.M. (2022) *State-Owned Entities and Human Rights: The Role of International Law* (Cambridge University Press)

Baumann-Pauly, D. (2020) 'Making Mining Safe and Fair: Artisanal Cobalt Extraction in the Democratic Republic of the Congo'

—— and Nolan J. (eds) (2016) *Business and Human Rights From Principles to Practice* (Routledge)

Baxi, U. (2015) 'Human Rights Responsibility of Multinational Corporations, Political Ecology of Injustice: Learning from Bhopal Thirty Plus?' 1 *Business and Human Rights Journal* 21

Bekker, G. (2003) 'The Social and Economic Rights Action Center and the Center for Economic and Social Rights/Nigeria' 47 *Journal of African Law* 126

Bernaz, N. (2013) 'Enhancing Corporate Accountability for Human Rights Violations: Is Extraterritoriality the Magic Potion?' 117 *Journal of Business Ethics* 493

—— (2016) *Business and Human Rights: History, Law and Policy-Bridging the Accountability Gap* (Routledge)

Bethlehem, B., McRae, D., Neufeld, R., and Van Damme, I. (eds) (2022) *The Oxford Handbook of International Trade Law* (2nd edn, Oxford University Press)

Bhatt, K., and Erdem Türkellí, G. (2021) 'OECD National Contact Points as Sites of Effective Remedy: New Expressions of the Role and Rule of Law within Market Globalization?' 6 *Business and Human Rights Journal* 423

Bilchitz, D. (2021) *Fundamental Rights and the Legal Obligations of Business* (Cambridge University Press)

Bingham, T. (2010) *The Rule of Law* (Penguin)

Birchall, D. (2019) 'Any Act, Any Harm, To Anyone: The Transformative Potential of "Human Rights Impacts" under the UN Guiding Principles on Business and Human Rights' *University of Oxford Human Rights Hub* 120

—— (2022) 'Reconstructing State Obligations to Protect and Fulfil Socio-Economic Rights in an Era of Marketisation' 71 *International and Comparative Law Quarterly* 227

Bird, D., Cahoy, D., and Darin Prenkert, J. (eds) (2014) *Law, Business and Human Rights: Bridging the Gap* (Edward Elgar)

Blackett, A., and Trebilcock, A. (eds) (2015) *Research Handbook on Transnational Labour Law* (Edward Elgar)

Blanpain, R. (ed.) (2014) *Protecting Labour Rights in a Multi-Polar Supply Chain and Mobile Global Economy* (Wolters Kluwer)

Boisson de Chazournes, L. (2020) 'The International Law Commission in a Mirror—Forms, Impact and Authority' in United Nations, Seventy Years of the International Law Commission (United Nations)

Bonnitcha, J., and McCorquodale, R. (2017) 'The Concept of 'Due Diligence' in the UN Guiding Principles on Business and Human Rights' 28 *European Journal of International Law* 899

Boyle, A., and Chinkin, C. (2007) *The Making of International Law* (Oxford University Press)

—— and Redgwell, C. (2021) *Birnie, Boyle and Redgwell's International Law and the Environment* (4th edn, Oxford University Press)

Brabant, S., and Savourey, E. (2020) 'All Eyes on France', www.cambridge.org/core/ blog/2020/01/24/all-eyes-on-france-french-vigilance-law-first-enforcement-cases-1-2-current-cases-and-trends/#_edn13

—— Savourey, E., and Michon, C. (2017) 'The Vigilance Plan: Cornerstone of the Corporate Duty of Vigilance Law' *Revue internationale de la compliance et de l'éthique des affaires* (14 December)

Bright, C., and Smit, L. (2022) 'The New European Directive on Corporate Sustainability Due Diligence' British Institute of International and Comparative Law, The New European Directive on Corporate Sustainability Due Diligence (BIICL)

British Academy (2019) *Reforming Business for the 21st Century* (British Academy)

Brown, B. (2020) *The Company: The Rise and Fall of the Hudson's Bay Empire* (Doubleday)

Brownlie, I. (1983) *System of the Law of Nations: State Responsibility, Part I* (Clarendon Press)

BSR and Centre for Democracy and Technology (2014) *Legitimate and Meaningful, Stakeholder Engagement in Human Rights Due Diligence: Challenges and Solutions for ICT Companies* (BSR)

Bueno, N., and Bright, C. (2020) 'Implementing Human Rights Due Diligence through Corporate Civil Liability' 69 *International and Comparative Law Quarterly* 789

Buhmann, K. (2016) 'Public Regulators and CSR: The Social Licence to Operate in Recent United Nations Instruments on Business and Human Rights and the Juridication of CSR' *Journal of Business Ethics* 136

—— (2017) *Changing Sustainability Norms through Communication Processes* (Edward Elgar)

—— (2022) *Human Rights: A Key Idea for Business and Society* (Routledge)

Buscemi, M., Lazzerini, N., Magi, L., and Russo, D. (eds) (2020) *Legal Sources in Business and Human Rights: Evolving Dynamics in International and European Law* (Brill)

Business and Human Rights Resource Centre

—— (2023) List of Large Businesses, Associations & Investors with Public Statements & Endorsements in Support of Mandatory Due Diligence Regulation

—— (2023) Towards an EU Mandatory Due Diligence & Corporate Accountability Law

—— (2023) Binding Treaty on Business & Human Rights

Cantú Rivera, H. (2019) 'National Action Plans on Business and Human Rights: Progress or Mirage?' 4 *Business and Human Rights Journal* 213

—— (2022) 'Binding Treaty Negotiations, Binding Treaty Negotiations: Considerations on Legal Liability and Access to Justice'

Capone, F., Hausler, K., Fairgrieve, D., and McCarthy,C. (2013) *Education and the Law of Reparations* (BIICL)

Cassel, D. (2016) 'Outlining the Case for a Common Law Duty of Care of Business to Exercise Human Rights Due Diligence' 1 *Business and Human Rights Journal* 179

Center for International Legal Cooperation (2019) Hague Rules on Business and Human Rights Arbitration

Centre for Effective Dispute Resolution (2021) 'Mediation for Business and Human Rights', Mediation for Business and Human Rights—CEDR

Centre for International Environmental Law and Others (2015) *The International Finance Corporation's Performance Standards and the Equator Principles: Respecting Human Rights and Remedying Violations?*

Chambers, R., and Berger-Walliser, G. (2021) 'The Future of International Corporate Human Rights Litigation: A Transatlantic Comparison' 58 *American Business Law Journal* 579

Charlesworth, H., and Chinkin, C. (2000) *The Boundaries of International Law: A Feminist Analysis* (Manchester University Press)

Chesterman, S. (2022) *We, The Robots: Regulating Artificial Intelligence and the Limits of Law* (Cambridge University Press)

Chimni, B.S. (2004) 'International Institutions Today: An Imperial Global State in the Making' 15 *European Journal of International Law* 1

Chiussi, L. (2019) 'The Role of International Investment Law in the Business and Human Rights Legal Process' 21 *International Community Law Review* 3

Cîrlig, R. (2016) 'Business and Human Rights: From Soft Law to Hard Law?' 6 *Juridical Tribune* 228

Clapham, A. (1993) *Human Rights in the Private Sphere* (Clarendon Press)
—— (2006) *Human Rights Obligations of Non-State Actors* (Oxford University Press)
—— (2008) 'Extending International Criminal Law beyond the Individual to Corporations and Armed Opposition Groups' 6 *Journal of International Criminal Justice* 899
Collins, H., Lester, G., and Mantouvalou, V. (eds) (2018) *Philosophical Foundations of Labour Law* (Oxford University Press)
Conley, J., and Williams, C. (2011) 'Global Banks as Global Sustainability Regulators?: The Equator Principles' 33 *Law & Policy* 542
Cook, R. (ed.) (1994) *Human Rights of Women: National and International Perspectives* (University of Pennsylvania Press)
Cossart, S., Chaplier, J., and Beau de Lomenie, T. (2017) 'The French Law on Duty of Care: A Historic Step Towards Making Globalization Work for All' 2 *Business and Human Rights Journal* 317
Crawford, E., and Pert, A. (2020) *International Humanitarian Law* (2nd edn, Cambridge University Press)
Crawford, J. (2002) *The International Law Commission's Articles on State Responsibility: Introduction, Text and Commentaries* (Cambridge University Press)
—— (2012) *Brownlie's Principles of Public International Law* (8th edn, Oxford University Press)
Croser, M., Day, M., Van Huijstee, M., and Samkalden, C. (2020) 'Vedanta v Lungowe and Kiobel v Shell: The Implications for Parent Company Accountability' 5 *Business and Human Rights Journal* 130
Crumpler, W. (2021) 'The Human Rights Risks and Opportunities in Blockchain' (CSIS)
Cryer, R., Friman, H., Robinson, D., and Wilmshurst, E. (2014) *An Introduction to International Criminal Law and Procedure* (3rd edn, Cambridge University Press)
Dalrymple, W. (2019) *The Anarchy: The Relentless Rise of the East India Company* (Bloomsbury)
Danish Institute for Human Rights (2013) *Talking the Human Rights Walk: Nestle's -Experience Assessing Human Rights Impacts in its Business Activities* (DIHR)
d'Aspremont, J., and Besson, S. (2017) (eds), *Oxford Handbook on the Sources of International Law* (Oxford University Press)
Davies, M., and Munro, V. (eds) (2016) *The Ashgate Companion to Feminist Legal Theory* (Routledge)
Davis, R. (2012) 'The UN Guiding Principles on Business and Human Rights and Conflict-Affected Areas: State Obligations and Business Responsibilities' 94 *International Review of the Red Cross* 961
Davitti, D. (2019) *Investment and Human Rights in Armed Conflict: Charting an Elusive Intersection* (Hart)
de Felice, D. (2015) 'Business and Human Rights Indicators to Measure the Corporate Responsibility to Respect: Challenges and Opportunities' 37 *Human Rights Quarterly* 511
De Feyter, K., and Gómez Isa, F. (eds) (2005) *Privatisation and Human Rights in the Age of Globalisation* (Intersentia)

De Schutter, O. (2015) 'Towards a New Treaty on Business and Human Rights' 1 *Business and Human Rights Journal* 41

de Sousa Santos, B. (2002) *Towards a New Legal Common Sense: Law, Globalization, and Emancipation* (Butterworths)

De Wet, E., and Vidmar, J. (eds) (2012) *Hierarchy in International Law* (Oxford University Press)

Debevoise and Plimpton (2021) UN Guiding Principles on Business and Human Rights at 10: The Impact of the UNGPs on Courts and Judicial Mechanisms'

Deva, S. (2014) *Regulation of Corporate Human Rights Violations: Humanising Business* (Routledge)

—— (2021) 'Business and Human Rights: Alternative Approaches to Transnational Regulation' 17 *Annual Review of Law and Social Science* 9

—— and Bilchitz, D. (eds) (2017) *Building A Treaty on Business and Human Rights: Context and Contours* (Cambridge University Press)

—— and Birchall, D. (eds) (2020) *Research Handbook on Business and Human Rights* (Edward Elgar)

—— and van Ho, T. (2023) 'Addressing (In)Equality in Redress: Human Rights-Led Reform of the Investor-State Dispute Settlement Mechanism' 24 *Journal of World Investment & Trade* 398

—— Ramasastry, A., Wettstein, F., and Santoro, M. (2019) 'Editorial: Business and Human Rights Scholarship: Past Trends and Future Directions' 4 *Business and Human Rights Journal* 201

Dupuy, P-M., Francioni, F., and Petersmann, E-U. (2009) *Human Rights in International Investment Law and Arbitration* (Oxford University Press)

Enneking, L. (2012) *Foreign Direct Liability and Beyond: Exploring the Role of Tort Law in Promoting International Corporate Social Responsibility and Accountability* (Eleven International Publishing)

Enodo Rights (2015) 'Assessment of Barrick Gold's Grievance Mechanism'

Erdem Turkelli, G., Gibney, M., Krajewski, M., and Vandenhole, W. (eds) (2021) *Handbook on Extraterritorial Human Rights Obligations* (Routledge)

ESCR-Net (2014) *Global Economy, Global Rights: A Practitioner's Guide for Interpreting Human Rights Obligations in the Global Economy*

European Coalition on Corporate Justice (2023) Comparative Table: Corporate due diligence laws and legislative proposals in Europe—ECCJ

European Commission, Shift and Institute for Human Rights and Business (2013) *ICT Sector Guide on Implementing the UN Guiding Principles on Business and Human Rights*

Evans, M. (2018) *International Law* (5th edn, Oxford University Press)

Falk, F., Rajagopal, B., and Stevens, J. (eds) (2008) *International Law and the Third World: Reshaping Justice* (Routledge)

Farringdon, F. (2002) *Trading Places: The East India Company and Asia 1600–1834* (British Library)

Fasterling, B. (2016) 'Human Rights Due Diligence as Risk Management: Social Risk Versus Human Rights Risk' 2 *Business and Human Rights Journal* 225

—— and Demuijnck, G. (2013) 'Human Rights in the Void? Due Diligence in the UN Guiding Principles on Business and Human Rights' 116 *Journal of Business Ethics* 799

Feminists for Binding Treaty (2021) Key Recommendations for a Binding Treaty, Key recommendations by Feminists for a Binding Treaty on the Third Revised Draft

Fleck, F. (2021) *The Handbook of International Humanitarian Law* (4th edn, Oxford University Press)

Ford, J., and Nolan, J. (2020) 'Regulating Transparency on Human Rights and Modern Slavery in Corporate Supply Chains: The Discrepancy Between Human Rights Due Diligence and the Social Audit' 26 *Australian Journal of Human Rights* 27

Fox, H., and Webb, P. (2015) *The Law of State Immunity* (3rd edn, Oxford University Press)

Frank Bold (2017) 'Comparing the Implementation of the Non-Financial Reporting' Directive

George, E., and Thomas, E. (2018) 'Bringing Human Rights into Bilateral Investment Treaties: South Africa and a Different Approach to International Investment Disputes' 27 *Transnational Law & Contemporary Problems* 403

Global Network Initiative (2017) GNI Principles on Freedom of Expression and Privacy

Gowar, C. (2012) 'The Alien Tort Claims Act and the South African Apartheid Litigation: Is the End Nigh?' *Speculum Juris* 4

Griffith, A., Smit, L., and McCorquodale, R. (2020) 'Responsible Business Conduct and State Laws: Addressing Human Rights Conflicts' 20 *Human Rights Law Review* 641

Hamdani, K., and Ruffin, L. (eds) (2015) *UN Centre on Transnational Corporations: Corporate Conduct and the Public Interest* (Routledge)

Hampson, F. (2007) 'An Overview of the Reform of the UN Human Rights Machinery' *Human Rights Law Review* 7

Harper Ho, V. (2012) 'Theories of Corporate Groups: Corporate Identity Reconceived' 42 *Seton Hall Law Review* 122

Heller, K., and Venzke, I. (eds) (2021) *Contingency in International Law: On the Possibility of Different Legal Histories* (Oxford University Press)

Hessbruegge, J. (2004) 'The Historical Development of the Doctrines of Attribution and Due Diligence in International Law' 36 *International Law and Politics* 265

Hestermeyer, H. (2007) *Human Rights and the WTO: The Case of Patents and Access to Medicines* (Oxford University Press)

Higgins, R. (1994) *Problems and Process: International Law and How We Use It* (Oxford University Press)

Horspool, M., Humphreys, M., and Wells-Greco, M. (2021) *European Union Law* (11th edn, Oxford University Press)

International Bar Association (2016) *Practical Guide on Business and Human Rights*

International Council on Mining and Metals (2015) 'Good Practice Guide: Indigenous Peoples and Mining' (2nd edn)

International Law Association (2010) *First Report of the Committee on Non-State Actors*
—— (2016) Study Group on Due Diligence in International Law, Second Report
International Law Commission (2001) Articles on the Responsibility of States for Internationally Wrongful Acts, Report of the International Law Commission on the Work of its 53rd session, UN Doc. A/56/10(SUPP)
—— (2006) 'Fragmentation of International Law: Difficulties Arising from the Diversification and Expansion of International Law'
International Organisation of Employers (2014) 'Consensus on Business and Human Rights is Broken with the Adoption of the Ecuador Initiative'
—— (2021) 'Input for the Roadmap for the Next Decade—Building Blocks for Realizing UNGPs Implementation toward 2030'
Jägers, N. (2002) *Corporate Human Rights Obligations: In Search of Accountability* (Intersentia)
Jackson, J. (1995) 'International Economic Law: Reflections on the "Boiler Room" of International Relations' 10 *American University Law Review* 595
Jefferson Bray, J. (1968) 'Possible Guidance from Roman Law' 3 *Adelaide Law Review* 145
Kamminga, M., and Scheinin, M. (eds) (2009) *The Impact of Human Rights Law on General International Law* (Oxford University Press)
—— and Zia-Zarifi, S. (eds) (2000) *Liability of Multinational Corporations under International Law* (Brill)
Karavias, M. (2014) *Corporate Obligations under International Law* (Oxford University Press)
Kaufman, J., and McDonnell, K. (2015) 'Community-Driven Operational Grievance Mechanisms' 1 *Business and Human Rights Journal* 125
Khoury, S., and Whyte, D. (2019) 'Sidelining Corporate Human Rights Violations: The Failure of the OECD's Regulatory Consensus' 18 *Journal of Human Rights* 363
Kinley, D. (2009) *Human Rights and Corporations* (Routledge)
Knop, K. (2002) *Diversity and Self-Determination in International Law* (Cambridge University Press)
Krajewski, M., Tonstad, K., and Wohltmann, F. (2021) 'Mandatory Human Rights Due Diligence in Germany and Norway: Stepping, or Striding, in the Same Direction?' 6 *Business and Human Rights Journal* 550
Kriebaum, U., Schreuer, C., and Dolzer, R. (2022) *Principles of International Investment Law* (3rd edn, Oxford University Press)
Kriebitz, A., and Lütge, C. (2020) 'Artificial Intelligence and Human Rights: A Business Ethical Assessment' 5 *Business and Human Rights Journal* 84
Krisch, N. (2022) 'Jurisdiction Unbound: (Extra)territorial Regulation as Global Governance' 33 *European Journal of International Law* 481
Krishnan, J. K. (2002) 'Bhopal in the Federal Courts: How Indian Victims Failed to Get Justice in the United States' 72 *Rutgers University Law Review* 101
Kube, V. (2019) *EU Human Rights, International Investment Law and Participation* (Springer)

Kyriakakis, J. (2017) 'Corporations before International Criminal Courts: Implications for the International Criminal Justice Project' 30 *Leiden Journal of International Law* 221

Lagoutte, S. (2015) 'New Challenges Facing States within the Field of Human Rights and Business' 33 *Nordic Journal of Human Rights* 158

Lapierre, D. and Moro, J. (2003) *Five Past Midnight in Bhopal* (Grand Central Publishing)

Lauterpacht, H. (1947) 'The Subjects of the Law of Nations' 63 *Law Quarterly Review* 438

LeBaron, G. (2020) *Combatting Modern Slavery: Why Labour Governance is Failing and What We Can Do About It* (Polity Press)

Lees, E., and Viñuales, J. (eds) (2019) *The Oxford Handbook of Comparative Environmental Law* (Oxford University Press)

Letnar Černic, J. (2008) 'Corporate Responsibility Human Rights: A Critical Analysis of the OECD Guidelines for Multinational Enterprises' 4 *Hanse Law Review* 71

—— (2019) 'The ILO Tripartite Declaration of Principles Concerning Multinational Enterprises and Social Policy Revisited: Is There a Need for Its Reform?' *European Yearbook of International Economic Law* 193

—— (2022) 'The Human Rights Due Diligence Standard-Setting in the European Union: Bridging the Gap Between Ambition and Reality' 10 *Global Business Law Review* 1

—— and Carrillo-Santarelli, N. (eds) (2018) *The Future of Business and Human Rights: Theoretical and Practical Considerations for a U.N Treaty* (Insentia)

Local Authority Pension Fund (2022) 'Mining and Human Rights: An Investor Perspective'

López, C. (2021) 'The Third Revised Draft of a Treaty on Business and Human Rights: Modest Steps Forward, But Much of the Same' *Opinio Juris* (3 September)

—— and Shea, B. (2015) 'Negotiating a Treaty on Business and Human Rights: A Review of the First Intergovernmental Session' 1 *Business and Human Rights Journal* 111

Maastricht Principles on Extraterritorial Obligations of States in the Area of Economic, Social and Cultural Rights (2013)

McBeth, A. (2004) 'Privatising Human Rights: What Happens to the State's Human Rights Duties when Services are Privatised?' 5 *Melbourne Journal of International Law* 133

—— (2010) *International Economic Actors and Human Rights* (Routledge)

McCorquodale, R. (2004) 'An Inclusive International Legal System' 17 *Leiden Journal of International Law* 477

—— (2013) 'Pluralism, Global Law and the Accountability of Corporations for Human Rights Violations' 2 *Global Constitutionalism* 287

—— and Neely, S. (2022) 'Director's Duties and Human Rights: A Comparative Approach' 22 *Journal of Corporate Legal Studies* 605

—— and Nolan, J. (2021) 'The Effectiveness of Human Rights Due Diligence for Preventing Business Human Rights Abuses' 68 *Netherlands International Law Review* 455

—— and Simons, P. (2007) 'Responsibility Beyond Borders: State Responsibility for Extraterritorial Violations by Corporations of International Human Rights Law' 70 *Modern Law Review* 599

—— Smit, L., Neely, S., and Brooks, R. (2017) 'Human Rights Due Diligence in Law and Practice: Good Practices and Challenges of Business Enterprises' 2 *Business and Human Rights Journal* 195

McDonald, N. (2019) 'The Role of Due Diligence in International Law' 68 *International and Comparative Law Quarterly* 1041

McGregor, L., Murray, D., and Ng, V. (2019) 'International Human Rights Law as a Framework for Algorithmic Accountability' 68 *International and Comparative Law Quarterly* 309

McLachlan, C., Shore, L., and Weiniger, M. (2017) *International Investment Arbitration* (2nd edn, Oxford University Press)

Macchi, C. (2020) 'The Climate Change Dimension of Business and Human Rights: The Gradual Consolidation of a Concept of 'Climate Due Diligence'' 5 *Business and Human Rights Journal* 93

—— and van Zeben, J. (2021) 'Business and Human Rights Implications of Climate Change Litigation: Milieudefensie et al. v Royal Dutch Shell' 30 *Review of European, Comparative & International Environmental Law* 409

Mann, F.A. (1984) *The Doctrine of International Jurisdiction Revisited After Twenty Years* (Brill)

Mares, R. (2010) 'The Limits of Supply Chain Responsibility: A Critical Analysis of Corporate Responsibility Instruments' 79 *Nordic Journal of International Law* 193

—— (2012) (ed.) *The UN Guiding Principles on Business and Human Rights—Foundations and Implementation* (Martinus Nijhoff)

Martin, J., and Bravo, K. (eds) (2015) *The Business and Human Rights Landscape—Looking Forward and Looking Back* (Cambridge University Press)

—— Bravo, K., van Ho, T. (eds) (2020) *When Business Harms Human Rights: Affected Communities that are Dying to be Heard* (Anthem)

Martin-Ortega, O. (2013) 'Human Rights Due Diligence for Corporations: From Voluntary Standards to Hard Law at Last?' 31 *Netherlands Quarterly of Human Rights* 44

—— and Methven O'Brien, C. (eds) (2019) *Public Procurement and Human Rights* (Edward Elgar)

Marx, A., Bright, C., and Wouters, J. (2019) 'Access to Legal Remedies for Victims of Corporate Human Rights Abuses in Third Countries' (European Parliament)

—— Van Calster, G., Wouters, J. with Otteburn K., and Lica, D. (2022) *Research Handbook on Global Governance, Business and Human Rights* (Edward Elgar)

Mattei, U., and Lena, J. (2000) 'US Jurisdiction over Conflicts Arising outside of the United States: Some Hegemonic Implications' 24 *Hastings International & Comparative Law Review* 381

Meeran, R. and Meeran, J. (eds) (2021) *Human Rights Litigation against Multinationals in Practice* (Oxford University Press)

Mégret, F (2008) 'The Disabilities Convention: Human Rights of Persons with Disabilities or Disability Rights?' 30 *Human Rights Quarterly* 494

Methven O'Brien, C. (2018) 'The Home State Duty to Regulate the Human Rights Impacts of TNCs Abroad: A Rebuttal' 3 *Business and Human Rights Journal* 47
—— (2022) 'Bounded Rationality, Metonymy, Humility: Further Arguments for a Framework-Style Business and Human Rights Treaty' *Völkerrechtsblog* (22 June)
Michalowski, S. (ed.) (2013) *Corporate Accountability in the Context of Transitional Justice* (Routledge)
Morgera, E. (2009) *Corporate Accountability in International Environmental Law* (Oxford University Press)
Muchlinski, P. (2021) *Multinational Enterprises and the Law* (3rd edn, Oxford University Press)
—— (2022) *Advanced Introduction to Business and Human Rights* (Edward Elgar)
Multi-Stakeholder Integrity (2020) *Not Fit-for-Purpose: The Grand Experiment of Multi-Stakeholder Initiatives in Corporate Accountability, Human Rights and Global Governance* (MSI)
Mutung'u, G. (2022) 'The United Nations Guiding Principles on Business and Human Rights, Women and Digital ID in Kenya: A Decolonial Perspective' 7 *Business and Human Rights Journal* 117
Mwanza, R. (2020) 'Toxic Spaces, Community Voices, and the Promise of Environmental Human Rights: Lessons on the Owino Uhuru Pollution Incident in Kenya' 38 *Nordic Journal of Human Rights* 279
Nagar, A. (2021) 'The Juukan Gorge Incident: Key Lessons on Free, Prior and Informed Consent' 6 *Business and Human Rights Journal* 377
Nolan, A. (2018) 'Privatization and Economic and Social Rights' 40 *Human Rights Quarterly* 815
Nortmann. M., and Ryngaert, C. (eds) (2010) *Non-State Actor Dynamics in International Law: From Law-Takers to Law-Makers* (Ashgate)
Oberg, D. (2005) 'The Legal Effects of Resolutions of the Security Council and the General Assembly in the Jurisprudence of the ICJ' 16 *European Journal of International Law* 879
OECD Watch (2015) Remedy Remains Rare
Omari Lichuma, C. (2021) '(Laws) Made in the "First World": A TWAIL Critique of the Use of Domestic Legislation to Extraterritorially Regulate Global Value Chains' *Zeitschrift für Ausländisches Öffentliches Recht und Völkerrecht* 81
Oppenheim, L. (1905) *International Law*, vol. 1 (Longmans)
Orrego Vicuña, F. (2004) 'Of Contracts and Treaties in the Global Market' (2004) 8 *Max-Planck-Yearbook of United Nations Law* 341
Pahuja, S. (2011) *Decolonizing International Law* (Cambridge University Press)
Palombo, D. (2022) 'Transnational Business and Human Rights Litigation: An Imperialist Project?' 22 *Human Rights Law Review* 1
Parella, K. (2023) 'International Law in the Boardroom' 108 *Cornell Law Review* 839
Partiti, E. (2021) 'Polycentricity and Polyphony in International Law: Interpreting the Corporate Responsibility to Respect Human Rights' 70 *International and Comparative Law Quarterly* 133
Patz, C. (2022) 'The EU's Draft Corporate Sustainability Due Diligence Directive: A First Assessment' 7 *Business and Human Rights Journal* 291

Paul, G. (2015) 'The treaty process can serve as a catalyst for effective reforms at domestic levels'

Pierce, S. (2015) 'Blacklisted: An Overview of Brazil's "Dirty List"' (11 May)

Pisillo Mazzechi, R. (2004) 'The Marginal Role of the Individual in the ILC's Articles on State Responsibility' 14 *Italian Yearbook of International Law* 39

Porter, M., and Kramer, M. (2011) 'Creating Shared Value', *Harvard Business Review*

Quijano, G. (2019) 'A New Draft Business and Human Rights Treaty and a Promising Direction of Travel'

—— and Lopez, C. (2021) 'Rise of Mandatory Human Rights Due Diligence: A Beacon of Hope or a Double-Edged Sword?' 6 *Business and Human Rights Journal* 241

Ra'ad Al Hussein, Z. (2015) 'Ethical Pursuit of Prosperity' *The Law Society Gazette* (23 March)

RAID (2021) 'The Road to Ruin? Electric Vehicles and Workers' Rights Abuses at DR Congo's Industrial Cobalt Mines'

Rajamani, L., and Peel, J. (eds) (2021) *The Oxford Handbook on International Environmental Law* (Oxford University Press)

Ramasastry, A. (2015) 'Corporate Social Responsibility versus Business and Human Rights: Bridging the Gap Between Responsibility and Accountability' 14 *Journal of Human Rights* 237

Ratner, S. (2001) 'Corporations and Human Rights: A Theory of Legal Responsibility' 111 *Yale Law Journal* 443

Roberts, A., and Sivakumaran, S. (2012) 'Lawmaking by Nonstate Actors: Engaging Armed Groups in the Creation of International Humanitarian Law' 37 *Yale Journal of International Law* 107

Rodríguez-Garavito, C. (ed.) (2017) *Business and Human Rights: Beyond the End of the Beginning* (Cambridge University Press)

Roht-Arriaza, N. (1990) 'State Responsibility to Investigate and Prosecute Grave Human Rights Violations in International Law' 78 *California Law Review* 449

Ronen, Y. (2015) 'Big Brother's Little Helpers: The Right to Privacy and the Responsibility of Internet Service Providers' 31 *Utrecht Journal of International and European Law* 72

Roorda, L. (2021) 'Broken English: A Critique of the Dutch Court of Appeal decision in Four Nigerian Farmers and Milieudefensie v Shell' 12 *Transnational Legal Theory* 144

Ruggie, J. (2013) *Just Business: Multinational Corporations and Human Rights* (Norton)

—— (2014) 'Global Governance and "New Governance Theory": Lessons from Business and Human Rights' 20 *Global Governance* 8

—— (2017) 'Comments on Thun Group of Banks Discussion Paper on the Implications of UN Guiding Principles 13 & 17 in a Corporate and Investment Banking Context'

—— (2017) 'Letter to OECD towards it Workshop on Understanding Relationships to Impact under the OECD Guidelines for Multinational Enterprises: Considering "Cause", "Contribute" and "Directly Linked"'

—— and Nelson, T. (2015) 'Human Rights and the OECD Guidelines for Multinational Enterprises: Normative Innovations and Implementation Challenges' Corporate Social Responsibility Initiative Working Paper No. 66

—— Rees, C., and Davis, R. (2021) 'Ten Years After: From UN Guiding Principles to Multi-Fiduciary Obligations' 6 *Business and Human Rights Journal* 179

Rühmkorf, A., and Walker, L. (2018) 'Assessment of the Concept of "Duty of Care" in European Legal Systems for Amnesty International' (European Institutions Office)

Saage-Maaß, M., Zumbansen, P., Bader, M., and Shahab, P. (2021) *Transnational Legal Activism in Global Value Chains* (Springer)

Santacroce, F. (2019) 'The Applicability of Human Rights Law in International Investment Disputes' 34 *ICSID Review—Foreign Investment Law Journal* 136

Santoro, M. (2012) 'Sullivan Principles or Ruggie Principles? Applying the Fair Share Theory to Determine the Extent and Limits of Business Responsibility for Human Rights' XXVIII/106 *Notizie di Politeia* 171

Saul, B., and Akande, D. (eds) (2020) *The Oxford Guide to International Humanitarian Law* (Oxford University Press)

Sauvant, K. (2015) 'The Negotiations of the United Nations Code of Conduct for Transnational Corporations: Experiences and Lessons Learned' 16 *The Journal of World Investment & Trade* 11

Savarian, A. (2021) 'The Ossified Debate on a UN Convention on State Responsibility' 70 *International and Comparative Law Quarterly* 769

Schabas, W. (2012) *International Criminal Law* (Edward Elgar)

Scheltema, M., and McCorquodale, R. (2022) "Supervisory Mechanisms and Directors Duties: Innovations in the Proposed EU Directive on Corporate Sustainability Due Diligence'

Schiff Berman, P. (2012) *Global Legal Pluralism: A Jurisprudence of Law Beyond Borders* (Cambridge University Press)

Schooner, S. (2005) 'Contractor Atrocities at Abu Ghraib: Compromised Accountability in a Streamlined, Outsourced Government' 16 *Stanford Law and Policy Review* 549

Schreuer, C. (1993) 'The Waning of the Sovereign State: Towards a New Paradigm for International Law' 4 *European Journal of International Law* 447

Scott, C. (ed.) (2001) *Torture as Tort* (Hart)

Scott, J. (2014) 'Extraterritoriality and Territorial Extension in EU Law' 62 *American Journal of Comparative Law* 87

Seck, S. (2016) 'Indigenous Rights, Environmental Rights, or Stakeholder Engagement: Comparing FC and OECD Approaches to Implementation of the Business Responsibility to Respect Human Rights' 12 *McGill International Journal of Sustainable Development, Law and Policy* 53

—— and Can, O. (2006) 'The Legal Obligations with Respect to Human Rights and Export Credit Agencies' (Schulich Law Scholars)

Sheeran, S., and Rodley, N. (eds) (2013) *Handbook of International Human Rights Law* (Routledge)

Shift (2014) 'Remediation, Grievance Mechanisms, and the Corporate Responsibility to Respect Human Rights'

Shue, H. (1996) *Basic Rights: Subsistence, Affluence, and US Foreign Policy* (2nd edn, Princeton University Press)

Simons, P. (2012) 'International Law's Invisible Hand and the Future of Corporate Accountability for Violations of Human Rights' 3 *Journal of Human Rights and the Environment* 5

—— (2023) 'Developments in Canada on Business and Human Rights; One Step Forward Two Steps Back' 36 *Leiden Journal of International Law* 1

—— and Handl, M. (2019) 'Relations of Ruling: A Feminist Critique of the United Nations Guiding Principles on Business and Human Rights and Violence against Women in the Context of Resource Extraction' 31 *Canadian Journal of Women and the Law* 113

—— and Macklin, A. (2015) *The Governance Gap: Extractive Industries, Human Rights, and the Home State Advantage* (Routledge)

Sinha, M.K. (ed.) (2013) *Business and Human Rights* (Sage)

Sivakumaran, S. (2012) *The Law of Non-International Armed Conflict* (Oxford University Press)

Skinner, G., with Chambers, R., and McGrath, S. (2020) *Transnational Corporations and Human Rights: Overcoming Barriers to Judicial Remedy* (Cambridge University Press)

—— McCorquodale, R., De Schutter, O., and Lambe, A. (2013) 'The Third Pillar: Access to Judicial Remedies for Human Rights Violations by Transnational Business' (ICAR)

Slot, P., and Bulterman, M. (eds) (2004) *Globalisation and Jurisdiction* (Kluwer)

Smit, L., Bright, C., McCorquodale, R., Bauer, M., Deringer, H., Baeza-Breinbauer, D., Torres-Cortés, F., Alleweldt, F., Kara, S., Salinier, C., and Tejero Tobed, H. (2020) Study on Due Diligence Requirements through the Supply Chain (European Commission)

—— Holly, G., McCorquodale, R., and Neely, S. (2020) 'Human Rights Due Diligence in Global Supply Chains: Evidence of Corporate Practices to Inform a Legal Standard' 25 *International Journal of Human Rights* 945

Smith, R. (2013) '"To See Themselves as Others See Them": The Five Permanent Members of the Security Council and the Human Rights Council's Universal Periodic Review' 35 *Human Rights Quarterly* 1

Soghoian, C. (2011) 'An End to Privacy Theater: Exposing and Discouraging Corporate Disclosure of User Data to the Government' 12 *Minnesota Journal of Science and Technology* 191

Sornarajah, M. (1997) 'Power and Justice in Foreign Investment Arbitration' 14 *Journal of International Arbitration* 103

Staggs Kelsall, M. (2019) 'Human Rights, Incorporated? Business & Human Rights in an Age of Neoliberalism' (PhD thesis, University of Nottingham, 2019, unpublished, with author)

Stein, M., and Bantekas, I. (2021) 'Including Disability in Business and Human Rights Discourse and Corporate Practice' 6 *Business and Human Rights Journal* 490

Tapias Torrado, N. (2022) 'Overcoming Silencing Practices: Indigenous Women Defending Human Rights from Abuses Committed in Connection to Mega-Projects: A Case in Colombia' 7 *Business and Human Rights Journal* 29

Taylor, M. (2011) 'The Ruggie Framework: Polycentric Regulation and the Implications for Corporate Social Responsibility' 5 *Nordic Journal of Applied Ethics* 9

—— (2021) 'Mandatory Human Rights Due Diligence in Norway—A Right to Know'

Thirlway, H. (2015) 'Human Rights in Customary Law: An Attempt to Define some of the Issues' 28 *Leiden Journal of International Law* 495

Thun Group of Banks (2013) Discussion Paper for Banks on Implications of Principles 16–21

—— (2017) Discussion Paper on the Implications of UN Guiding Principles 13 & 17 in a Corporate And Investment Banking Context

Toope, S. (2023) *A Rule of Law for Our New Age of Anxiety* (Cambridge University Press)

Tripathi, S. (2020) 'Companies, Covid and Respect for Human Rights' 5 *Business and Human Rights Journal* 252

Turner, J. (2018) *Robot Rules: Regulating Artificial Intelligence* (Springer)

Van Dam, C. (2011) 'Tort Law and Human Rights: Brothers in Arms—On the Role of Tort Law in the Area of Business and Human Rights' *Journal of European Tort Law* 221

van Ho, T. (2019) 'General Comment No. 24 (2017) on State Obligations Under the International Covenant on Economic, Social and Cultural Rights in the Context of Business Activities (CESCR)' 58 *International Legal Materials* 872

—— (2021) 'Defining the Relationships: "Cause, Contribute, and Directly Linked to" in the UN Guiding Principles on Business and Human Rights' 43 *Human Rights Quarterly* 625

Villalta Puig, G. (2007) 'Unethical Conduct in the Performance of International Government Contracts: AWB Ltd and the United Nations Oil-For-Food Programme' 37 *Public Contract Law Journal* 59

Vogt, J., Subasinghe, R., and Danqua, P. (2022) 'A Missed Opportunity to Improve Workers' Rights in Global Supply Chains' *Opinio Juris* (18 March)

Walk Free (2020) *Beyond Compliance in the Finance Sector*

Wallace, S. (2016) 'Private Security Companies and Human Rights: Are Non-Judicial Remedies Effective' 35 *Boston University International Law Journal* 69

Weidemaier, M., and Gauthier, M. (2017) 'Venezuela as a Case Study in Limited (Sovereign) Liability' 12 *Capital Markets Law Journal* 215

Weissbrodt, D., and Kruger, M. (2003) 'Norms on the Responsibilities of Transnational Corporations and Other Business Enterprises' 97 *American Journal of International Law* 901

Wesche, P., and Saage-Maaß, M. (2016) 'Holding Companies Liable for Human Rights Abuses Related to Foreign Subsidiaries and Suppliers before German Civil Courts: Lessons from Jabir and Others v KiK' 16 *Human Rights Law Review* 370

Wettstein, F. (2012) 'Silence as Complicity: Elements of a Corporate Duty to Speak Out Against the Violation of Human Rights' 22 *Business Ethics Quarterly* 37

—— (2022) *Business and Human Rights: Ethical, Legal, and Managerial Perspectives* (Cambridge University Press)
Williams, Z. (2016) 'Investor-State Arbitration in Domestic Mining Conflicts' 16 *Global Environmental Politics* 32
Wolfrum, R. (ed.) (2012) *Max Planck Encyclopedia of Public International Law* (Oxford University Press)
Wright, C. (2012) 'Global Banks, the Environment, and Human Rights: The Impact of the Equator Principles on Lending Policies and Practices' 12 *Global Environmental Politics* 56
Zerk, J. (2010) 'Extraterritorial Jurisdiction: Lessons for the Business and Human Rights Sphere from Six Regulatory Areas'
—— (2014) 'Corporate Liability for Gross Human Rights Abuses' (OHCHR),
Zhao, J. (2015) 'Human Rights Accountability of Transnational Corporations: A Potential Response From Bilateral Investment Treaties' 8 *Journal of East Asia and International Law* 47

Index

For the benefit of digital users, indexed terms that span two pages (e.g., 52–53) may, on occasion, appear on only one of those pages.

access to remedies 124–56, 200–1
Argentina 15–16
Artificial Intelligence *see* technology

banks *see* financial institutions
barriers to access to remedies 135–37
Bhopal 1–3, 197
bilateral investment treaties 15, 23–24, 73–74
Brazil "Dirty List" 161
business
  definition 4–5, 89–90
  direct obligations 11–12, 34–35, 86–87, 192–93
  domicile 70–71
  international law history 6–14, 17–18
  responses 46–47, 118, 153, 157–59
business associations standards 46
Business and Human Rights Treaty 10, 35, 72, 75, 106, 188–95

California Transparency in Supply Chains Act 161–62, 174
cases
  domestic law cases 137–45
  international cases 148–50
cause 95–96
climate change 176–77, 180–85, 197, 200
colonial 8–9, 10–11, 63, 107, 128, 186, *see also* Third World Approaches
communication 117–19
conflict areas 72–73, 121–22
consultation with stakeholders 109–11, 118
contribute to 95–96, 100–1
corporate responsibility to respect human rights

beyond domestic law 87–89
definition 83–85
distinction from state obligations 86–87
general 81–123
criminal law 143–44

defences 119, 162, 170–71, 174
definitions
  business 4–5, 89–90
  business and human rights 4–6
  cause, contribute to, directly linked 95–101
  corporate responsibility 83–85, 86–87
  grievance mechanism 132–33
  human rights 91–94
  human rights due diligence 103–8
  leverage 99, 101–2
  remedy 129–32
  respect 85–86
directly linked 95–101
disabilities, persons with 93, 114, 131, 191–92
due diligence
  business due diligence 105–6
  human rights *see* human rights due diligence
  state due diligence 59–60, 62, 79
duty of care 124–26, 139–41, 176–77

effectiveness 115, 126–27, 129–30, 131–32, 151
environment and due diligence 107–8
Equator Principles 39–40
European Union Corporate Sustainability Due Diligence Directive (draft) 40–41, 158–59, 168–71, 174
extraterritorial jurisdiction *see* transnational jurisdiction

222 Index

feminist approaches 22, 34–35, 93–94, 194, *see also* gender
financial institutions 81–83, 90, 97, 148–50
forum non conveniens 128
French Duty of Vigilance Act 40, 157, 162–64, 173–74

gender 73, 94, 112–14, 115, *see also* feminist approaches
German Corporate Due Diligence Obligations in Supply Chains Act 40, 157, 166–67, 173–74
governance gap 6
grievance mechanisms
 general 132–33
 operational grievance mechanisms 151–54

history 6–14, 17–18, 199
human rights
 definition 91–94
 impacts 94–95
human rights due diligence
 application 108–19
 contrast to business due diligence 105–6
 contrast to state due diligence 103–4
 definition 103–8
 heightened 72–73, 121–22
human rights impact assessment 108–11

indigenous peoples 60–63, 93, 110–11, 114, 129, 144, 153, 172
integration 111–14
international environmental law 28–29, 182, 198
International Finance Corporation Performance Standards 38–39
international humanitarian law 26–28, 198, 199
international investment law 23–25, 73–76, 197–98, 199
International Labour Organisation Multinational Enterprises Declaration
 general 11, 37–38, 154
 Fundamental Principles and Rights at Work 92–94, 184
 legal nature 46
international law impact 198, 199–201
International Law Commission Articles on the Responsibility of States for Internationally Wrongful Acts 18–20, 50–54, 56
international organizations 75–76

judicial mechanisms
 barriers 135–37
 types 133–35

legislation *see* regulation
leverage 99, 101–2

Modern Slavery Acts 172, 173–74
Multinational Enterprises *see* transnational corporations

National Contact Points 145–51
Netherlands
 cases 41, 45, 124–26, 141, 176–77
 Child Labour Due Diligence Act 40, 164–66, 173–74
Nigeria 48–49, 61, 124–26, 197
Norms on the Responsibilities of TNCs and Other Business Enterprises with regard to Human Rights 11–12
Norwegian Transparency Act 40, 167–68, 173–74

operational grievance mechanisms *see* grievance mechanisms
Organisation for Economic Cooperation and Development Guidelines for Multinational Enterprises
 general 10–11, 16–17, 35–37, 96–99, 101–2, 106–8, 172, 174, 182
 legal nature 45–46
 National Contact Points 145–51

participation in international law 22–23, 25, 30
prioritise 119–20

regulation 71–73, 197–98
remediation 122
remedy
 case law 137–45
 definition 129–32
 effectiveness 129–30, 131, 132, 151
 general responsibility 122
 right to a remedy 126–27
reporting 173
Royal Dutch Shell *see* Shell
Ruggie, John 12, 31–32, 33–34, 35–36, 43, 82–83, 86, 123, 159

"safe harbour" 119, 162
salience 120
severity 119–20
Shell 124–26, 137–38, 140–38, 176–77, 197
Sierra Leone Customary Land Rights Act and Land Commission Act 40, 172
social auditing 115–16
social expectation 83–85
social licence to operate *see* social expectation
soft law 43–45, 199
South African Broad-Based Black Empowerment Act 160–61
state-based judicial mechanisms 133–37
state-based non-judicial mechanisms 145–51
state duty to protect human rights *see* state obligations
state obligations 48–80
state responsibility
  attribution 51–59
  complicity 56–59
  general 18–20, 50–52
state-owned entities 76–79
state sovereignty 3–4, 5, 63, 68, 79, 128, 198, 199, 200
"subjects" of international law *see* participation
supply chain *see* value chain

technology 116–17, 185–88, 200
terminating a business relationship 102
third world approaches 8, 22, 93–94, *see also* colonial
tracking 114–17
trade 73–76

transnational corporations 16–17, 20–21, 193–94
transnational jurisdiction 63–70, 127–29, 199, 200
treaty *see* business and human rights treaty

United Kingdom 138–41
United Nations Commission on Transnational Corporations 8–11
United Nations Global Compact 12–13
United Nations Guiding Principles on Business and Human Rights
  criticism 34–35
  general 32–33
  history 3–4, 13
  influence on cases 41–42
  influence on international regulation 35–40, 197–98, 199
  influence on national regulation 40–42
  legal nature 42–45, 47
  process 33–34
  progress 178–80
  structure 32–33
United States 1–2, 54–55, 119, 137–38

value chain 12–13, 35–37, 76–77, 96–97, 98–99, 101–2, 107–8, 109, 114–15, 116–17, 118–19, 120–21, 173, 186
vulnerable groups 94, 112–14

women 34–35, 112–14, *see also* feminist approaches
Working Group on Business and Human Rights 31, 57–58, 72–73, 76–78, 94, 112–14, 121–22, 129–30, 131–32, 155, 178–79, 195, 200–1